Beginning Equity and Trusts

Whether you're new to higher education, coming to legal study for the first time or just wondering what Equity and Trusts is all about, **Beginning Equity and Trusts** is the ideal introduction to help you hit the ground running. Starting with the basics and an overview of each topic, it will help you come to terms with the structure, themes and issues of the subject so that you can begin your Equity and Trusts module with confidence.

Adopting a clear and simple approach with legal vocabulary explained in a detailed glossary, Mohamed Ramjohn breaks the subject of Equity and Trusts down using practical, everyday examples to make it understandable for anyone, whatever their background. Diagrams and flowcharts simplify complex issues, important cases are identified and explained and on-the-spot questions help you recognise potential issues or debates within the law so that you can contribute in classes with confidence.

Beginning Equity and Trusts is an ideal first introduction to the subject for LLB, GDL or ILEX students, and especially international students, those enrolled on distance-learning courses or on other degree programmes.

Mohamed Ramjohn is Principal Lecturer in Law at The University of West London.

Beginning the Law

A new introductory series designed to help you master the basics and progress with confidence.

Publishing Spring 2013:

Beginning Constitutional Law, Nick Howard
Beginning Contract Law, Chris Monaghan and Nicola Monaghan
Beginning Criminal Law, Claudia Carr and Maureen Johnson
Beginning Equity and Trusts, Mohamed Ramjohn

Following in Spring 2014:

Beginning Employment Law, James Marson
Beginning Evidence, Chanjit Singh Landa
Beginning Human Rights, Howard Davis

www.routledge.com/cw/beginningthelaw

Beginning
Equity and Trusts

MOHAMED RAMJOHN

Routledge
Taylor & Francis Group

LONDON AND NEW YORK

First published 2013
by Routledge
2 Park Square, Milton Park, Abingdon, Oxon OX14 4RN

Simultaneously published in the USA and Canada
by Routledge
711 Third Avenue, New York, NY 10017

Routledge is an imprint of the Taylor & Francis Group, an informa business

British Library Cataloguing in Publication Data
A catalogue record for this book is available from the British Library

Library of Congress Cataloging in Publication Data
A catalog record for this book has been requested

ISBN: 978–0–415–52859–7 (hbk)
ISBN: 978–0–415–52860–3 (pbk)
ISBN: 978–0–203–38735–1 (ebk)

Typeset in Vectora LH
by RefineCatch Limited, Bungay, Suffolk

Printed and bound in Great Britain by
TJ International Ltd, Padstow, Cornwall

Contents

Table of Cases   ix
Table of Legislation   xvii
Preface   xix
Guide to the Companion Website   xxi

1   Introduction to the law of trusts   1
Introduction   1
Trust concept   1
Equitable remedies   8
Basic study skills   8
Examination technique   10
Issues to think about further   13
Summary   13
Case law summary   13
Further reading   14
Companion website   14

2   Origin of the trust   15
Learning outcomes   15
Introduction   15
Historical development of equity   15
Development of the trust   18
Maxims of equity   20
Case law summary   25
Issues to think about further   25
Summary   26
Further reading   26
Companion website   26

3   Nature of a trust   27
Learning outcomes   27
Introduction   27
Characteristics of a trust   27
Classification of trusts   32
Trusts compared with other relationships   35
Case law summary   36
Issues to think about further   37
Summary   37
Further reading   37
Companion website   38

4 The 'three certainties' **39**
Learning outcomes 39
Introduction 39
Certainty of intention 40
No binding precedent 42
Precatory words 43
Commercial transactions 44
Effect of uncertainty of intention 45
Certainty of subject matter 46
Trust property 47
Beneficial interest 47
Certainty of objects 48
Powers of appointment 51
Case law summary 55
Issues to think about further 56
Summary 57
Further reading 58
Companion website 59

5 Constitution of a trust and formalities **61**
Learning outcomes 61
Introduction 61
Modes of creation 61
Last act theory 64
Multiple trustees, including the settlor 67
Future property 68
Choses in action 68
Inter vivos dispositions of equitable interests 69
Effect of creating a trust 70
Exceptions to the rule that 'equity will not assist a volunteer' 71
Case law summary 73
Issues to think about further 74
Summary 74
Further reading 75
Companion website 76

6 Private purpose trusts **77**
Learning outcomes 77
Introduction 77
Private purpose trusts 77
Perpetuity rule 79
Exceptions to the beneficiary principle 80
Denley approach 81

Unincorporated associations   82
Case law summary   89
Issues to think about further   90
Summary   91
Further reading   91
Companion website   92

7   Charitable trusts   **93**
Learning outcomes   93
Introduction   93
Privileges enjoyed by charitable status   93
Public benefit   97
Charitable purposes   99
Political purposes   107
Activities outside the UK   107
Cy-près doctrine   109
Case law summary   112
Issues to think about further   114
Summary   114
Further reading   114
Companion website   115

8   Resulting trusts   **117**
Learning outcomes   117
Introduction   117
What is a resulting trust?   117
Abolition of the presumption of advancement   122
Rebuttal of the presumption   122
Intended unlawful transactions   122
Winding-up of unincorporated associations   124
Case law summary   126
Issues to think about further   127
Summary   128
Further reading   128
Companion website   129

9   Constructive trusts   **131**
Learning outcomes   131
Introduction   131
Constructive trusts   132
Recognised categories of constructive trusts   134
Case law summary   151
Issues to think about further   152

Summary   153
Further reading   154
Companion website   154

10 Breach of trust   **155**
Learning outcomes   155
Introduction   155
Appointment, retirement and removal of trustees   155
Duties of trustees   158
Powers of trustees   160
Variation of the terms of a trust   162
Breach of trust   163
Proprietary remedies   168
Case law summary   172
Issues to think about further   173
Summary   173
Further reading   174
Companion website   175

11 Specific performance and injunctions   **177**
Learning outcomes   177
Introduction   177
Specific performance   178
Injunctions   180
Case law summary   188
Issues to think about further   190
Summary   190
Further reading   191
Companion website   191

Index   193

Table of Cases

Abbott Fund Trusts, *Re* [1900] 2 Ch 326 .... 119, 127
Abou Ramah v Abacha [2006] EWCA Civ 1492, CA 153
Adams and the Kensington Vestry, *Re* (1884) 27 Ch D 394.. 43, 55
Air Jamaica v Charlton [1999] 1 WLR 1399 .... 126, 127
American Cyanamide Co v Ethicon Ltd [1975] AC 396,
    [1975] 1 All ER 504, HL.. 184, 185, 189
Ames Settlement, *Re* [1946] Ch 217 .... 118, 119, 127
Anton Piller KG v Manufacturing Processes Ltd [1976] Ch 55,
    [1976] 1 All ER 779 187–9
Armitage v Nurse [1998] Ch 241, [1997] 3 WLR 1046 .... 167, 172
Astor's Settlement Trusts, *Re* [1952] Ch 534..78, 79, 81, 89
Attorney-General v Charity Commission [2012] WTLR 977.. 100
Attorney General for Hong Kong v Reid [1994] 1 AC 324, [1994] 1 All ER 1 .... 137, 151
Attorney-General of the Bahamas v Royal Trust Co [1986] 1 WLR 1001 .... 94, 95

Baden, *Re* Delvaux v Société General [1983] BCLC 325... 48
Baden, *Re, See* McPhail v Doulton (*sub nom, Re* Baden)—
Baden's Deed Trusts (No 2), *Re* [1973] Ch 9, [1972] 2 All ER 1304,
    [1972] 3 WLR 250, CA 53, 57, 58
Bahin v Hughes (1886) 31 Ch D 390... 159, 164, 172
Baldry v Feintuck [1972] 2 All ER 81... 101
Bank of Credit and Commerce International Ltd v Akindele [2000]
    3 WLR 1423, [2000] 4 All ER 221 .... 149, 152
Barclays Bank v Quistclose Investments Ltd [1970] AC 567,
    [1968] 3 All ER 651, HL...118–20, 126, 128, 129
Barlow Clowes v Eurotrust [2006] 1 All ER 333, PC.. 150, 152, 153
Barlow Clowes International Ltd (In Liquidation) and Others v Vaughan and
    Others [1992] 4 All ER 22.. 171, 173
Barlow's Will Trusts, *Re* [1979] 1 All ER 296, [1979] 1 WLR 278.................................. 54, 56, 58
Barnes v Addy (1874) LR 9 Ch App 244 .... 148, 152
Belmont Finance Corp v Williams Furniture (No.2) [1980] 1 All ER 393 149
Benjamin, *Re* [1902] 1 Ch 723 53
Beswick v Beswick [1968] AC 58, HL 178, 188
Biscoe v Jackson (1887) LR 35 Ch D 460... 100, 110–12
Bishopsgate Investment Management Ltd v Homan [1994] 3 WLR 1270 171
Blackwell v Blackwell [1929] AC 318.. 147, 152
Boardman v Phipps [1967] 2 AC 46 .... 135, 151, 158
Bourne v Keane [1919] AC 815 81
Bowden, *Re* [1936] Ch 71 .... 29, 36

Boyce v Boyce (1849) 16 Sim 476 48

Boyes, *Re* (1884) LR 26 Ch D 531 .... 144, 145

Bristol and West Building Society v Mothew [1996] 4 All ER 698 134

Broadway Cottages, *See* IRC v Broadway Cottages Trust—

Brown v Burdett (1882) 21 Ch D 667 77

Bucks Constabulary Widows and Orphans Fund Friendly Society (No 2)
   [1979] 1 WLR 936 .... 124, 127, 128

Burns v Burns [1984] 2 WLR 582 140

Chillingworth v Chambers [1896] 1 Ch 685 164

Choithram (T) International SA v Pagarani [2001] 1 WLR 1,
   [2001] 2 All ER 492 .... 67, 73, 76

Clayton's Case, Devaynes v Noble (1816) 1 Mer 529 .... 171, 173

Cocks v Manners (1871) LR 12 Eq 574 .... 84, 90

Comiskey and Others v Bowring-Hanbury and Another [1905] AC 84 .... 43, 55

Compton, *Re* [1945] 1 All ER 198, ... 98, 112

Conservative and Unionist Central Office v Burrell [1982] 1 WLR 522 83

Cook's Settlement Trusts, *Re* [1965] Ch 902 68

Co-operative Insurance v Argyll Stores [1997] 3 All ER 297,
   [1998] AC 1 .... 180, 189

Corbyn, *Re* [1941] Ch 400 106

Cottam, *Re* [1955] 1 WLR 1299 .... 100, 112

Coxen, *Re* [1948] Ch 747 .... 95, 112

Cranstoun, *Re* [1949] 1 Ch 523 104

Crippen, *Re* [1911] P 108 .... 22, 25

Davis v Richards and Wallington Industries Ltd [1990] 1 WLR 1511,
   [1991] 2 All ER 563 126

Day v Brownrigg (1878) 10 Ch D 294 .... 181, 189

Delius' Will Trusts, *Re* [1957] 1 All ER 854 .... 101, 112

Denley's Trust Deed, *Re* [1969] 1 Ch 373 .... 81, 82, 90, 91

Dingle v Turner [1972] AC 601 .... 100, 101, 112

Don King Productions Inc v Warren [1998] 2 All ER 608 68

Driffill, *Re* [1950] Ch 92 106

Earl of Oxford case (1615) 1 Rep Ch 1 16

Endacott, *Re* [1960] Ch 232 .... 81, 89

Edlington Properties Ltd v JH Fenner Ltd [2006] 1 WLR 1583 9

Ellenborough, *Re* [1903] 1 Ch 697 68

Family Planning Association (1969) Ch Comm Rep 111 103

Farley v Westminster Bank [1939] 3 All ER 491 103

Fisher v Brooker (2009) *The Times*, 12 August 167, 172

Fletcher v Fletcher (1844) 4 Hare 67 .... 68, 73, 74
Fry, *Re* [1946] Ch 312 .... 65, 73

Gaudiya Mission v Brahmachary [1997] 4 All ER 957 108
Good, *Re* [1950] 2 All ER 653 106
Goodman v Gallant [1986] 2 WLR 236 140
Goodman v Saltash Corporation (1882) 7 App Cas 633 107
Grant's Wills Trusts, *Re* [1980] 1 WLR 360 .... 87, 90
Greasley v Cooke [1980] 3 All ER 710 72
Grey v IRC [1960] AC 1, [1959] 3 All ER 603, [1959] 3 WLR 759, HL 69, 73, 75
Grove-Grady, *Re* [1929] 1 Ch 557 106
Guild v IRC [1992] 2 AC 310, [1992] 2 All ER 10 .... 105, 112
Gulbenkian's Settlement Trusts, *Re* [1970] AC 508 50

Halifax Building Society v Thomas [1996] 2 WLR 63 .... 132, 133, 151
Hallet's Estate, *Re* (1880) 13 Ch D 696 .... 169, 170, 173
Hanchett-Stamford v Attorney General [2008] EWHC 330 (Ch),
    [2009] 2 WLR 405, [2008] All ER (D) 391 (Feb), Ch D 86, 90, 124, 128
Harding, *Re* [2007] EWHC 3 107
Hay's Settlement Trusts, *Re* [1982] 1 WLR 202 53
Hetherington (Deceased), *Re* [1990] Ch 1, [1989] 2 All ER 129 .... 103, 112
Hillier, *Re* [1944] 1 All ER 480 105
Hodgson v Marks [1971] Ch 892 121
Holder v Holder [1968] Ch 353 .... 136, 151
Hooper, *Re* [1932] 1 Ch 38 81
Hopkins, *Re* [1965] Ch 669 .... 101, 112
Hopkinson, *Re* [1949] 1 All ER 346 107
Horley Town Football Club, *Re*, Hunt v McLaren [2006] EWHC 2386 (Ch),
    [2006] All ER (D) 34 (Oct), Ch D 85, 86, 90
Hunter v Moss [1994] 1 WLR 452 .... 47, 56, 58

ICLR v Attorney-General [1971] 3 All ER 1029 101
Independent Schools Council v Charity Commission [2011] UKUT 421 97
IRC v Baddeley [1955] AC 572 .... 98, 112
IRC v Broadway Cottages Trust [1955] Ch 20; [1954] 1 All ER 878 .... 49, 50, 56
IRC v City of Glasgow Police Athletic Association [1953] AC 380,
    [1953] 1 All ER 747 .... 94, 104, 112
IRC v McMullen [1981] AC 1 .... 104, 112
IRC v Pemsel [1891] AC 531 .... 99, 100
IRC v Yorkshire Agricultural Society [1928] 1 KB 611 106–8

Jacobs, *Re* (1970) 114 SJ 515 108
Jaggard v Sawyer [1995] 1 WLR 269 .... 182, 189

Jeffreys v Jeffreys (1841) Cr & Ph 138 .... 24, 25
Jones v Kernott [2011] UKSC 53, [[2012] 1 All ER 1265, (2011) *Times*,
    10 November, SC 131, 140, 141, 151
Jones v Lock (1865) LR 1 Ch App 25 ....25, 41, 55, 63
Joseph Rowntree Memorial Trust Housing Association v AG [1983] Ch 159 105

Kayford, *Re* [1975] 1 All ER 604, [1975] 1 WLR 279, HC... 44, 55
Keech v Sandford (1726) Sel Cas Ch 61...............................30, 36, 135, 151, 153, 158
Keen, *Re* [1937] Ch 236.. 145
Keren Kayemeth Le Jisroel v IRC [1932] AC 650... 108
Khoo Cheng Teow, *Re* [1932] Straits Settlement Reports 226................................... 81
Knight v Knight (1840) 3 Beav 148.. 40
Koeppler's Will Trusts, *Re* [1986] Ch 423 .... 101, 112

Laskar v Laskar [2008] 1 WLR 2695... 140
Leahy v Attorney General for New South Wales
    [1959] AC 457, PC 88, 90
Learoyd v Whiteley (1887) 12 AC 727 158
Lepton's Charity, *Re* [1972] Ch 276 .... 110, 114
Letterstedt v Broers (1884) 9 AC 371.. 157, 172
Lewis, *Re* [1954] 3 All ER 257... 98
Lipinski's Wills Trusts, *Re* [1976] Ch 235, [1977] 1 All ER 33.............................. 89, 90
Lister v Stubbs (1890) 45 Ch D 1 .... 136, 137, 151
Littlewood v Caldwell (1822) 11 Price 97 .... 183, 184, 189
London Wine Co (Shippers) Ltd, *Re* [1986] PCC 121... 47, 56
Lysaght, *Re* [1966] Ch 191 .... 112, 114
Lysaght v Edwards (1876) 2 Ch D 499.. 139

McGovern v Attorney General [1982] Ch 321, [1981] 3 All ER 493..................... 107, 114, 115
McPhail v Doulton (*sub nom, Re* Baden) [1971] AC 424, HL, *Reversing*
    Baden's Deed Trusts, *Re*, Baden v Smith [1969] 2 Ch 388, CA,
    Affirming, [1967] 3 All ER 159, Ch D 48, 50–3, 56, 57
Manisty's Settlement, *Re* [1974] Ch 17, [1973] 3 WLR 341 53
Mareva Compania Naviera SA v International Bulk Carriers SA,
    The Mareva [1980] 1 All ER 213, [1975] 2 Lloyd's Rep 509, CA 186, 189–91
Marquess of Abergavenny v Ram [1981] 2 All ER 643 161
Mason v Farbrother [1983] 2 All ER 1078 163
Mellody, *Re* [1918] 1 Ch 228 107
Mettoy Pensions Trustees Ltd v Evans [1990] 1 WLR 1587;
    [1991] 2 All ER 513... 51, 125
Milroy v Lord (1862) 31 LJ Ch 798, (1862) 4 De GF & J 264................32, 61, 64, 73, 74
Moggridge v Thackwell (1807) 13 Ves 416.. 95
Montagu's Settlement Trusts, *Re* [1987] Ch 264.. 149, 152

Morice v Bishop of Durham (1805) 10 Ves Jr 522...78
Moss, *Re* [1949] 1 All ER 495 106

Nail v Punter (1832) 5 Sim 555 165
National Anti-Vivisection Society v IRC [1948] AC 31...106, 107, 112
Neville Estates v Madden [1962] Ch 832 83
New, *Re* [1910] 2 Ch 524..162
Newland v Attorney-General (1809) 3 Mer 684..107
Nightingale v Goulbourn (1849) 5 Hare 484..107

OT Computers Ltd v First National Tricity Finance Ltd [2003] EWHC 1010...........................50
Oatway, *Re* [1903] 2 Ch 356..170, 173
Oppenheim v Tobacco Securities Trust Co Ltd [1951] AC 297................................98, 101, 112
O'Rourke v Darbishire [1920] AC 581..160, 172
Osoba, *Re* [1979] 1 WLR 247..120, 127
Ottaway v Norman [1972] Ch 698..145, 152
Oughtred v IRC [1960] AC 206..69, 74, 75
Oxley v Hiscock [2004] EWCA Civ 546, [2005] Fam 211, CA 140, 141, 152

Palmer v Simmonds (1854) 2 Drew 221..47, 56
Paragon Finance v DB Thakerar & Co [1999] 1 All ER 400 134
Partington, *Re* (1887) 57 LT 654..164
Patel v Ali [1984] Ch 283, [1984] 1 All ER 978..179, 188
Paul v Constance [1977] 1 WLR 527, CA..40, 55
Pemsel's case, *See* IRC v Pemsel—
Pennington v Waine [2002] All ER (D) 24 (Mar), [2002] 1 WLR 2075 ....65, 66, 73, 75
Perrins v Bellamy [1899] 1 Ch 797 ....166, 172
Pettingall v Pettingall (1842) 11 LJ Ch 176 ....80, 81, 89
Pettitt v Pettitt [1970] AC 777 139
Pinion, *Re* [1965] 1 Ch 85..101, 102
Printers and Transfers Society, *Re* [1899] 2 Ch 84 124
Pullan v Koe [1913] 1 Ch 9..70, 74

R v District Auditor No 3 Audit District of West Yorkshire Metropolitan
    County Council, *ex p* West Yorkshire Metropolitan County Council
    (1986) 26 RVR 24..53, 56
R v Ghosh [1982] 2 All ER 689 153
Raikes v Lygon [1988] 1 WLR 281 163
Ralli's Will Trusts [1964] Ch 288 ....63, 64, 73
Recher's Will Trusts, *Re* [1972] Ch 526 85
Rees Wills Trust, *Re* [1950] Ch 204 146
Remnant's Settlement Trusts, *Re* [1970] Ch 560..163
Resch's Will Trust, *Re* [1969] 1 AC 514 ....103, 112

Richards v Delbridge (1874) LR 18 Eq 11 ....63, 64, 73, 74
Rochefoucauld v Boustead [1897] 1 Ch 196, CA..............................9, 10, 13, 14, 139
Roscoe v Winder [1915] 1 Ch 62 .... 170, 171, 173
Rose, *Re* [1952] Ch 499 .... 65, 73, 75
Royal Brunei Airlines Sdn Bhd v Tan [1995] 2 AC 378 ....149, 150, 152, 154
Royal Choral Society v IRC [1943] 2 All ER 101 101

Salusbury v Denton (1857) 3 K & J 529 .... 95, 96, 112
Saunders v Vautier (1841) 4 Beav 115, (1841) Cr & Ph 240..........................31, 36, 90, 157, 162
Scarisbrick, *Re* [1951] Ch 622.. 100
Schmidt v Rosewood [2003] 2 WLR 1442, [2003] 3 All ER 76 .... 160, 172
Scottish Burial Reform and Cremation Society v Glasgow City
    Corporation [1968] AC 138, [1967] 3 All ER 215, HL 107, 114
Series 5 Software Ltd v Clarke (1996) 1 All ER 853.. 185, 189
Shaw, *Re* [1957] 1 WLR 729, [1958] 1 All ER 245 .... 77, 89
Shelfer v City of London Electric Lighting Co [1895] 1 Ch 287...................... 183, 189
Shelley v Shelley (1868) LR 6 EQ 540 42
Sinclair Investments Ltd v Versailles Ltd [2011] EWCA Civ 347,
    [2012] Ch 453, CA.. 137, 138, 151
Smith, *Re* [1932] 1 Ch 153 107
South Place Ethical Society, *Re* [1980] 1 WLR 1565................................. 102, 107, 112
Southwood v Attorney-General [2000] WTLR 1199 107
Sprange v Barnard (1789) 2 Bro CC 585 .... 47, 55
Stack v Dowden [2007] 2 AC 432 ....140, 142, 151, 154
Stead, *Re* [1900] 1 Ch 237 146
Steel's Will Trusts, *Re*, National Provincial Bank Ltd v Steele
    [1948] Ch 603, [1948] 2 All ER 193, Ch D... 42, 55
Strong v Bird (1874) LR 18 Eq 315 ....61, 64, 71, 72, 75

Target Holdings v Redferns [1995] 3 All ER 785...................................... 163, 164, 172
Taylor v Plumer (1815) 3 M & S 562 .... 169, 172
Tempest, *Re* (1866) LR 1 Ch App 485 157
Third Chandris Shipping Corp v Unimarine SA [1979] 2 All ER 972 .... 186, 189, 190
Thompson, *Re* [1934] Ch 342 .... 81, 89
Timpson's Executors v Yerbury [1936] 1 KB 645 69
Tinker v Tinker [1970] 1 All ER 540 .... 122–4, 127, 128
Tinsley v Milligan [1993] 3 All ER 65; [1994] 1 AC 340............117, 122–4, 127, 128
Tuck's Settlement Trusts, *Re* [1978] Ch 49 .... 54, 56, 58
Twinsectra v Yardley [2002] UKHL 12, [2002] 2 All ER 377 152

United Grand Lodge of Freemasons in England and Wales v
    Holborn Borough Council [1957] 1WLR 1090 102
University of London v Yarrow (1857) 1 De G & J 72 106

Vandervell v IRC [1967] 2 AC 291 ....70, 73, 75, 119
Vandervell's Trusts (No 2), *Re* [1974] Ch 269; [1974] 1 All ER 47 .... 118, 127
Vinogradoff, *Re* [1935] WN 68... 121, 128

Wallgrave v Tebbs (1855) 2 K & J 313 .... 144, 152
Wedgwood, *Re* [1915] 1 Ch 113.. 106
West Sussex Constabulary's Widows, Children and Benevolent
    (1930) Fund Trusts, *Re* [1971] Ch 1.. 124, 127
Westdeutsche Landesbank Girozentrale v Islington Borough Council
    [1996] AC 669.. 127
Wheeler and De Rochow, *Re* [1896] 1 Ch 315 156
Whicker v Hume (1858) 7 HL Cases 124.. 101
White's Will Trust, *Re* [1951] 1 All ER 528 103
Williams v IRC [1947] AC 447.. 98, 112
Wokingham Fire Brigade Trusts, *Re* [1951] Ch 373, [1951] 1 All ER 454 .... 103, 106
Wolverhampton Corp v Emmons [1901] 1 KB 515....................................... 180, 189
Wrotham Park Estate Co Ltd v Parkside Homes Ltd [1974] 1 WLR 798,
    [1974] 2 All ER 321 .... 182, 189

Young, *Re* [1951] Ch 344 .... 143, 152

Table of Legislation

Statutes

Administration of Estates Act 1925 34

Chancery Amendment Act 1858 (Lord
    Cairns' Act) 183
Charitable Uses Act 1601 (Statute of
    Elizabeth 1) 99
Charities Act 1993—
    s 13(1)(a)–(e). 110
    s 14 112
Charities Act 2006
    . . . . 5, 33, 65, 93, 99, 114, 115
Charities Act 2011
    . . . . 5, 33, 93, 97, 99, 102, 106, 114
    s 1(1)(a) 94
    s 1(1)(b) 108
    s 2(1)(b) 97
    s 3(1) 99, 114
    s 3(1)(a)–(m). 99
    s 3(1)(a)–(l) 99, 106
    s 3(1)(a) 99
    s 3(1)(b) 101
    s 3(1)(c). 102
    s 3(1)(d) 103
    s 3(1)(e) 103
    s 3(1)(f). 104
    s 3(1)(g) 104
    s 3(1)(h) 105
    s 3(1)(i) 105
    s 3(1)(j) 105
    s 3(1)(k). 106
    s 3(1)(l) 106
    s 3(1)(m). 99, 106
    s 3(1)(m)(i) 99, 106
    s 3(1)(m)(ii) 106
    s 3(1)(m)(iii). 106
    s 3(2)(a) 102
    s 3(2)(b) 103
    s 3(2)(d) 104

s 3(2)(e) 105
s 3(3) 99
s 4(2) 97
s 4(3) 97
s 5 104
s 5(1) 104
s 5(3) 104, 105
s 17 97
s 30 99
s 37 99
s 62 110
ss 63–66. 112
Civil Liability (Contribution) Act 1978. . . . 164
Civil Procedure Rules 1998,
    SI 1998/3132 186
Contracts (Rights of Third Parties)
    Act 1999. 71, 75
Criminal Justice Act 1988. 133

Equality Act 2010—
    s 199 122

Forfeiture Act 1982. 22

Human Rights Act 1998 . . . . 9, 191
    Sch 1, European Convention
    on the Protection of Human
    Rights and Fundamental
    Freedoms 1950 122

Judicature Act 1873 . . . 3, 17, 18, 25, 26, 177
    s 25(11) 17
Judicature Act 1875 . . . 3, 17, 18, 25, 26, 177

Law of Property Act 1925—
    s 53(1)(b) 9, 13, 62, 140
    s 53(1)(c). 69, 70, 73–5, 127
    s 53(2) 13, 74, 140
    s 60(3) 121

Law of Property (Miscellaneous
Provisions) Act 1989—
  s 2(6) 62
Limitation Act 1980 . . . . .23, 133
  s 21(1) 166
  s 21(3) 166

Matrimonial Causes Act 1973—
  s 23–25 140
  s 24 163
Matrimonial Proceedings and
Property Act 1970—
  s 37 140

Pensions Act 1995 126
Pensions Act 2004 126
Perpetuities and Accumulations
  Act 1964 80
  s 2(2) 96

Recognition of Trusts
  Act 1987 37
  s 1 27
  Sch 1 27
  Sch 1, Art 2 .27
Recreational Charities
  Act 1958 104

Sale of Goods Act 1979 191
Senior Courts Act 1981—
  s 37 186
  s 50 183
Settled Land Act 1925—
  s 64(1) 163
Statute of Frauds 1677—
  s 7 . . . . .9, 10, 13
  s 8 13
Statute of Uses 1535 . . . . .19, 26

Stock Transfer Act 1963 65

Trustee Act 1925 156
  s 14 6
  s 14(1) 161
  s 18(1) 156
  s 19 . . . . .6, 161
  s 20 161
  s 31 . . . . .6, 161
  s 32 . . . . .6, 161
  s 36(1) .156, 157
  s 36(6) 156
  s 39 157
  s 41 . . . . .156, 157
  s 53 163
  s 57(1) 162
  s 61 . . . . .165, 166, 172
  s 62 165
Trustee Act 2000 . . . . .9, 158
  ss 1–10 160
  s 1(1) 158
  s 3(1) 160
  ss 11–23 159
  s 11(2) 159
  Sch 1 158
Trusts of Land and Appointment
  of Trustees Act 1996 34
  s 14 . . . . .141, 142
  ss 19–21 156
  s 19 157
  s 20 157

Variation of Trusts Act 1958 163
  s 1 163

Wills Act 1837 . . . . .28, 142, 143, 147
  s 9 . . . . .143, 144, 147
  s 15 . . . . .143, 152

Preface

Equity has a reputation for being a subject with a collection of complex property law concepts and a vast array of cases with subtle distinctions that create confusion in the minds of readers. Nothing could be further from the truth. Equity is a stimulating and dynamic property-based subject with a wealth of case law designed to achieve fair results for the parties in this ever-changing world.

The aim of writing *Beginning Equity and Trusts* is to give the reader an overview of the subject as a 'taster' before embarking on a more in-depth study of the subject at undergraduate, postgraduate or professional level. It is expected that the book will be read before the commencement of the module or fairly early on in the course. The book has been written in plain and simple English, and is split into 11 chapters. Each chapter commences with a list of learning outcomes to be achieved by the end of the chapter, an introduction to the issues that will be analysed within the chapter, clear headings under which the information is presented, regular 'on-the-spot' questions that focus on the issues under discussion, a summary of the main points, 'issues to think about further' – which may take the form of examination questions – and a list of entries for further reading with annotations on each article or book listed.

Finally, I wish to acknowledge the enormous debt of gratitude that I owe to Fiona Briden, Damian Mitchell and the team at Routledge, Taylor & Francis for their support and effort in the production of this book.

Mohamed Ramjohn – LLB, LLM, CIOT, JP, Barrister at law
A principal lecturer in Ealing Law School
University of West London

Guide to the Companion Website

www.routledge.com/cw/beginningthelaw

Visit the *Beginning the Law* website to discover a comprehensive range of resources designed to enhance your learning experience.

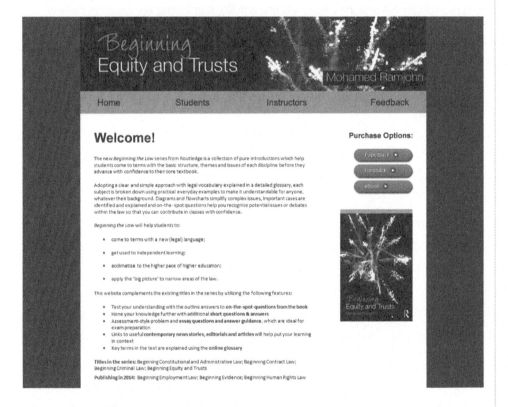

Answers to on-the-spot questions

Podcasts from the authors provide pointers and advice on how to answer the on-the-spot questions in the book.

Online glossary

Reinforce your legal vocabulary with our online glossary flashcards. The flashcards can be used online, or downloaded for reference on the go. Key terms are emboldened throughout the book, and you will find a deck of simple and easy-to-understand definitions of all these terms for each chapter of the book here.

Case flashcards

Test your knowledge of the key cases with this deck of flash cards which could be used to identify either the case name from the precedent set or the precedent from the case name. The Flashcards can be used online, or downloaded for revision on the go.

Weblinks

Discover more with this set of online links to sources of further interest. These include links to contemporary news stories, editorials and articles, illuminating key issues in the text.

Updates

Twice a year, our authors provide you with updates of the latest cases, articles and debates within the law, so you can be confident you will always be on track with the very latest developments.

Chapter 1
Introduction to the law of trusts

INTRODUCTION

This book introduces you to the law of equity and trusts. The study of the subject at undergraduate, postgraduate or professional levels can be a daunting prospect. The purpose of this book is to introduce you to the subject and simplify it to such an extent that you may feel confident to progress further and embark on a more detailed examination of the subject. The book is written in plain, simple and user-friendly language with key definitions, bullet point analyses of key cases, diagrams, 'on-the-spot' questions and chapter summaries in an effort to promote a quick understanding of the subject.

This chapter will comprise a summary of the component elements of trusts law. These elements will be covered in more detail in subsequent chapters. The subject is essentially based on case law developed from the fourteenth century, but tempered occasionally by statutory intervention. Throughout this book, reference will be made to key definitions of concepts, key cases including the underlying reasons for the decisions, and relevant statutory provisions. Finally, in this chapter advice will be given on basic study skills and the technique of optimising your performance in examinations.

TRUST CONCEPT

The subject will be analysed by reference to the following elements:

Origin of the trust

The trust under the broad jurisdiction of **equity** owes its origin to the bold steps taken initially by the **Lord Chancellor** in the fourteenth century and subsequently by the **Court of Chancery**. The origin of the trust is intertwined with the intervention of equity as a means of preventing a person who has control of property from abusing his position by taking an unfair advantage.

Example

Selwyn wishes to benefit Bertrand and conveys a plot of land, known as Blackacre, to Thomas to hold on trust for Bertrand absolutely. This illustration is intended as an example of an express trust. Selwyn is treated as a settlor, Thomas acquires the **legal title** to Blackacre and is treated as a trustee, and Bertrand is called a beneficiary or *cestui que trust* and acquires an **equitable interest** in the same property.

The trust institution (its predecessor was the '**use**') was developed by equity as a means of addressing some of the grievances felt by disappointed litigants. By the thirteenth century, the King's courts applied principles of law on a strict basis. The only interest that was recognised as subsisting in property was the legal title.

If this example had taken place in the thirteenth century, transferring title to Thomas on the understanding that he would use the property for the benefit of Bertrand would have meant that, if Thomas neglected his moral duties towards Bertrand, there was very little that the latter could do about it at law. The common law courts would have recognised Thomas as the legal owner and he would have been entitled to do as he pleased with the property. The understanding or assurance made to Selwyn to provide for Bertrand was at that time not recognised at law. The effect was that injustice to Bertrand and Selwyn was, in effect, condoned by the courts.

This situation was not rectified until about the fourteenth century with the introduction of equity. From that time, Bertrand and/or Selwyn could petition the Chancellor and subsequently the Court of Chancery in order to compel Thomas to carry out his moral obligations and recognise Bertrand's interest in the property. As a result, Bertrand would acquire an equitable interest in the property.

A broad understanding of how the rules of equity and trusts developed will assist in appreciating the nature of the modern law of trusts. This process will be considered further in Chapter 2.

Key Definitions

Equity comprised a distinct and separate body of rules that owed its origin to the intransigence of the common law. The rigidity and practice of the common law created enormous injustices for subjects, which were mainly alleviated by principles of equity. The institution of the trust was created exclusively by equity.

The **Chancellor** (later referred to as **Lord Chancellor**) was the King's leading minister. He headed the 'Chancery' (which was responsible for the issue of writs) and was an important member of the King's Council whose duties included consideration and adjudication of petitions addressed to the Council by aggrieved subjects who sought justice.

The **Court of Chancery**, headed by the Lord Chancellor, was set up to deal with the surfeit of petitions by aggrieved litigants. These petitions were originally dealt with by the Chancellor, but by the fifteenth century the petitions became so numerous that the Chancellor adapted the Chancery to constitute a special court to adjudicate on the petitions. This court remained distinct from the Courts of Common Law (King's Courts) until the Judicature Acts 1873–75, when the administration of law and equity was fused. The principles laid down by the Court of Chancery were referred to as 'equity'.

The **legal title** is ownership of property that is recognised by the world at large. The acquisition of the legal title to property varies with the nature of that property and the particular mode of transfer.

Cestui que trust is the person for whose benefit a trust was created. This is the technical expression for a beneficiary under a trust.

Equitable interest is the interest enjoyed by a beneficiary under a trust. This interest was enforceable against third parties with the exception of a *bona fide* transferee of the legal estate for value without notice.

The **use** was the forerunner to the trust institution and was introduced into English jurisprudence by the Normans in the eleventh century. Its development was promoted as a device to avoid certain laws in feudal England.

The nature of a trust

In Chapter 3 we will consider the underlying features of a trust to enable you to readily recognise and classify this property concept. A trust is a device by which the legal ownership of property is separated from the equitable interest. The legal ownership involves the acquisition of control of the property in the hands of the trustee(s). But the equitable interest is vested in the beneficiary(ies) and in many ways this interest is associated with the ownership of the property. Thus, the beneficiary(ies) will be beneficially entitled to the **income** and **capital** of the trust and may sell or make a gift of their interest to another. The powers and duties of the trustees are exercisable in a representative capacity in order to maintain the trust property, and these are identified by reference to the terms of the trust and the law. In this chapter we will classify the various types of trusts that exist and also focus our attention on distinguishing the trust concept from a variety of similar, but distinct, property concepts.

On-the-spot question

 Would you say that from the fourteenth century the Chancellor and, subsequently, the Court of Chancery had consciously set out to undermine the jurisdiction of the King's Courts?

Key Definitions

Income: May be identified as the recurring profits derived from property, for example, dividends payable in relation to the ownership of shares in a company. Likewise, interest earned on sums paid into a building society account.

Capital: Involves the corpus of funds originally paid by the settlor to the trustees and from which income may be derived. An analogy that has been drawn by the courts is to treat capital as a tree and its fruits as equivalent to income.

The 'three certainties' test

The essential elements of a trust are well settled. An express trust is required to be validly declared, which will be achieved if the settlor satisfies the 'three certainties' test; namely certainty of intention, subject matter and objects. Certainty of intention will be manifested if the words and conduct of the settlor are construed as imposing a trust obligation on the trustees in respect of a transfer of property to them; for example, a transfer of £50,000 to Terry 'on trust for Barry absolutely'. The subject matter or trust property is required to be sufficiently certain so that the court may identify the relevant property that will be subject to the trust. In the above example, this is £50,000. In addition, the courts are required to be able to ascertain the beneficiaries in order to prevent strangers to the trust unlawfully enjoying benefits. In the example above, Barry is the sole beneficiary. This subject will be considered in Chapter 4.

Constitution and formal requirements of a trust

In Chapter 5 we will examine the methods and consequences of creating an express trust. This overlaps with the declaration of trust or 'three certainties' test as stated above. An express trust is created where either a transfer of the property is made to the trustees subject to a declaration of trust, or by way of a self-declaration of trust. The first method requires the settlor to ensure that the appropriate property has been conveyed to the nominated trustee and also that a trust had been validly declared or the terms of the trust specified. The second method of creation involves the settlor declaring that he holds the relevant property on trust for the beneficiary; for example, Sam declares that he holds 5,000 shares in BP plc upon trust for Brenda absolutely. In this event the settlor makes himself a trustee. Occasionally, Parliament imposes a formal requirement of writing concerning the declaration of trust or transfer of the property. This is also included in Chapter 5.

Private purpose trusts

A private purpose trust is void for lack of a beneficiary to enforce the intended trust. Accordingly, an intended trust to board up the windows of a designated house in private ownership may be void for the beneficiary (purpose) is incapable of ensuring that the trust will be validly administered. This principle is subject to a number of exceptions that will be examined in Chapter 6.

Charitable trusts

An express trust may be created for the benefit of the public and will be treated as promoting charitable objects. The law of charities has been developed ever since the sixteenth century and the main principles were consolidated in the Charities Act 2006, the forerunner to the Charities Act 2011. There are a number of privileges that have been accorded to charities because of their public nature. Examples of charities include trusts that relieve poverty such as Oxfam, trusts that advance education such as universities, entities that advance religion such as churches, the promotion of the arts such the Royal Shakespeare Society, etc. The Charities Act 2011 lays down 13 purposes that are recognised as charitable. These will be considered in Chapter 7.

Implied trusts

Resulting and constructive trusts will be considered in Chapters 8 and 9 respectively. These are implied trusts that are created by the courts in pursuance of distinct objectives. A resulting trust arises when the transferor is treated as having impliedly retained an interest in the property in the event of the transfer failing for any reason. The resulting trust is distinct from an express trust because the transferor did not expressly state who would be entitled to the property in the event of a failure of the trust. In these circumstances the court will return the property to the transferor by implication. For example, Sunil transfers 50,000 shares in BP plc to Terry to hold 'upon trust for Brendon for life', but fails to make provision for what will happen when Brendon dies. In this event, the property will be held on trust but the beneficial interest will result to Sunil, or his estate after his death.

A constructive trust is created by the court whenever it is **unconscionable** for the legal owner to deny an equitable interest to the claimant. The intention of the parties is irrelevant, for the trust is created in order to maintain a balance between the parties. A common example of a constructive trust arises on the sale of land. Let us assume that Victor agrees in writing to sell his house, Twelve Oaks, to Peter, the purchaser for £250,000. If Peter paid the purchase price in whole or in part, Victor will then retain the legal estate in the land, but will hold it on constructive trust for Peter until the sale has been completed. Constructive trusts form a residuary category of trusts which is called into play whenever the other types of trusts (express or resulting) are inappropriate. The circumstances that give rise to a constructive trust are determined by the court in its discretion.

> **Key Definition**
>
> **Unconscionable:** This is a technical expression used in equity to mean unfairness or an abuse of position.

Breach of trust

The trust institution is one where the trustees have acquired the legal title to, and control over, the trust property for the benefit of the beneficiaries. The effect is that there is a certain degree of inequality between the parties. In order to maintain the balance between the trustee and beneficiary, the courts and Parliament accorded a number of powers to the trustees. Thus, the trustees have the power to insure trust property (s 19 of the Trustee Act 1925), a power to give a valid receipt (s 14 of the Trustee Act 1925), the power to maintain infant beneficiaries from the trust income (s 31 of the Trustee Act 1925) and the power to advance up to 50% of the trust capital for the benefit of the beneficiaries (s 32 of the Trustee Act 1925).

In addition, trusteeship involves a **fiduciary** relationship with the beneficiaries requiring the trustee to ensure that his interests do not conflict with his duties. Accordingly, any unauthorised profits obtained by the trustees are required to be paid to the trust. For example, if the trustee receives a secret profit or a bribe from a third party, the profit is required to be paid to the trust. Likewise, the trustees have a duty to invest the trust funds in appropriate investments in order to maintain the trust capital and income.

Key Definition

A **fiduciary** relationship is one of confidence or good faith imposed on a party, such as a trustee. The fiduciary is not entitled to act in a way that allows his personal interest to conflict with his duties. Thus, he is not entitled to obtain an unauthorised profit for himself.

Trustees' duties and powers of management, as well as the notion of the breach of trust and the remedies available to an aggrieved beneficiary, will be explored in Chapter 10.

The remedies that may be obtained by a successful claimant against a trustee may be personal and/or proprietary. A personal remedy, such as damages, is an obligation that is imposed upon a defendant personally. If a trustee is liable to pay damages to a successful claimant (beneficiary), he is required to pay the monetary amount from his own resources, and not from the trust fund. The trustee may even become bankrupt as a result of the successful claim. If the trustee becomes bankrupt prior to the claim by the beneficiaries, the latter will be entitled to claim against the trustee, along with the other creditors. This may prove to be of little value to the claimant.

On the other hand, a proprietary claim entitles the claimant to trace his property into the hands of the defendant and claim the specific property, or to have the property charged with the amount of the claim. For example, the title to a valuable painting may be vested in Tom, a trustee, to hold upon trust for the beneficiaries – Bert for life with remainder to Brenda absolutely. Unknown to the beneficiaries, Tom conspired with Hank, a crooked art collector, to sell the painting to Hank at a knock-down price. The sale was completed and Hank took possession of the painting. By the time that the beneficiaries became aware of the facts, Tom had disappeared with the proceeds of sale. The beneficiaries will be entitled to trace their property into the hands of Hank and obtain a court order requiring him to transfer the painting to Bert and Brenda. These principles will be explored in Chapter 10.

EQUITABLE REMEDIES

The general principles applicable to the variety of equitable remedies, including injunctions, specific performance, rectification and rescission, will be outlined in Chapter 11.

An analysis of the various aspects of the subject may be presented in the form of a diagram as follows:

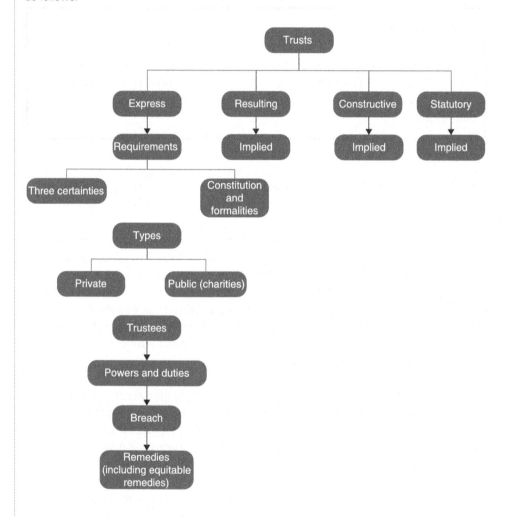

BASIC STUDY SKILLS

It should be emphasised from the outset that trusts law is very much a case law subject with only a thin layer of statutes. This is understandable as trusts law has been moulded by the courts for over 600 years. A significant feature of trusts law is that, in an effort to achieve justice for the parties, the judges have regularly distinguished precedents that they regarded as undesirable. The effect is that there has been a great deal of detachment from predictable outcomes in the cases. However, the modern tendency is to develop aspects of equity in accordance with settled principles of law as per Lord Neuberger in *Edlington Properties Ltd v JH Fenner Ltd* [2006] 1 WLR 1583:

> The fact that a particular type of right or relief is equitable does not . . . operate as a green light to invent new general or specific rules in order to achieve what one judge might regard as a fair result in a particular case or, to put it another way, to achieve a form of palm tree justice . . .

In this section we will briefly consider some of the elementary rules about what to look for in reading a case or statute.

Reading cases

A law report may contain a number of catchwords at the head. These briefly describe the nature of the case and are followed by the headnote, which is a summary of the facts of the case and what was decided. The headnote is not part of the judgment, but is simply the reporter's interpretation of the facts and decision of the court. Generally, the headnote represents an accurate version of the case and, if this is so, the reader may then proceed to consider the judgment(s). It is, of course, the principle(s) of law on which the decision is based that represents the *ratio(nes) decidendi* of the case. One of the objectives of analysing a law report is to extract the *ratio* of the case. Any other statements of law are *obiter dicta*, which are only of persuasive authority.

An Act of Parliament, such as the Trustee Act 2000, openly creates new law. It is distinct from a judgment in that no reason for the principle is stated in the statute and the Act of Parliament is imperative. Subject to the Human Rights Act 1998, an Act of Parliament is supreme and supersedes any conflicting case law. A related principle is that 'equity will not allow a statute to be used as an engine of fraud', and in exceptional circumstances may suspend the operation of a statute if its strict application may promote a clear case of fraud. A classic case on the point is *Rochefoucauld v Boustead* in which s 7 of the Statute of Frauds 1677 (the precursor to s 53(1)(b) of the Law of Property Act 1925) was involved. This provision lays down that a declaration of trust (terms of a trust) respecting land is required to be reduced into writing.

KEY CASE ANALYSIS: *Rochefoucauld v Boustead* **[1897] 1 Ch 197, Court of Appeal**

Background

- The claimant owned land subject to a mortgage.
- The mortgagees sold the land to the defendant subject to the mortgage.
- The defendant orally agreed to hold the land upon trust for the claimant.
- The defendant subsequently became bankrupt and his trustee in bankruptcy then acted in breach of trust by selling the land and claiming the proceeds in contradiction of the trust.
- The claimant brought a claim against the defendant for an **account** of the proceeds of sale held on trust.
- The defendant pleaded that the claimant could not rely on the trust of land as it was not evidenced in writing.

The question in issue was whether the trust was enforceable, despite its lack of writing as laid down by s 7 of the Statute of Frauds 1677.

Principle established

The court decided in favour of the claimant and gave effect to the oral evidence of the trust in order to prevent the defendant denying the existence of the trust and committing a fraud on the claimant. It would have been counterproductive if a statute that was designed to prevent fraud could have been utilised by the defendant to promote a fraud on the claimant.

Key Definitions

An **account** is an equitable remedy requiring a fiduciary or trustee to reinstate to the trust the original capital and make full disclosure of all the profits derived from it.

EXAMINATION TECHNIQUE

The essence of a good answer to an examination question is one that has a sound structure with sub-headings, and addresses the issues posed in the question. You should bear in mind that the period spent in the examination hall is the most valuable time you may spend on equity and trusts. For these purposes your knowledge of the law is measured by what you have written in your examination script. What follow are useful tips in presenting good examination answers under examination conditions.

Reading the exam paper

(a) Take some time to read all the questions on the examination paper and select the ones with which you are most comfortable. If you are required to answer four questions from eight, then it is prudent to select the four questions that you wish to answer before you start writing. This process has the advantage of avoiding a late change of heart and consequent time-wasting as well as planning structured answers. As the examination progresses, tiredness steps in and it becomes progressively more difficult to think clearly.

(b) Having selected the questions, it is most important that you are fully conversant with the facts of the problem or the focus of the essay. If necessary, re-read the question and underline or highlight key words or phrases. Every word of the question needs to be carefully read. These words have been inserted for a particular purpose. When words such as 'oral' or 'verbal' communication have been used, it is a prompt that you will need to consider the formal requirements for the creation of a trust.

Planning your answers

(c) Plan your answers as quickly as possible by jotting down notes (cases, phrases, sections of statutes and articles) on the exam paper. These notes should be as brief as possible and are designed to be an *aide memoire* for you when you commence writing the answers.

(d) Assemble the points in a logical order. This involves the structure of your answer. With a sound structure it is possible to present the relevant points in a logical manner. Too often, examinees present confused or disorganised answers that could have been avoided with a little care in planning the answer.

Writing your answers

(e) Get stuck into the issues posed by the questions. Avoid writing vague introductions or preambles to your answers. This is distinct from identifying the issues in the first paragraph. Identifying the issues goes some way in presenting the structure to your answer. It indicates to the examiner that you appreciate what he is asking you to deal with.

(f) Avoid rewriting the question. Many students believe (mistakenly) that they can, in effect, alter the emphasis of a question or even change it completely. Answer the specific question set. You will not score any marks by dealing with irrelevant points. Indeed, you may incur the wrath of the examiner in being penalised for dealing with irrelevant material. This is different from dealing with a gap in the facts of the problem that you have identified. If you have unearthed a fact that has been omitted from the problem, it is prudent to deal with the issue. Much depends on your alertness and judgment.

(g)   You should not assume that the examiner knows everything pertaining to the question. He or she probably does, but it is up to you to prove to him or her that you do too. If you omit to deal with relevant issues, you run the risk of losing marks.

(h)   Trusts law is a fairly fluid subject in that very often the statement of a principle may be met with a counter-proposition. It is imperative that you be as objective as possible and deal with all the possible permutations of principles that you can identify. You should distinguish questions of fact (such as questions of intention) from issues of law (such as certainty of subject matter) and bear in mind that with issues of fact you should assume both ways. For example, if an issue is whether the settlor intended to create a trust, you should deal with the consequences on the assumption that he did and, conversely, that he did not.

(i)   Apportion the time to be spent on each question carefully and try to stick to this plan. If, per chance, you miscalculate your time and feel that you are likely to run short, then, as a last resort, present your answer in note form. This is better than nothing. In any event, you are more likely to be rewarded with five marks of a new question than the last five marks of an earlier one.

(j)   One of the skills that the examiner is looking for is your ability to analyse the issues posed by the question, and the application of the relevant principles of law. Accordingly, it is advisable to present your arguments as clearly as possible, in neat and legible handwriting. It is good practice to use subheadings and present your answers in short paragraphs, each of which involves a distinct point.

(k)   You should adopt the habit of defining the relevant principle of law, in legal language, and apply the same to the facts of the problem. This may be followed by a discussion of the relevant principles of law. Very often, problem scenarios are set on issues that are not covered by decided cases. The examiner is trying to assess your ability to present relevant arguments on points of law as coherently as possible. Where the law is obscure or eccentric, you should have the courage to say so and, more importantly, give the reason(s) for your analysis.

(l)   Cases should be cited by underlining the names of the parties. The dates of decided cases are not necessary, but the short titles and dates of statutes must be stated.

(m)   Where questions are divided into parts, you must clearly identify each part of the question to which you present your answer.

(n)   Your answer to each question should be presented on a separate page.

(o)   In your concluding paragraph you should try to address the issues raised by the question. It is advisable to relate back to the instructions set out in the question, such as: 'In the light of the arguments set out above, my advice to A is as follows . . .'

ISSUES TO THINK ABOUT FURTHER

Section 53(1)(b) of the Law of Property Act 1925 and its predecessor, s 7 of the Statute of Frauds 1677, require a declaration of trust respecting land or any interest therein to be evidenced in writing. This subsection was enacted as a means of protection against fraudulent transactions concerning land. If A orally declares a trust in respect of land in favour of B, and B detrimentally changes his position to the knowledge of A, would a court be entitled to uphold the oral declaration of trust concerning the land, despite non-compliance with the statutory provision? If so, on what basis may the court give effect to the trust?

Read *Rochefoucauld v Boustead* in the law report and consider whether the court decided that it was a genuine case of:

(i)   an express trust created by the settlor but excluded from the formal requirements of s 7 of the Statute of Frauds (now s 53(1)(b) of the Law of Property Act 1925), or

(ii) a constructive trust created by the court that was exempt from the requirements of writing under s 8 of the Statute of Frauds 1677 (now s 53(2) of the Law of Property Act 1925)?

SUMMARY

- We can see that the origin of equity is significant to an understanding of the introduction of the trust to legal jurisprudence in English law.
- The different elements that comprise trusts law have been introduced and will be discussed in depth throughout this text.
- The skills necessary to study the subject have been briefly explained and various techniques for performing well in examinations have been identified.

CASE LAW SUMMARY

Rochefoucauld v Boustead – An oral undertaking made between a mortgagor and mortgagee creates an express trust and is binding on the successor in title to a mortgagee in order to prevent a fraud.

FURTHER READING

Finch E and Fafinski S, *Legal Skills* (Oxford University Press, 2011).
[This book explains in simple English how the law student may enhance his or her study, research, writing, mooting and negotiation skills.]

Hanson S, *Legal Method, Skills and Reasoning*, 3rd edn (Routledge-Cavendish, 2009).
[This book identifies and explains the techniques for perfecting the academic and practical skills of law students. It is an invaluable aid to the law student who is keen to develop a deeper understanding of the law.]

Ramjohn M, *Q&A Equity and Trusts 2011 & 2012* (Routledge, 2011).
[A revision guide that deconstructs 50 examination questions with answers to help students through the examination.]

Ramjohn M, Q&A Equity and Trusts 2013 & 2014 (Routledge, 2012).

Ramjohn M, 'Text, Cases and Materials on Equity and Trusts', 4th edn (Routledge-Cavendish, 2008).
[A combined text and casebook that examines the subject in more depth.]

Ramjohn M, 'Unlocking Trusts', 4th edn (Routledge, 2013.
[A comprehensive and up to date text written in simple, clear language that de-mystifies complicated concepts in trusts law.]

Webley L, *Legal Writing*, 2nd edn (Routledge-Cavendish, 2009).
[A student guide to writing impressive essays. The book guides students on the techniques of conducting sound legal research in order to answer examination questions.]

Williams G, *Learning the Law*, 14th edn (London: Sweet & Maxwell, 2010).
[Essential reading for all potential lawyers. The book includes an overview of the fundamentals of English law in student-friendly language and a consideration of the legal skills that are invaluable in the academic and professional world.]

COMPANION WEBSITE

An online glossary compiled by the author is available on the companion website:
www.routledge.com/cw/beginningthelaw

Chapter 2
Origin of the trust

LEARNING OUTCOMES

At the end of this chapter, you should be able to:

- Outline the historical and contextual development of equity
- Identify the maxims of equity

INTRODUCTION

The creation and development of the trust under the huge umbrella of equity is a fascinating subject of study in its own right. Equity, including the trust institution, has been regarded as a unique feature of English law, created out of the need to suppress a variety of unfair practices. The origin and growth of equity was connected with the office of the Chancellor and the Court of Chancery's response to the harsh and inflexible rules that were meted out to some litigants by the King's judges. In this chapter, we will outline some of the key factors that contributed to the growth of equity and the maxims of equity.

HISTORICAL DEVELOPMENT OF EQUITY

Following the Norman invasion in 1066, the colonisers did not radically change the local customs that characterised English law. Instead, the Normans created a system that crystallised the law. This was achieved by the introduction of a 'circuit system'. The King's judges travelled around the country and moulded the various customs into a coherent system of law applicable to the country as a whole. This system was called the **common law**.

Over the next 300 years, the judges developed and consolidated the common law. During this period they were in close contact with the King to such an extent that the common law reflected the King's notions of law. By the fourteenth century, the judges became more self-conscious of their work and attempted to assert a degree of independence from the King. At this stage the common law became rigid and a number of defects surfaced.

- The inflexible nature of the **writ**. A common law action may only be commenced by means of a writ and there were only a limited number of these available. A writ was only issued if the cause of action fell squarely within one of the limited **forms of action** that existed at this time. Any variation, however slight, was not tolerated. The effect was that a new or different claim or grievance was disregarded by the common law courts.

- The courts operated at a leisurely pace. Some actions took about 20 years before the matter went to trial.
- Bribery and corruption of officials were commonplace.
- The only remedy available at law was **damages**.

Disappointed litigants and aggrieved parties sought redress by petitioning the King, as the 'Fountain of Justice'. These petitions or bills were initially passed on to the Chancellor and, by the fifteenth century, were made directly to the Chancellor. Owing to the abundance of petitions, a separate court was created called the Court of Chancery, which was headed by the Chancellor. The principles upon which the Chancellor decided disputes came to be known as **equity**.

Initially, the rules of equity were based on ideas of **natural justice** as opposed to the strict rules of law. These rules were not intended to be independent principles of fairness, but merely supplements to the common law. The effect was that two separate systems of law had begun to co-exist and litigants were required to be careful to choose the correct court to commence their suit. At first, the relations between the common law courts and the Court of Chancery were amicable but relations became strained by the Chancery Court's frequent use of the **common injunction** as a means of frustrating the judgments of the courts of common law.

Example

If Alexander, by undue influence, had forced Bill to transfer title to his land to him, Bill's claim in the common law courts would not have been recognised and Alexander would have been declared the sole owner of the property. If Bill had appealed to the Court of Chancery, the Chancellor would have issued a common injunction suspending the operation of the court order and may have decided ultimately in favour of Bill, thus requiring Alexander to return the property to Bill.

The influence of the Court of Chancery was finally recognised in the *Earl of Oxford* case (1615) 1 Rep Ch 1, with a firm decision that where the principles of law and equity conflict, equity prevailed. Following this decision, the two systems of law went their separate ways and the Court of Chancery developed the rules of equity until the great reforms in the nineteenth century (see below).

In a nutshell, the intervention of the Court of Chancery was based on inadequacies of the common law courts. Common occurrences were:

- occasions when the common law courts failed to recognise injustices based on fraud, undue influence, mistake and the institution of the trust (see later);
- situations when the common law remedy of damages were inappropriate; and
- cases of abuse of process, for example where one of the parties was powerful and unscrupulous and wielded his influence over the common law court.

A legal system based on two independent streams of rules, law and equity, promoted its own share of difficulties and was far from being an ideal basis for resolving legal disputes. What was needed was an all-embracing uniform system of administering the law. This was achieved by the great reform Acts, the Judicature Acts 1873–75. The result was a fusion of the administration of the common law and equity. This meant that any court may apply common law or equitable principles. In particular, claims, defences and rights were required to be recognised in the same manner as existed before the Judicature Acts 1873–75. In addition, s 25(11) of the Act provided that in the event of a conflict between law and equity, the latter will prevail. Section 25(11) of the Judicature Act 1873 provides:

> 25(11) Generally, in all matters not hereinbefore mentioned in which there is any conflict or variance between the rules of equity and the rules of common law with reference to the same matter, the rules of equity shall prevail.

Key Definitions

Common law in this context means the legal rules that were common to all the subjects of England and Wales and administered in the Common Law Courts.

Writ – This expression was used to describe the means of commencing an action in a court of law. An action was required to fit a specific writ and, until the seventeenth century, there were a limited number of writs.

Forms of action – These were means of bringing claims in the common law courts. Actions were divided into real, personal and mixed. Real actions were those for the specific recovery of land or other realty. Personal actions existed for the recovery of debts, chattels or damages. Mixed actions are those for the recovery of real property together with damages for wrongs connected therewith.

Damages – Monetary compensation payable by a defendant for loss suffered by the claimant. This was the only common law remedy that was available before the enactment of the Judicature Acts 1873–75.

Equity – The body of rules created originally by the Chancellor and subsequently by the Court of Chancery.

Natural justice – These are principles of fairness and justice that may be interpreted and applied by judges.

Common injunction – This was an order issued by the office of the Chancery preventing a litigant from pursuing a judgment issued by the court of common law.

On-the-spot question

 How did equity develop as a separate system of principles? What major changes were made by the Judicature Acts 1873–75?

DEVELOPMENT OF THE TRUST

As a single institution, the trust was arguably the most important institution exclusively created by equity. Its forerunner, the 'use', was adopted as a device to separate the legal ownership of property from its beneficial interest.

Example

Simon, the legal owner of an estate called Blueacre, wished to benefit his daughter, Belinda. He was concerned about making a gift of Blueacre directly to Belinda, as he believed that she was financially immature. As an alternative, Simon transferred the legal title to Blueacre to his friends, Mary and Norman, subject to an understanding that they would maintain the land 'to the use' of Belinda. If Mary and Norman set out to defraud Simon and Belinda and claim the profits and the land for themselves, back in the fourteenth century, the claims of Simon and Belinda would have been brought in the common law courts, which only recognised the legal title to Blueacre. Thus, the moral obligations imposed on Mary and Norman would have been of no effect at law. The aggrieved parties,

Simon and/or Belinda, could have petitioned the Chancellor to give effect to the commitment made by Mary and Norman. The Court of Chancery, after verifying the facts of the case, would have recognised Belinda's beneficial interest and created an equitable interest in her favour as the beneficiary (referred to as a *cestui que* trust).

The effect was that a duality of ownership in property was created: the legal title, which would have been recognised by both courts of law and equity, and the equitable interest, which was recognised originally only by a court of equity. The legal title was vested in the trustee/s and the equitable interest was enjoyed by the beneficiary/beneficiaries.

The use became a popular device to avoid the feudal dues or financial obligations that were payable by a tenant to his lord and the king. In the sixteenth century, Parliament attempted to deal with this form of tax avoidance by passing the Statute of Uses 1535. This attempt at abolishing the use was an unmitigated failure. First, the Act was limited to apply only to land. Thus, any use over **personalty** was outside the statute. Second, the Act was construed as not affecting a 'use upon a use'. It was only capable of operating once (i.e. in respect of a 'use to Bert'). In such a case, the use was executed by the 1535 statute. This meant that the Act regarded Bert as the holder of the legal title. In order to avoid the Act, it became the practice of conveyancers to create an additional use or a 'use upon a use'. For example, a transfer may be made to 'Thomas to the use of Bert to the use of Charlie'. The first use to Bert will be executed, which means that Thomas and Bert will hold the legal title to property to the use of Charlie. From the late sixteenth century, this second use became known as a trust. Owing to the changeover from 'use' to 'trust', it was acceptable for Sam, referred to as a settlor, to transfer land or any other property to 'Alfred and Archie upon trust for Betty absolutely'. Alfred and Archie would acquire the legal title to the property, and were referred to as **trustees**. Betty would acquire the equitable interest and was referred to as a **beneficiary**.

Key Definitions

Personalty – An expression that refers to personal property such as tangible, moveable property (books, cars, furniture) and intangible, personal property known as choses in action (shares, royalties, debts).

Trustee – A person to whom the legal title to property has been transferred subject to trust obligations in favour of another called a beneficiary (or *cestui que trust*).

Beneficiary – A person who enjoys an equitable interest in property under the control of a trustee.

MAXIMS OF EQUITY

There are a number of maxims or mottos that represent certain principles that contributed to the development of equity over the centuries. The maxims lay down broad statements of policies, as opposed to narrow or watertight principles to be derived from the cases. Some of these are highlighted below.

Equity follows the law

The court of equity endorsed the legal principles or the common law where such principles were recognised as consistent with rules of equity. However, the court of equity intervened to supplement the common law in an effort to achieve justice or fairness in the dispute. The only remedy that was available at common law was damages, but in a dispute regarding a clear breach of contract for the sale of land, monetary compensation or damages may prove to be an inadequate remedy. What was needed was an order from the court requiring the defendant to complete his part of the bargain, namely, specific performance. Before 1873 this order was only obtained in a court of equity. The same approach applies to the equitable remedies of **injunctions**, **rectification**, **rescission** and **account**.

Key Definitions

Injunction – A court order requiring a defendant to refrain from pursuing a course of conduct.

Rectification – An equitable remedy that seeks to amend a document so that it reflects the true intentions of the parties.

Rescission – Involves the termination of a contract and restoring the parties to the position they would have been, had there not been a breach of contract.

Account – An order of disclosure to explain how funds received have been dealt with and requiring any loss to the trust to be made good.

Equity will not suffer a wrong to be without a remedy

This maxim represents the **exclusive** and **concurrent** jurisdictions of equity. As part of its exclusive jurisdiction, the maxim illustrates the contribution of equity in creating the institution of the trust. Equity intervened in order to recognise a moral obligation that was not enforceable at law. The common law did not give effect to the promise made by the legal owner to deal with property entrusted to him for the benefit of another. The court of equity regarded the assurance made by the legal owner as creating a fiduciary relationship and a consequential equitable interest in the beneficiary.

In addition, the variety of equitable remedies mentioned above (specific performance, etc.) in order to remedy wrongs reflects equity's concurrent jurisdiction. Occasions existed where both equity and the common law recognised that the defendant committed a breach of his duties and that the common law remedy of damages was inappropriate. In these circumstances, equity was prepared to devise a remedy to suit the facts of the case.

Example

Victor agreed to sell a valuable plot of land, Whiteacre, to Peter who paid a deposit of 10% of the purchase price. Subsequently, Victor unlawfully refused to sell the land. Peter will be entitled to force Victor to complete the transaction through the remedy of specific performance.

Key Definitions

Exclusive jurisdiction of equity – This contribution of equity in the development of the law refers to institutions and concepts that were created solely by equity, such as the trust.

Concurrent jurisdiction of equity – This refers to occasions when equity supplemented the law by affirming the relevant legal principles but creating new remedies.

He who seeks equity must do equity

The policy here is based on the premise that a person who petitions the court of equity for assistance must demonstrate that he is prepared to act with due fairness. One example is that a **proprietary** remedy would not be imposed on a defendant if the latter can demonstrate that he has *bona fide* changed his position to such an extent that it would be inequitable to require him to disgorge a benefit obtained by him by the use of trust property.

Key Definition

Proprietary remedy – A remedy that attaches to the relevant property and may require the defendant to hold the property upon trust for the claimant.

He who comes to equity must come with clean hands

This maxim takes into consideration the claimant's past conduct in determining whether relief in equity would be available to him. A classic illustration of the principle is to the effect that a murderer or person guilty of manslaughter may not profit from his crime.

KEY CASE ANALYSIS: *Re Crippen* [1911] P 108

Background

- Mr Crippen murdered his wife, who died intestate.
- Mr Crippen was executed and, in his will, left property to his mistress, X.
- The issue was whether Mrs Crippen's estate was inherited by her husband and devolved on his mistress.

Principle established

The court decided that X was not entitled to Mrs Crippen's estate because Mr Crippen was never beneficially entitled to it.

- If, however, the killer had acquired title to the property, there was room for the imposition of the constructive trust in order to prevent unjust enrichment.
- This rule has now been modified by the Forfeiture Act 1982 to the effect that, subject to an exception for convicted murderers, the court has the discretion to grant relief to the claimant and/or his heirs.

Delay defeats equity

Traditionally, courts of equity refused to lend assistance to claimants who unreasonably delayed in pursuing their claims. The technical name for such delays is 'laches'. Substantial prejudice and manifest injustice to the defendant are significant factors to be taken into consideration by the court. In order to raise a successful defence, the defendant is required to establish the following three elements:

- That there has been unreasonable delay in bringing the action by the claimant.
- That there has been consequent substantial prejudice or detriment to the defendant.
- That the balance of justice requires the claimant's cause of action to be withheld.

Limitation periods were introduced by Parliament. These refer to the maximum period during which a claimant may bring an action. The current provision, the Limitation Act 1980, makes express provision for some equitable claims, and in others the 1980 statute may be applied by analogy. In such cases, there will be no room for the doctrine of laches.

Equity looks to the intent rather than the form

Equity had never considered grievances in blinkers and was not obsessed with technicalities or form, but instead unearthed injustices by reference to the substance of transactions. Accordingly, in trusts law, a settlor may create a trust without using the expression 'trust'. The test has always been whether the settlor, in substance, intended to create a trust.

Equity does not allow a trust to fail for want of a trustee

The court has an inherent jurisdiction to appoint trustees where the settlor has failed to appoint one or where the appointed trustee is dead and the settlor had not given the power to another person to appoint new trustees. Thus, the policy of equity is that the trust will not fail merely because no trustee exists. As a last resort, the court will appoint a trustee

Equity regards as done that which ought to be done

The approach by equity is where a person (say a party to a contract) is under an obligation to perform an act that is specifically enforceable, the parties acquire the same rights and liabilities as if the obligation had been performed. For example, in conveyancing law, where the vendor and purchaser have exchanged contracts, the vendor will be treated as a constructive trustee for the purchaser until the formal completion of the contract.

Equity will not assist a volunteer

Generally, a volunteer is a person who has not provided consideration for the promise. Consideration for these purposes mean the price of the promise measured in money or money's worth or marriage consideration. The claimant is therefore required to demonstrate that he has provided consideration as a pre-condition to an equitable remedy to enforce an agreement.

KEY CASE ANALYSIS: *Jeffreys v Jeffreys* (1841) Cr & Ph 138

Background

- A father **covenanted** to settle certain copyholds on trust for the benefit of his daughters but failed to do so.
- On his death, an application was made to compel the father's personal representatives to perform the covenant.

Principle established

The court refused to compel performance of the covenant in equity. In the eyes of equity, the agreement was treated as a voluntary promise (i.e. it lacked consideration).

The effect of this rule is that no equitable assistance will be available to a volunteer.

Key Definition

Covenant – An agreement in writing where originally a seal was attached to the document and was treated as notional consideration. Today, the requirement of a seal has been dispensed with and the document may be referred to as a deed.

Equity will not perfect an imperfect gift

The principle here is that where an intended donor fails to complete a gift, the intended donee (volunteer) is not entitled to enlist the assistance of the court of equity in order to have the intended gift completed.

KEY CASE ANALYSIS: *Jones v Lock* **(1865) LR 1 Ch App 25**

Background

- A father received a cheque for £900 drawn in his favour.
- He intended to make a gift of the funds to his infant child.
- Before his death, he failed to endorse the cheque in favour of the child and failed to transfer the fund for the child's benefit.
- The child's representative brought a claim against the father's estate seeking to complete the gift.

Principle established

The court decided against the child and, subject to exceptions, refused to complete the gift.

CASE LAW SUMMARY

Jeffreys v Jeffreys – A 'voluntary' agreement (i.e. lacking consideration) to create a trust that has not been fully constituted will not be enforced in equity.

Re Crippen – In equity, the successor in title of a convicted murderer will not be allowed to inherit the deceased person's estate on the death of the murderer on the grounds that the convicted person will not become beneficially entitled to his victim's property.

Jones v Lock – A failure to transfer property to a donee will not be construed as an effective self-declaration of trust by the intended donor.

ISSUES TO THINK ABOUT FURTHER

Aggrieved litigants who felt a sense of injustice at the outcome of the common law courts' decisions petitioned the king, who passed these on to the Chancellor. The Chancellor studiously analysed these petitions and issued rulings based on broad notions of fairness and justice. At a later date, the Court of Chancery was set up to entertain such claims and proceeded to lay down a separate set of legal principles, known as equity. Some of these rules were symbolised in a set of maxims that, in a broad sense, encapsulated some of the equitable principles. The Judicature Acts 1873–75 fused the administration of law and equity, and today the rules of equity have become as rigid as the common law.

Do you think that the maxims of equity serve any useful purpose in contemporary trusts law?

SUMMARY

- We have considered that in the fourteenth century, the common law became an inflexible body of rules unwilling to react to abuses of process
- Equity, through the Lord Chancellor and the Court of Chancery, intervened in order to protect the interests of aggrieved litigants
- The use (predecessor to the trust) was arguably the most significant institution created by equity
- Conflict developed between the common law courts and the court of equity
- The Statute of Uses 1535 proved to be ineffective to stem the expansion of the jurisdiction of equity and the institution of the trust was developed by equity
- The Judicature Acts 1873–75 fused the administration of the two streams of law and equity and provided that, in the event of a conflict, equity prevailed
- The maxims of equity are broad-based policies that give recognition to equitable principles

FURTHER READING

Gardner S, 'Two maxims of equity' [1995] *CLJ* 60.
[The author analyses the two maxims, 'equity regards as done that which ought to be done' and 'equity follows the law' in the context of recent cases.]

Martin J, 'Fusion, fallacy and confusion' [1994] 58 *Conv* 13.
[This article considers the extent to which the 'fusion' debate, introduced by the Judicature Acts, was capable of stultifying the development of equitable principles and concludes that there is no inconsistency in seeking to achieve logical and coherent doctrines, while at the same time acknowledging that law and equity remain separate.]

Ramjohn M, 'Text, Cases and Materials on Equity and Trusts', 4th edn (Routledge-Cavendish, 2008).
[A combined text and case book that examines the subject in more depth.]

Ramjohn M, 'Unlocking Trusts', 4th edn (Routledge, 2013).
[A comprehensive and up to date text written in simple, clear language that de-mystifies complicated concepts in trusts law.]

COMPANION WEBSITE

An online glossary compiled by the author is available on the companion website:
www.routledge.com/cw/beginningthelaw

Chapter 3
Nature of a trust

LEARNING OUTCOMES

At the end of this chapter, you should be able to:

- Describe a trust and identify its main features
- Identify the various types of trusts that exist
- Distinguish trusts from related concepts

INTRODUCTION

The trust institution possesses a number of unique features that were moulded by equity over the centuries. An understanding of these features will assist you in recognising a trust and analysing its constituent elements. This chapter introduces you to the main characteristics of a trust and, at this early stage, we will outline the various types of trusts so that you may become familiar with the terminology employed by the courts over the centuries. Finally, we will identify the distinguishing features of a trust and compare it with a number of similar concepts.

CHARACTERISTICS OF A TRUST

The fundamental features of a trust were laid down in s 1 of the Recognition of Trusts Act 1987, which declared that the 'Provisions of the Convention [on the Law applicable to Trusts and on their Recognition] set out in the Schedule to this Act shall have the force of law in the United Kingdom'. Article 2 of the Schedule declares:

> For the purposes of this Convention, the term 'trust' refers to the legal relationship created – *inter vivos* or on death – by a person, the settlor, when assets have been placed under the control of a trustee for the benefit of a beneficiary or for a specified purpose.

A trust has the following characteristics:

> (a) the assets constitute a separate fund and are not part of the trustee's own estate;

    (b)   title to the trust assets stands in the name of the trustee or in the name of another person on behalf of the trustee;

    (c)   the trustee has the power and the duty, in respect of which he is accountable, to manage, employ or dispose of the assets in accordance with the terms of the trust and the special duties imposed upon him by law.

The reservation by the settlor of certain rights and powers, and the fact that the trustee may himself have rights as a beneficiary, are not necessarily inconsistent with the existence of a trust.

A number of these characteristics require further discussion.

Inter vivos or on death

A trust may be created during the lifetime of the settlor. This is referred to as an *inter vivos* trust. For example, during his lifetime a settlor, Saeed, transfers £50,000 to trustees, Tariq and Abdul, to hold upon trust for Xavier for life with remainder to Yolanda absolutely. Xavier will enjoy the income from the capital fund (£50,000) during his lifetime and, after his death, Yolanda will acquire the capital and future income absolutely. Note that during Xavier's lifetime, Yolanda will enjoy a vested interest in the capital of the fund.

Alternatively, a trust may be created by will on the death of the **testator** (or **testatrix**). A legacy of £10,000 may be bequeathed by Sam, a testator, under his **will** to Lester, a legatee. The **executors** are required to collect and realise the assets of the testator, settle the debts owed by the estate and distribute the net estate, including the **legacy**, to Lester in accordance with the will.

Key Definitions

Testator – A person who makes a valid will that disposes of his property after his death. The female equivalent is a testatrix.

Will – A formal document executed under the Wills Act 1837 (as amended) that distributes property on the death of the testator or testatrix.

Executor – A person appointed by will and acts as the living representative of the deceased. He has fiduciary duties imposed on him akin to a trustee.

Legacy – Personal property that has been distributed under a will. Real property (land) distributed under a will is referred to as a 'devise'.

Settlor

The creator of an express trust is called a settlor. He is the original owner of the property and specifies the terms of the trust, which, in addition to the principles laid down by the general law, identify the duties that are imposed on the trustees.

On the creation of an express trust, the settlor drops out of the picture and becomes a stranger to the trust unless he has retained an interest as a trustee or beneficiary, illustrated by *Re Bowden*.

KEY CASE ANALYSIS: *Re Bowden* [1936] Ch 71

Background

- The settlor had expected to receive an inheritance from the will of her father.
- She wished to become a nun, which would require her to undertake a vow of poverty.
- Shortly before entering a convent, she executed a covenant in which she undertook to transfer her property (existing and future) to trustees on trust for specified beneficiaries.
- On the death of her father, his executors transferred the relevant property to the trustees, subject to the trust, with her approval.
- Having spent many years (some 60 years) at the convent, she decided to leave and attempted to reclaim the property for her own benefit.

Principle established

The court held that, since the property was transferred to the trustees subject to the approval of the settlor, a trust was created. The effect was that, as settlor, the claimant had lost all interest in the property and therefore lacked the capacity to recover that property.

Trustees

The trustees are the legal owners of the property entrusted to them. They control and manage the property solely for the benefit of the beneficiaries. This responsibility is treated as giving rise to fiduciary duties – a relationship of confidence and trustworthiness to act for the benefit of the beneficiary and a duty not to act for their (the trustees') own advantage.

KEY CASE ANALYSIS: *Keech v Sandford* (1726) Sel Cas Ch 61

Background

- The defendant, a trustee, held the profits of a lease of Romford market on trust for a minor.
- Before the expiration of the lease, the defendant requested a renewal of the lease in favour of the beneficiary personally, but this was refused.
- The defendant then attempted to renew the lease in his capacity as trustee for the infant, but this was also refused.
- The lessor agreed to renew the lease in favour of the trustee personally and this was done.
- A claim was brought on behalf of the beneficiary for an assignment of the lease.

Principle established

The court decided that the lease was held by the trustee on constructive trust for the beneficiary.

Although there was no suggestion that fraud or unconscionable behaviour had been practised by the trustee, the court was reluctant to run the risk of finding it difficult in many cases to ascertain accurately whether or not an unfair advantage has been taken by the trustee. Unfairness to the trustee is not the major concern; the primary consideration of the courts is to ensure that there is no possibility of injustice to the beneficiaries.

Breaches of trustees' duties give rise to personal liability on the part of the trustees and they become liable to restore the trust funds to the state they would have been, but for the breach.

A trust fund may be managed by a sole trustee but a minimum of two trustees is required for the disposal of land.

Beneficiaries

The beneficiaries (as owners of the equitable or beneficial interest) are given the power to compel the due administration of the trust. Normally, the trustees may bring or defend claims on behalf of the trust. But in the event of an alleged breach of trust by the trustees, the beneficiaries are entitled to sue the trustees and any third party for damages.

In addition, the beneficiaries may trace the trust property into the hands of third parties, with the exception of the bona fide **transferees of the legal estate for value without notice**. Through this process, the beneficiaries may be able to recover the trust property that had been wrongly transferred to another. The notion of the *bona fide* purchaser of the legal estate for value without notice (known as 'equity's darling') is based on the assumption that, as between two innocent parties – the beneficiary under the trust and an innocent third party who acquired the legal estate for consideration without notice of a trust – the court of equity favoured the latter. It follows that the interest of a beneficiary under a trust will give way to the interest belonging to the purchaser in good faith.

Example

Terry, a trustee, holds a valuable painting on trust for Bret, a beneficiary, and Terry attempts to defraud Bret by conducting an unauthorised sale of the painting to Xavier. Bret would be entitled to recover the painting from Xavier, provided that he is not a *bona fide* purchaser of the legal estate for value without notice. In any event, Terry will be required to account to the trust for any profits received by him and to compensate the trust for any loss suffered.

As the equitable owners of the trust property, the beneficiaries are entitled to assign the whole or part of such interest to others. They are also entitled to terminate the trust by directing the trustees to transfer the legal title to them, provided that they have attained the age of majority (18 years), are *compos mentis* (mentally sound) and absolutely entitled to the trust property. This is known as the rule in *Saunders v Vautier* (1841) 4 Beav 115. Thus, assuming that Tom and Fred hold property upon trust for Bertha for life with remainder to Calvin absolutely, then if Bertha and Calvin are adults and are of sound mind, they can act collectively and terminate the trust by directing Tom and Fred to transfer the legal estate to them.

Key Definitions

***Bona fide* transferee of the legal estate for value without notice** is an innocent party who acquires the legal title to property without notice of the existence of a trust. This person's estate defeats the interest of the beneficiary under a trust.

On-the-spot question

?

Trevor holds 5,000 shares in Barclays Bank plc upon trust for David absolutely. The shares are currently valued at £8,000. David is 17 years old and wishes to purchase a car for £7,500. The trustee has refused a request from David to sell the shares and distribute the proceeds to him. Would David be entitled to direct Trevor to transfer the legal title to the shares to him, and thereby terminate the trust?

CLASSIFICATION OF TRUSTS

There are a variety of ways of classifying trusts. One approach involves the distinction between express and implied trusts.

An **express** trust (or a completely constituted trust) is one created in accordance with the express intention of the settlor. There are two modes of creation, namely a self-declaration of trust or a transfer and declaration of trust. This principle is referred to as the rule in *Milroy v Lord* (1862) 4 De GF&J 264.

A self-declaration of trust requires the settlor to declare himself a trustee on behalf of the beneficiaries. A valid declaration of trust requires the 'three certainties' test to be satisfied. These are certainty of intention, certainty of subject matter (trust property and beneficial interest) and certainty of objects (beneficiaries). Subject to statutory provisions to the contrary, this may be done orally, in writing or by conduct. In this event, the settlor becomes the trustee.

Example

Sam, the absolute owner of 50,000 BT plc shares, declares that henceforth he holds the entire shareholding upon trust for Bert, a beneficiary, absolutely. Sam retains the legal title as trustee for Bert absolutely. The latter acquires an equitable interest and is accordingly entitled to all the dividends as well as the capital. Indeed, if Bert has attained the age of majority and has the mental capacity, he may terminate the trust.

Sam (legal title) ⟶ Bert (equitable interest)

A transfer and declaration of trust mode requires the settlor to transfer the trust property to a trustee, subject to a declaration of trust (the 'three certainties' test above). The requirements for the transfer of the legal title vary with the nature of the property. For example, Seb, the settlor, has transferred the legal ownership of a car to Terry to hold on trust for Bert absolutely. The additional question that arises is whether Seb had effectively declared a trust. This involves the 'three certainties' test referred to above.

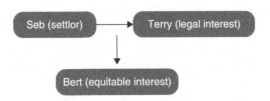

Express trusts may be classified into private or public (charitable) trusts. Charitable trusts are public trusts that benefit society as a whole in a number of different ways, as laid down in the Charities Act 2011 (which repealed and replaced the Charities Act 2006). This Act consolidated the purposes (13 in total) that have been recognised as charitable over the centuries, such as the relief of poverty (Oxfam), advancement of education (Oxford University) and so on. A non-charitable trust is regarded as private.

Another classification of express trusts is into fixed and discretionary trusts. A fixed trust is one where the settlor has initially quantified the precise interest that has been acquired by the beneficiary, such as an absolute interest, a life interest, an interest for a number of years, etc. A discretionary trust, on the other hand, is one where the beneficiary does not have a measured, precise interest but is a member of a class of objects in whose favour the trustees are required to exercise their discretion. Before the discretion is exercised in their favour, the objects of the trust enjoy a 'spes' or hope of acquiring an interest. Thus, an object may become a beneficiary only after the trustees exercise their discretion in his favour.

Example

£75,000 is held by trustees, Thomas and Terence, upon trust (as to the income and capital) for such of Sandra's children – Albert, Bernard and Charles – as the trustees may decide in their absolute discretion to be in need. In this case, Albert, Bernard and Charles are the objects of the trust and, if the trustees decide to distribute £10,000 to Albert to provide for his education, Albert becomes a beneficiary.

Non-express or **implied** trusts may be classified into resulting, constructive and statutory trusts. A resulting trust is one that arises in accordance with the implied intention of the transferor. This may be based on the presumed intention of the transferor, such as where Seymour voluntarily transfers the bare legal title to property in the name of Theo without declaring a trust. Theo will be presumed to hold the property on resulting trust for Seymour. Thus, Seymour is treated as having retained the equitable interest in the property. Alternatively, a resulting trust may be treated as automatic in the sense that the court may fill a gap in beneficial ownership and declare that the equitable interest results in favour of the transferor. For example, Sunil (settlor) transfers property to Tim (trustee) to hold on trust in favour of Brad (beneficiary) absolutely. Prior to the creation of the trust and unknown to Sunil, Brad died from a drug overdose. In these circumstances, the intended express trust becomes void and Tim will hold on resulting trust for Sunil and/or his estate.

Constructive trusts are created by the courts and are independent of the intentions of the transferors. These are imposed by operation of law where it would be inequitable or unfair for the transferee to deny the claimant an interest in the property. For example, if a sale of land has been agreed and the purchaser has paid part of the consideration, the vendor will hold the legal title to the land on constructive trust for the purchaser until completion of the sale. This principle is based on the premise that the purchaser may be able to obtain an order of specific performance.

A statutory trust is one created by Parliament in special circumstances. If land is conveyed to more than one legal owner, the real property will be held upon statutory trust for them under the Trusts of Land and Appointment of Trustees Act 1996. Likewise, where a person dies intestate, the personal representatives of the deceased hold his estate on a statutory trust for distribution to his heirs under the Administration of Estates Act 1925.

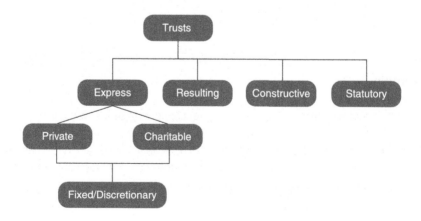

On-the-spot questions

How would you distinguish an express trust from an implied trust?
How would you distinguish a resulting trust from a constructive trust?

TRUSTS COMPARED WITH OTHER RELATIONSHIPS

There are a number of relationships that *appear* to be similar to the trust concept but are, in reality, distinct from the trust.

Agency

The agency relationship arises where one party (agent) is authorised by another party (principal) to act on behalf of the latter. The effect is that the authorised acts of the agent bind the principal. Agency, like trusteeship, creates a fiduciary relationship and the agent must not allow a conflict of duty and interest. However, the agency relationship is distinct from the trust in that the agent will rarely be the owner of property belonging in equity to the principal. In addition, the agent, unlike the trustee, will not be personally liable in respect of transactions made with third parties on his principal's behalf. The relationship between the agent and principal is contractual, whereas the trustee/beneficiary relationship is proprietary.

Contracts

The basic principle at common law is that only parties to a contract may enforce it, subject to statutory modifications. Accordingly, third parties do not have rights or interests in the property. Under a trust, a beneficiary not only has an equitable proprietary interest, but may compel the performance of the trust, despite not being a party to the creation of the trust. Further, a contract is based on a consensual bargain between the parties, whereas the creation of an express trust may reflect the unilateral intention of the settlor.

Personal representatives

The duties of the executor of a will and the administrator of an intestate's estate (collectively referred to as the personal representatives of the deceased) are in many ways similar to the obligations of trustees. They owe fiduciary duties to those entitled under the estate as a whole. However, the functions of the personal representatives are different from those of the trustees. The personal representatives acquire both legal and beneficial ownership of the deceased's estate and are required to distribute the property in accordance with the will or rules of intestacy. Of course, on completion of the estate, the personal representatives often become trustees of a trust created by will, unless different trustees are appointed.

Bailment

This concept involves the delivery of goods to someone (bailee) on condition that they will be returned to the bailor when the purpose of the bailment is completed (e.g. the delivery of a suit to the dry-cleaners). The bailment transaction, unlike the trust, involves the law of contract. It is restricted to chattels, the bailee does not acquire legal title and this arrangement was created at common law.

Gifts

Gifts, as distinct from trusts, involve the transfer of both legal and equitable interests to the donee. Accordingly, when the gift is completed, the donee becomes the absolute owner of the property. If, however, the gift is imperfect, the intended donee would find it difficult to maintain a claim to complete the gift. On the other hand, a trust involves the separation of the legal title from the equitable interest.

CASE LAW SUMMARY

Re Bowden – A feature of an express trust is that, on creation, it becomes irrevocable and binding on the settlor, and the property is separated from his estate. The trustee acquires the property for the benefit of the beneficiaries. It follows that once the trust is created, the settlor is not entitled to reclaim the property in his capacity as the original owner of the property.

Keech v Sandford – The trustee, as the legal owner of the property for the benefit of the beneficiaries, has onerous duties imposed on him and is not allowed to place himself in a position of conflict between his duties and personal interest. If the trustee obtains an unauthorised profit, such as acquiring the trust property for his own benefit, he is required to hold the same upon trust for the beneficiaries.

Saunders v Vautier – Where the beneficiaries are of full age (the age of majority) and sound mind (not mentally deficient) and absolutely entitled to the trust property, they may collectively terminate the trust or rewrite the terms of the trust as they wish.

ISSUES TO THINK ABOUT FURTHER

A settlor who creates an express trust in law is treated as having dispossessed his interest under the trust. The trustee is regarded as the owner of the property on behalf of the beneficiaries. Under the trust, the interests are divided between the trustees, who acquire legal ownership, and the beneficiaries, who acquire equitable interests. Once the trust is created, the settlor – as settlor – is treated as a stranger to the trust and has no *locus standi* to enforce the trust or to recover his original property.

Why would a person who wishes to benefit another enlist the trust institution?

SUMMARY

- We can see that there are several distinctive features of a trust identified in the Recognition of Trusts Act 1987.
- The main parties that feature in the trust relationship are the trustees and beneficiaries.
- The trustees acquire the legal title and control the trust property whilst the beneficiaries enjoy the equitable interest in the property.
- Trusts law comprises four distinct types of trusts: express, resulting, constructive and statutory.
- A trust may be distinguished from an agency relationship, a contract, the office of the personal representatives, a bailment transaction and a gift.

FURTHER READING

Duggan A, 'Is equity efficient?' (1997) 113 LQR 601.
[An analysis of equitable doctrines from an economic point of view. The purpose is designed to show that there is correlation between economic sentiment and equitable outcomes.]

Mason A, 'The place of equity and equitable remedies in the contemporary common law world' (1994) 110 LQR 238.
[The author explores the extent to which the common law and equitable principles have converged and concludes that the differences in origin between the principles may become of decreasing importance.]

Millett P, 'Equity's place in the law of commerce' (1998) 114 LQR 214.
[This article analyses the reasons responsible for equity making a significant contribution to the development of commercial law and consideration of two concepts – the fiduciary duty and the constructive trust.]

Ramjohn M, 'Text, Cases and Materials on Equity and Trusts', 4th edn (Routledge-Cavendish, 2008)
[Student text and case book that provides more detailed treatment of the subject.]

Ramjohn M, 'Unlocking Trusts', 4th edn (Routledge, 2013).
[A comprehensive and up to date text written in simple, clear language that de-mystifies complicated concepts in trusts law.]

Sands A, 'Learning to trust' [2006] 150 SJ 758
[Explores personal injury trusts and the process and effect of claimants holding their damages in personal injury trusts.]

COMPANION WEBSITE

An online glossary compiled by the author is available on the companion website: www.routledge.com/cw/beginningthelaw

Chapter 4
The 'three certainties'

LEARNING OUTCOMES

At the end of this chapter, you should be able to:

- Define the tests that are applicable to each of the 'three certainties'
- Appreciate the three certainties test as a pre-requisite for a valid declaration of trust
- Understand the consequences that follow when a trust fails for lack of each of the certainties
- Distinguish between a discretionary trust and a power of appointment
- Comprehend the distinctions between linguistic (conceptual), evidential and administrative unworkability
- Identify the various judicial approaches to the 'any given postulant' test

INTRODUCTION

A valid declaration of trust requires the settlor to satisfy the three certainties test – certainty of intention, subject matter (trust property and beneficial interests) and objects (beneficiaries). A declaration of trust is equivalent to the settlor manifesting not only his *intention* to create a trust, but also specifying the *details* of the trust with such precision that the terms may be objectively identified by the courts. If this requirement is not satisfied, it follows that the intended express trust will fail. The courts will be powerless to enforce the obligations intended for the trustees and, consequently, no rights will be obtained by the intended beneficiaries.

Example

Sarah transfers 5,000 shares in BP plc, 10,000 shares in BT plc and 15,000 shares in Barclays Bank plc to Terry and June and declares that 'some' of the shares are to be held upon trust for Bertram absolutely. It would be extremely difficult to enforce an express trust in these circumstances because of the vague nature of identifying the intended trust property.

The three certainties test was laid down by Lord Langdale MR in *Knight v Knight* (1840) 3 Beav 148, as follows:

> First, if the words were so used, that upon the whole, they ought to be construed as imperative; secondly, if the subject of the recommendation or wish be certain; and thirdly, if the objects or persons intended to have the benefit of the recommendation or wish be also certain.

Additional difficulties have been created with regard to discretionary trusts. The primary concern is whether the test for certainty of objects, known as the 'any given postulant' test, will be satisfied. A number of approaches to the test have been advocated by the judges and it is difficult to say with certainty which approach will be adopted in the future.

CERTAINTY OF INTENTION

The issue here is whether, on construction of the facts and surrounding circumstances (words spoken and written, and the conduct of the settlor), the courts are able to ascertain that the settlor intended to benefit another by way of a trust. In this regard, the courts adopt a practical approach to the question of the settlor's intention as summarised in the maxim, 'equity looks at the intent and not the form'. The test is whether the relevant facts are consistent with an intention to impose a trust on the property. There is no need for the settlor to use the expression 'trust'. But if that expression has been used, the courts will consider it in the context of the facts of the case. Alternative expressions will be construed by reference to the surrounding circumstances. This involves a question of degree, see *Paul v Constance*.

KEY CASE ANALYSIS: *Paul v Constance* [1977] 1 WLR 527, CA

Background

- Ms Paul and Mr Constance lived together as a couple.
- Mr Constance received £950 compensation for an industrial injury and both parties agreed to put the money in a deposit account in Mr Constance's name.
- On numerous occasions, both before and after the opening of the account, Mr Constance told Ms Paul that the money was as much hers as his.
- The funds were paid into an account opened in Mr Constance's sole name to avoid Ms Paul's embarrassment in having a joint account with a person whilst they were unmarried.
- After Mr Constance's death intestate, Ms Paul claimed the fund as beneficiary from Mrs Constance, the administrator of Mr Constance's estate.

Principle established

The court decided that Mr Constance, by his words and deeds, declared himself a trustee for himself and Ms Paul of the fund. The absence of the word, 'trust' was not decisive and the court was impressed by the regular assurance by Mr Constance to Ms Paul that the money was 'as much yours as mine' as to the creation of the trust. Accordingly, 50 percent of the fund was held upon trust for Ms Paul.

Distinction between an intention to create a trust and an intention to benefit another

To establish the existence of a trust, the burden of proof will lie on the party making such an allegation, usually the claimant. In this respect, the courts draw a distinction between an intention to create a trust on the one hand, and a broad intention merely to benefit another. The latter will be treated as too ambiguous to support the existence of a trust. This may be illustrated by *Jones v Lock*.

KEY CASE ANALYSIS: *Jones v Lock* (1865) LR 1 Ch App 25

Background

- Robert Jones placed a cheque for £900 (drawn in his favour) into the hand of his nine-month-old baby in the presence of the child's nanny.
- He said, 'I give this to baby.'
- He then recovered the cheque and said, 'I am going to put it away for him.'
- He took the cheque from the child and told his nanny: 'I am going to put this away for my son.'
- He put the cheque in his safe.
- A few days later, he told his solicitor: 'I shall come to your office on Monday to alter my will, that I may take care of my son.' He died the same day.

The question in issue was whether the cheque funds belonged to the child or the residuary legatees under Robert Jones's will.

Principle established

(a) No valid gift of the funds was made in favour of the child, for the funds were not paid over to him or on his behalf.

(b) Further, no trust had been declared in favour of the child, for Robert Jones had not made himself a trustee for his child. The circumstances were too ambiguous to spell out the existence of a trust and Robert Jones would have been surprised had he been told that he could no longer deal with the property for his own benefit during his lifetime.

NO BINDING PRECEDENT

Each case is determined on its own facts and, strictly, the doctrine of binding precedent is not applicable in this context. However, where the facts of a previously decided case have been used as a template to draft a trust deed for a settlor, the court is entitled to infer that the settlor intended to achieve the same result as the precedent. This approach was laid down in *Re Steele's Will Trust*.

KEY CASE ANALYSIS: *Re Steele's Will Trust* [1948] 1 Ch 603

Background

- S, a testatrix, left a diamond necklace to her son, to be held by him for his eldest son and so on 'as far as the rules of law and equity will permit'.
- The testatrix added, 'I request my said son to do all in his power by his will or otherwise to give effect to this, my wish.'
- The wording of the will was reproduced in precise terms from a previously decided case, *Shelley v Shelley* (1868) LR 6 EQ 540, where the court decided that a trust was intended.

The question in issue was whether the testatrix intended to create a trust of her necklace.

Principle established

The court decided that in the present case a trust was created. In choosing to adopt the precise wording that existed in *Shelley v Shelley*, the testatrix intended to achieve the same result, namely a trust of the necklace binding on the son.

On-the-spot question

 Is it a matter of some speculation as to whether a settlor may intend to create a trust?

PRECATORY WORDS

Words in a will that express a hope, confidence, desire or wish are known as 'precatory' words, and they may or may not be sufficient to create a trust. Much depends on the construction of the will as a whole and the surrounding circumstances as to whether a trust was intended or not (see *Re Adams and Kesington Vestry*).

KEY CASE ANALYSIS: *Re Adams and Kesington Vestry* (1884) 27 Ch D 394

Background

A testator left his property by will 'unto and to the absolute use of my wife . . . in full confidence that she will do what is right as to the disposal thereof between my children'.

The issue was whether a trust had been created by the will.

Principle established

The court decided that on construction of the facts no intention to impose a trust had been imposed on the testator's widow for the benefit of the children, so the wife was entitled to the property absolutely.

Conversely, in *Comiskey v Bowring-Hanbury,* the House of Lords decided that on construction of the precatory words and the surrounding circumstances, a trust was intended.

KEY CASE ANALYSIS: *Comiskey v Bowring-Hanbury* [1905] AC 84

Background

- The testator transferred his property by his will to his widow, subject to the following terms:

   . . . in full confidence that she will make such use of it as I should have made myself and that at her death she will devise it to such one or more of my nieces as she may think fit and in default of any disposition by her thereof by her will, I hereby direct that all my estate and property . . . shall at her death be equally divided among the surviving said nieces.

- The widow asked the court to determine whether she took the property absolutely or subject to a trust in favour of the nieces.

Principle established

The court decided that the intention of the testator was to transfer the property absolutely to his widow for life and, after her death, on trust for one or more of his nieces subject to a selection by his widow. Failing such selection, the nieces were entitled to the property equally.

On-the-spot question

What are precatory words and what is the effect of the use of such expressions in wills?

COMMERCIAL TRANSACTIONS

Trusts law may also extend to the field of commerce. The added difficulty here concerns the claims of creditors, both secured and unsecured, in the event of insolvency of the company. The question arises as to who would be entitled to recover funds from the company, and the order of recovery, in the event of a liquidation of the company. If trust funds are held by the company, then the beneficiaries will be entitled to claim those funds in priority over the creditors. This principle is based on the premise that trust funds are not shared by the company or its creditors, but exist for the benefit of the beneficiaries.

KEY CASE ANALYSIS: *Re Kayford Ltd* [1975] 1 All ER 604, HC

Background

- A mail-order company received in-house advice from accountants as to the methods of protecting advance payments of the purchase price or deposits for goods ordered by customers.
- The company was advised to open a separate bank account to be called 'Customer Trust Deposit Account' into which future sums of money received for goods not yet delivered to customers were to be paid.

- The company accepted the advice and its managing director gave oral instructions to the company's bank but, instead of opening a new account, a dormant deposit account in the company's name was used for this purpose.
- A few weeks later the company was put into liquidation.

The question in issue was whether the sums paid into the bank account were held upon trust for customers who had paid wholly or partly for goods that were not delivered or whether the funds formed part of the general assets of the company.

Principle established

The High Court decided that a valid trust had been created in favour of the relevant customers in accordance with the intention of the company and the arrangements effected. The position remained the same even though payments were not made into a separate bank account. The company became the settlor and the trustee for customers (beneficiaries). The beneficiaries therefore gained priority over the creditors (both secured and unsecured).

On-the-spot question

 Would a trust be more efficient to protect customers as opposed to the law of contract?

EFFECT OF UNCERTAINTY OF INTENTION

The effect of a ruling by the court that the intention to create a trust has not been achieved varies with the nature of the transaction. If no transfer has taken place, the legal owner is entitled to retain his property: in short, nothing happens. For example, if Sam expresses himself ambiguously to the effect that he will hold property for the benefit of Bret, and the court decides that no trust was declared, Sam is entitled to retain the property for his own use.

But if a transfer to another has taken effect, and no intention to create a trust can be ascertained, the transferee will be entitled to retain the property beneficially.

Example

Sarah transfers property to Tom but does not effectively manifest an intention to create a trust for Bill. Tom will be entitled to retain the property beneficially. In other words, Sarah will be treated as making a gift to Tom. He will therefore acquire both legal and equitable interests.

CERTAINTY OF SUBJECT MATTER

A trust is required to have an identifiable subject matter in respect of which a trust obligation may be imposed. The expression 'subject matter' for these purposes involves both the trust property and the beneficial interest. The importance of this distinction lies in the consequences of failure to satisfy the test. If the trust property is uncertain, a 'reflex' action on intention automatically arises and no trust will have been intended. The effect is as stated above where there is uncertainty of intention. For example, Sid transfers £50,000 to Tim and declares that 'some' of the money is to be held on trust for Black. If the court decides that the trust property is uncertain, this will impact on the intention to create a trust and Tim will be allowed to keep the property beneficially.

On the other hand, if the trust property is certain but the beneficial interest is uncertain, then although the express trust will fail, the transferee will hold the property on resulting trust for the transferor. For example, two valuable paintings are to be held by Terry on trust as to one of the paintings for Xavier and the other on trust for Yolanda. If there is an unresolved dispute as to which painting is to be enjoyed by each beneficiary, a resulting trust for the transferor may arise.

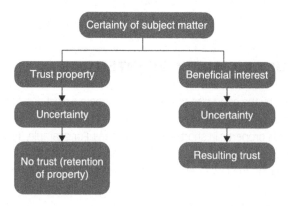

The test for certainty of subject matter is whether the trust property and the beneficial interest are ascertained or are ascertainable to such an extent that the court may attach an order on the relevant property. This is a question of law for the judge to decide and this issue is determined objectively.

TRUST PROPERTY

As was indicated above, the question here is whether the property that is subject to the trust obligation may be identified. If this question cannot be resolved, no intention to create a trust will be discerned.

In *Sprange v Barnard* (1789) 2 Bro CC 585, funds were transferred to T for his 'sole use' subject to a declaration that the 'remaining part of what was left that he does not want for his own use to be divided' between B and C equally. The court decided that no trust was intended and T was allowed to retain the property in his estate.

In *Palmer v Simmonds* (1854) 2 Drew 221, the 'bulk' of property acquired under a will was required to be transferred by will to others. The court decided that no trust was intended.

In *Re London Wine Co Ltd* [1986] PC 121, the court decided that unascertained goods (wine) bought, but stored by the sellers, did not give rise to a trust when the selling company went into liquidation.

But, in *Hunter v Moss* [1994] 1 WLR 452, the Court of Appeal distinguished *Re London Wine* and decided that the quantification of shares (5 percent) of one type (1,000 shares) was sufficient to identify the trust property, namely 50 shares. There was no need to list the reference numbers of the shares in order to identify the subject matter of the trust.

On-the-spot question

 How would you reconcile *Re London Wine Co* with *Hunter v Moss*?

BENEFICIAL INTEREST

Where the trust property is certain, but the interest to be acquired by the beneficiaries is uncertain, the express trust will fail and the property will be held on resulting trust for the transferor. This will be the case where trust property has been acquired subject to a distribution to the beneficiaries that is incapable of achievement.

KEY CASE ANALYSIS: *Boyce v Boyce* (1849) 16 Sim 476

Background

A testator devised two houses to trustees on trust to provide one for Maria, whichever she might choose, and the other to Charlotte.

Maria died before the testator and had failed to make a selection.

The question in issue was whether Charlotte may acquire one of the properties.

Principle established

The court decided that a personal obligation to select was imposed on Maria. No other person could have made the selection and the intended express trust failed but a resulting trust was set up for the testator's estate.

On-the-spot question

 What is the effect of the distinction between uncertainty of trust property and beneficial interest?

CERTAINTY OF OBJECTS

There are two separate tests for certainty of objects in respect of private trusts: a narrow test that is applicable to fixed trusts (referred to as the 'list' test or 'Broadway Cottages' test, or the class ascertainability test); and, since 1971, a broader test that is applicable to discretionary trusts (referred to as the 'is or is not' test, 'any given postulant' test, '*Re Baden*' test or the individual ascertainability test).

A 'fixed' (or non-discretionary) trust is one where the beneficiaries have fixed or immutable interests in the trust property, laid down from the beginning when the trust was created. In this respect, the beneficiaries have equitable interests in the trust property, which, subject to capacity, they are allowed to sell, exchange or gift away (e.g. 'on trust for Alvin, Bert and Calvin equally', 'on trust for Alice for life with remainder to Brenda').

A discretionary trust, on the other hand, is one where the trustees are granted discretion to distribute property in favour of any or all of a group of objects as the trustees may decide. A discretionary trust is obligatory in the sense that the trustees are required to exercise their discretion, but have the flexibility in deciding who should benefit and by what amount. Before the discretion is exercised in their favour, the members of the class of objects do not have an interest in the property but merely a hope or expectation of acquiring an interest. It follows that an object becomes a beneficiary of the amount of funds only when a distribution has been made to him. For example, trustees hold £50,000 upon trust to 'distribute to income to such of the children of Xeros as the trustees may decide in their absolute discretion'. If the trustees decide to distribute 75 percent of the income to Yannis, a child of Xeros, only then does Yannis acquire an interest in the fund and only by reference to the amount of the distribution.

Fixed trusts

The test for certainty of objects has always been the 'list' test; namely, whether the trustees are capable of drawing a comprehensive list of all the objects. Another way of expressing the principle is to consider whether the objects are ascertained or ascertainable. Until 1971, this test was also applicable to discretionary trusts.

KEY CASE ANALYSIS: *IRC v Broadway Cottages Trust* [1955] Ch 20

Background

- A settlement was created whereby trustees held property upon trust to apply the income for the benefit of all or any of a class of objects including, *inter alia*, the settlor's wife, specific relations of the settlor and the Broadway Cottages Trust, a charitable institution.
- The trustees paid income to the Broadway Cottages Trust and claimed exemption from income tax in respect of this.
- It was not possible to ascertain all the persons who might fall within the class of objects but it was possible to determine with certainty whether a particular person was a member of the class.

The question in issue was whether the trust was valid or void.

Principle established

The court decided that the trust was void for uncertainty of objects, and the claim for a repayment of income tax failed.

In a recent case, *OT Computers Ltd v First National Tricity Finance Ltd* [2003] EWHC 1010, the High Court decided that an intended trust in favour of 'urgent suppliers' failed because the formula for identifying the objects was too vague. A resulting trust had arisen.

Discretionary trusts

The narrow *Broadway Cottages* test for certainty of objects was regarded as unsuitable for the broader discretionary trusts and was discarded by the House of Lords. The modern test for certainty of objects in respect of discretionary trusts was laid down in *McPhail v Doulton* (*sub nom Re Baden*) in favour of the broader 'any given postulant' test that was applicable to a related concept, known as 'powers of appointment'. The test is whether the trustees may say with certainty that any given postulant is or is not a member of a class of objects, and that there is no need to draw up a list of all the objects. This means that if the question posed to hypothetical trustees is whether any given named person is a member of the class of objects and the answer is 'yes' or 'no', the test is satisfied. If, however, the trustees are unclear as to whether a person is within the class, the test will not be satisfied and the intended trust will fail with the consequence that a resulting trust will arise.

KEY CASE ANALYSIS: *McPhail v Doulton* [1971] AC 424, HL

Background

- The settlor, Bertram Baden, transferred property to trustees to apply the net income, in their absolute discretion, to the officers, ex-officers, employees and ex-employees of a company or their relatives or dependants.
- The question in issue was whether the trust was valid as satisfying the test for certainty of objects.
- At this time the test for certainty of objects for all private trusts was the 'list' test, as declared in the *Broadway Cottages* case. The trust objects were too broad to satisfy this narrow test.

Principle established

The House of Lords decided that the trust was valid and further changed the test for certainty of objects in respect of discretionary trusts. The new test for such trusts is whether the trustees may say with certainty that any given postulant is or is not a member of a class of objects, and that there is no need to draw up a list of the objects. This 'any given postulant' test was applicable to powers of appointment as illustrated in the House of Lords decision in *Re Gulbenkian's Settlement Trusts* [1970] AC 508. The court decided that, despite fundamental differences between a power of appointment and a discretionary trust, there were such similarities between the two concepts that the test for certainty of objects for powers of appointment ought to be extended to discretionary trusts.

On-the-spot question

What justification, if any, was there in *McPhail v Doulton (sub nom Re Baden)* to change the test for certainty of objects?

POWERS OF APPOINTMENT

A power of appointment (vested in the donee of the power or trustee) is an authority, as distinct from an obligation, to dispose of property in favour of a class of objects; for example, '£50,000 to my wife in the knowledge that she may distribute the funds to any or all of my children as she may decide in her absolute discretion'. This gift bears a similarity in appearance to a discretionary trust but it is fundamentally different from the latter because there is no duty to distribute the fund in favour of any of the objects. The donee of the power is merely empowered to consider distributing the property in favour of the objects, but is not required to do so.

On failure to distribute the property, the donee of the power is entitled to retain the fund for her own benefit. The reason is because a 'personal power' of appointment had been created (i.e. one created by virtue of the personal qualities of the donee of the power, namely the settlor's wife). If the property had been transferred to the appointor as a fiduciary (such as a trustee) and the fiduciary fails to distribute the property, a resulting trust in favour of the settlor will arise. This is referred to as a 'fiduciary power'. An exception to this rule was created in *Mettoy Pension Trustees Ltd v Evans* [1990] 1 WLR 1587, where the court decided that a 'fiduciary power in the full sense' was created by a company in respect of an occupational pension scheme. On the liquidation of the scheme, leaving a surplus of funds, the court decided that the power was not capable of being released.

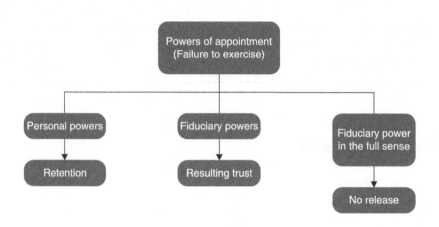

On-the-spot question

How does a power of appointment differ from a discretionary trust?

'Any given postulant' test

In extending the 'any given postulant' test from powers of appointment to discretionary trusts in *McPhail v Doulton*, Lord Wilberforce laid down three limitations: linguistic uncertainty, evidential uncertainty and administrative unworkability.

Linguistic uncertainty

Also known as conceptual uncertainty, linguistic uncertainty involves vagueness in defining the class of objects to such an extent that the class is incapable of legal definition. In this event, the gift will fail for uncertainty of objects and a resulting trust for the settlor will arise (e.g. on trust to distribute to persons with a moral claim on the settlor as the trustees may decide in their absolute discretion). This principle is applicable to both powers of appointment and discretionary trusts.

Evidential uncertainty

This principle applies to both trusts and powers but does not invalidate the gift. It involves practical difficulties in ascertaining the whereabouts of one or more members of the class of objects. In other words, it is clear *who* the member of the class is, but it is unclear whether the member is still alive or where he may be located. In this respect an application may be made to the court for directions as to how the trustees may proceed and it is advisable for the protection of the trustees. This is referred to as a 'Benjamin' order. The court may authorise a distribution on the assumption that the missing beneficiary is dead (see *Re Benjamin* [1902] 1 Ch 723).

Administrative unworkability

This refers to a definition of the class of objects that is so hopelessly wide as not to form 'anything like a class' (e.g. 'all the residents of Greater London'). This rule is restricted to discretionary trusts and, where it cannot be resolved by the court, the trust will be void. A mere power of appointment will not be invalidated solely because the size of the class of objects is excessive. In *R v District Auditors ex p West Yorkshire County Council* (1986) 26 RVR 24, county councillors attempted to set up a trust for the benefit of 'any or all or some of the inhabitants' of West Yorkshire (population numbering 2.5 million). The court decided that the gift was void owing to the size of the class of objects and a resulting trust had arisen. The reason for this approach stems from the obligatory nature of trusts. If the trust was valid in the first place and the trustees omitted to exercise their discretion, the court would have had enormous difficulty repairing the breach by exercising the discretion. However, in *Re Manisty's Settlement* [1974] Ch 17, Templeman J suggested in an *obiter* pronouncement that a power of appointment will be void for capriciousness if the terms of the power negative any sensible exercise of the discretion, such as ascertainment of the beneficiaries by height or colour. Whereas, in *Re Hay's Settlement* [1982] 1 WLR 202, Megarry VC reverted to the orthodox approach and regarded the issue of administrative unworkability as one concerning the size of the class of objects.

On-the-spot question

 Why did the court restrict the principle of administrative unworkability to discretionary trusts as distinct from powers of appointment?

Judicial approaches to the 'any given postulant' test

To date, there has been a wide-ranging series of judicial approaches to the 'any given postulant' test. In *McPhail v Doulton*, having changed the test for certainty of objects, the House of Lords remitted the case back to the High Court to determine whether the test was satisfied. The High Court and the Court of Appeal decided in favour of validity in *Re Baden (2)* [1972] 3 WLR 250. Each of the three Lords Justices of Appeal (Sachs, Megaw and Stamp LJJ) adopted a separate approach to the test.

Sachs LJ's approach is based on the assumption that the claimant is required to prove that he comes within the class. If he fails to discharge this burden of proof, then it follows that he is not within the class. This approach may be viewed as a practical method for the trustees to exercise their discretion, but for validity purposes this approach may have limited effect.

Megaw LJ's flexible approach requires the trustees to determine whether a substantial number of objects are clearly within the class of objects. If so, the gift is valid. What constitutes a substantial number is for the court to decide. This would vary with the facts of each case. Thus, the court has the power to decide what will be treated as the minimum number of objects in order to assess the validity of the gift. Having found this quota, it is immaterial whether it is unclear as to who else is within the class.

Stamp LJ's view heralds the traditional approach. The test will only be satisfied if the criterion for defining the class of objects is so clear that it is possible to say of 'any' given individual that he is within or outside the class. There is no room for doubt on this issue. In addition, if there are several classes of objects and one of these classes is unclear, the entire gift becomes void. There is no possibility of severance and validating part of the gift (e.g. a discretionary trust to relatives and friends) means that the gift is void if the expression 'friends' cannot be legally defined.

Further, the Court of Appeal in *Re Tuck Settlement Trust* [1978] Ch 49 laid down two further interpretations – the 'dictionary' and 'gifts subject to a condition precedent' approaches. The 'dictionary' approach requires the settlor to define, in part, the class of objects and leave it to an arbitrator to deal with any difficulties concerning the definition of the class. Thus, in *Re Tuck*, the meaning of 'an approved wife' was left to the arbitrator, the Chief Rabbi, to clarify. Therefore the gift was valid. The court also declared that a 'gift subject to a condition precedent' entitles the court to interpret the condition in a flexible manner. A gift subject to a condition precedent is one where the donee does not acquire an interest in the property until the condition is satisfied. Accordingly in *Re Barlow's Will Trust* [1979] 1 All ER 296, a testatrix bequeathed a collection of valuable paintings to 'family members and friends of mine'. The court decided that the gift was subject to a condition precedent and, despite the fact that the word 'friend' could not be legally defined, the quantum of the gift did not vary with the size of the class. Thus, once it was possible to find a number of friends (10 friends) equivalent to the number of paintings (10 paintings), the gift was valid.

On-the-spot question

Would the approach in *Re Barlow* be applicable in respect of a gift of £1,000:

(a) 'to my friends in equal shares'?
(b) '£10 to each of my friends'?

CASE LAW SUMMARY

Paul v Constance – The question of certainty of intention to create an express trust was satisfied when the settlor orally expressed his intention, and by his conduct indicated that a trust of a sum of money was created for the benefit of himself and partner in equal shares. His partner was a beneficiary of half of the fund under the *inter vivos* trust and, on the settlor's death, his estranged spouse became beneficially entitled to his half share as the next of kin.

Jones v Lock – An intended *inter vivos* gift of the proceeds of a cheque became imperfect because the donor failed to transfer the fund to his infant son, the intended donee. On the donor's death, the court decided that a trust by way of self-declaration was not created because there was little evidence that the donor intended to make himself a trustee of the fund for his son.

Re Steele's Will Trust – The question of certainty of intention is an objective question that is determined by reference to the facts of each case. The effect is that the doctrine of binding precedent is not applicable in determining this question. However, where it was clear that the settlor had relied on a legal precedent to express his intention, the court is entitled to conclude that the settlor's intention should be treated as the same as that which existed in the precedent.

Re Adams and Kensington Vestry – The use of precatory words in a will may or may not be sufficient to create an express trust. Much depends on the construction of the remaining clauses in the will and the surrounding circumstances. In this case the court decided that, on construction of the will and surrounding circumstances, no trust had been intended and the property had been acquired beneficially by the testator's widow.

Comiskey v Bowring-Hanbury – The use of precatory words on the facts of this case imported an intention to create an express trust of specified property for his widow for life, with remainder to his nieces as the widow may select in her will. In default of selection by the widow, the nieces were entitled to the estate equally.

Re Kayford – The question of certainty of intention to create an express trust was considered in the context of a commercial transaction. The evidence indicated that an express trust was intended for the benefit of customers of a mail order company. The company took advice on the means of protecting deposits paid by customers from the claims of creditors and acted on such advice before it went into liquidation. The effect was that the company acted as the settlor and trustee for the customers.

Sprange v Barnard – The test for certainty of subject matter (trust property) was not satisfied on these facts because of the vagueness in identifying the intended trust property.

Palmer v Simmonds – The intended trust property that was required to be subject to the trust was too imprecise to create an express trust. The effect was that the transferee acquired the property beneficially with no more than a moral obligation to devote part of the fund to the stated objects.

Re London Wine Co – Quantities of wine bought by customers, but stored by the vendor, were not subject to trusts before the vendor went into liquidation, the reason being that property in the wine had not passed to the purchasers in commercial law and the property was too uncertain in trusts law. The company's creditors were therefore entitled to the goods.

Hunter v Moss – In the case of fungibles where the property is indistinguishable, such as one type of shares in a company, the strict test in trust law for the specific allocation of the property is not necessary. Accordingly, the indication of a percentage of the shares, say 5 percent, was sufficient to satisfy the test for certainty of subject matter.

IRC v Broadway Cottages – The test for certainty of objects was the narrow 'list' test, which was not satisfied on the facts of this case. At this time the 'list' test was applicable to both fixed and discretionary trusts.

McPhail v Doulton (sub nom Re Baden) – The House of Lords changed the test for certainty of objects in respect of discretionary trusts by adopting the broader 'any given postulant' test.

R v District Auditors ex p West Yorkshire County Council – In judicial review proceedings, the High Court decided that an intended discretionary trust was void owing to administrative unworkability. The class of objects was so hopelessly wide that the courts would find it difficult to decide whether the discretion was validly exercised.

Re Tuck – The Court of Appeal decided that a potentially vague objects clause in a will was saved by virtue of a valid arbitration clause.

Re Barlow – The High Court decided that a potentially uncertain trust clause in a will was valid. In this case the gift was made subject to a condition precedent and the court was entitled to construe such condition in a generous manner.

ISSUES TO THINK ABOUT FURTHER

The broad 'any given postulant' test introduced by the House of Lords in *McPhail v Doulton* assimilated the test for certainty of objects for powers of appointment with the test for certainty of objects for discretionary trusts. In a sense, the purpose was to simplify the test for discretionary trusts, but the multitude of decisions of the courts, and at times the inconsistent approaches to the test, may be sufficient to justify a comment that the test is so unclear that only a decision of the Supreme Court may instil a degree of certainty in this area of the law.

To what extent has the *Baden* litigation clarified the law of certainty of objects in respect of discretionary trusts?

SUMMARY

- We can see that the three certainties test (intention, subject matter and objects) exists to determine whether a valid declaration of trust was made by the settlor.
- The settlor need not use the word 'trust' as the approach of the court is that 'equity looks at the intent rather than the form'.
- The test for certainty of intention is whether, on construction of all the relevant facts (words and conduct), the settlor intended to impose trust duties on the relevant property. This is a question of degree and not subject to binding precedent.
- Certainty of intention to create a trust is narrower and distinct from an intention to benefit another. The court will not lightly impose a trust on property.
- Precatory words may or may not manifest a trust intention. The will and surrounding circumstances are required to be construed in order to determine the true intention of the testator.
- The effect of uncertainty of intention to create a trust is that the intended settlor or transferee is entitled to deal with the property as he wishes and may retain it beneficially.
- Certainty of subject matter includes certainty of trust property and beneficial interest.
- The test for certainty of subject matter is whether the subject is identified or is identifiable to such an extent that the court may attach a court order on the relevant property.
- Uncertainty of trust property creates a reflex action on intention with the consequence that no trust exists.
- The effect of uncertainty of beneficial interest is that, although the intended express trust fails, a resulting trust for the transferor will be created.
- There are two separate tests for certainty of objects:

  - The test for fixed trusts is the 'list' test (or 'class ascertainability' test) requiring the trustees to be able to draw up a comprehensive list of all the objects.
  - The test for certainty of objects regarding discretionary trusts is the same as that for powers of appointment.

- The test for discretionary trusts and powers of appointment is the 'any given postulant' (or the 'individual ascertainability') test:

  - This test is subject to 'conceptual', 'evidential' and 'administrative unworkability' limitations.
  - The courts have advocated a variety of approaches to the 'any given postulant' test – proof of entitlement (Sachs LJ), substantial number (Megaw LJ), strict (Stamp LJ) in *Re Baden (2)*, dictionary, gifts subject to conditions precedent (*Re Tuck* and *Re Barlow*).

- The effect of uncertainty of objects is that the intended express trust fails and a resulting trust arises.

FURTHER READING

Battersby G, 'A reconsideration of "Property" and "Title" in the Sale of Goods Act' [2001] JBL 1. [Analysis of the concepts of 'title', 'property' and 'ownership' in the Sale of Goods Act 1979.]

Emery C, 'The most hallowed principle – certainty of beneficiaries in trusts and powers of appointment' (1982) 98 LQR 551.
[Analyses the test for certainty of objects in respect of discretionary trusts and powers of appointment, and argues that the cardinal principle here is whether the settlor has imposed duties on his trustees that are capable of being exercised by them or, in default, by the courts.]

Hayton D, 'Uncertainty of subject-matter of trusts' (1994) 110 LQR 335.
[A critical analysis of the principle laid down in *Hunter v Moss* and the unjustified way in which the principle in *Re London Wine* was distinguished.]

Jones A, 'Creating a trust over an unascertained part of a homogeneous whole' [1993] Conv 466.
[Analysis of *Hunter v Moss* and consideration of how far a declaration of trust of part of property that has not been ascertained may be sufficient to identify the trust property.]

Martin J, 'Certainty of objects – what is heresy?' [1984] Conv 304.
[In reply to an article written by Paul Matthews, where that author sought to establish that the 'list' test is a heresy, Jill Martin maintains that the test for certainty of objects for fixed trusts is the list test. The issue is whether a comprehensive list of objects is capable of being drawn to reflect the maximum quantum of shares that may be taken by the beneficiaries.]

Martin J, 'Certainty of subject-matter: a defence of *Hunter v Moss*' [1996] Conv 223.
[In defence of the *Hunter v Moss* principle, Martin argues that the solution is fair, sensible and workable. The case did not involve claims by unsecured creditors to gain priority on insolvency, and to uphold a declaration of trust of part of a shareholding or bank balance would not prejudice creditors. Such a trust may justifiably involve a separation of interests in the same way as a trust of the entire shareholding or bank balance.']

Ramjohn M, 'Text, Cases and Materials on Equity and Trusts', 4th edn (Routledge-Cavendish, 2008).
[Detailed text and materials on the subject.]

Ramjohn M, 'Unlocking Trusts', 4th edn (Routledge, 2013).
[A comprehensive and up to date text written in simple, clear language that de-mystifies complicated concepts in trusts law.]

Worthington S, 'Sorting out ownership interests in a bulk: gifts, sales and trusts' (1999) JBL 1.
[Case law analysis of when an individual acquires ownership of an interest in part of a bulk, be it tangible or intangible property.]

COMPANION WEBSITE

An online glossary compiled by the author is available on the companion website:
www.routledge.com/cw/beginningthelaw

Chapter 5
Constitution of a trust and formalities

LEARNING OUTCOMES

At the end of this chapter, you should be able to:

- Identify the essential tests laid down in *Milroy v Lord* for the creation of an express trust
- Recognise whether the formal requirements are satisfied
- Understand the effect of creating a perfect trust
- Appreciate the maxim, 'equity will not assist a volunteer'
- Comprehend the principles established in the *Strong v Bird* rule, *donatio mortis causa* and proprietary estoppel

INTRODUCTION

In Chapter 4 we considered the 'three certainties' test as a means of establishing a valid declaration of trust. In this chapter we will progress to put together the essential building blocks for the creation of an express trust. The theme here is to ascertain whether the trust property has been vested in the trustee and its effect. When the property has been acquired by the trustee subject to a valid declaration of trust, the trust is said to be 'perfect' or 'completely constituted'. Occasionally, the settlor is required to comply with specific formal requirements as laid down by Parliament.

MODES OF CREATION

There are generally two modes of creation of an express trust. These methods were laid down by Turner LJ in *Milroy v Lord*, as a transfer and declaration of trust and a self-declaration of trust. The policy behind the test is that no express trust may be created without the trustee acquiring control of the trust property for the stated purposes. We have already considered whether the settlor has validly declared a trust (i.e. the three certainties test).

Milroy v Lord (1862) 31 LJ Ch 798, **Turner LJ**:

> . . . in order to render a voluntary settlement valid and effectual, the settlor must have done everything which, according to the nature of the property

comprised in the settlement, was necessary to be done in order to transfer the property and render the settlement binding upon him. He may, of course, do this . . . if he transfers the property to a trustee for the purposes of the settlement, or declares that he himself holds it in trust for those purposes . . . but, in order to render the settlement binding, one or other of these modes must . . . be resorted to, for there is no equity in this court to perfect an imperfect gift.

Self-declaration of trust

A settlor may create an express trust by making himself a trustee of the property for the beneficiary. This intention is required to be expressly manifested by reference to the words stated by the settlor and the surrounding circumstances. This principle was examined in Chapter 4 by reference to the three certainties test.

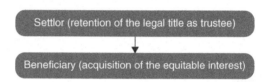

Figure 5.1 Illustration of a self-declaration of trust

Indeed, a sub-trust (i.e. a secondary trust created out of a primary trust) may be created by an original beneficiary in respect of his equitable interest. For example, Terry, a trustee, holds the legal title to property upon trust for Barry, a beneficiary. Barry may declare himself a trustee for Charles. In this case, Barry is the beneficiary under the head trust, but he is a settlor and trustee for Charles under the sub-trust.

If the trust property consists of land, the declaration of trust is required to be evidenced in writing in order to comply with s 53(1)(b) of the Law of Property Act 1925, which declares as follows:

> A declaration of trust respecting any land or any interest therein must be manifested and proved by some writing signed by some person who is able to declare such trust or by his will.

Section 2(6) of the Law of Property (Miscellaneous Provisions) Act 1989 defines 'an interest in land' as 'any estate, interest or charge in or over the land'. Thus all rights in or over the land involve interests in land. But s 53(1)(b) is purely evidential in the sense that it is concerned with proof of the terms of the trust, not the validity of the trust. For example, Sam may orally declare himself a trustee of a plot of land, Whiteacre, for Betty absolutely. The declaration of trust does not become void, but merely unenforceable in law for lack of evidence in writing.

Transfer and declaration

It is an elementary rule of trusts law that no trust may be created without the trustee acquiring the relevant property. Accordingly, if a settlor wishes to create a trust by this mode, it is incumbent upon him to transfer the property to the trustee, subject to the terms of the trust. A failure to transfer the property to the nominated trustee will not be construed as an effective self-declaration of trust, with the settlor as the trustee. This was laid down in *Jones v Lock* (see Chapter 4). This classic rule may be illustrated by *Richards v Delbridge*.

KEY CASE ANALYSIS: *Richards v Delbridge* (1874) LR 18 Eq 11

Background

- A grandfather attempted to assign a lease of business premises to his grandson, R.
- The assignment was ineffective because a deed was not executed.
- The grandfather delivered the legal lease to R's mother to hold on his behalf.

The question in issue was whether the business premises were acquired by the grandson, R, during the grandfather's lifetime.

Principle established

The court decided that the intended transfer was imperfect because a deed was not executed. Further, no trust had been created, as the grandfather had not declared himself a trustee of the lease for the grandson. In addition, the court will not imply that an ineffectual transfer will be converted into a valid declaration of trust.

Both modes may be expressly adopted by the settlor

The settlor is entitled to declare a trust by adopting both modes of creation (i.e. a self-declaration and a transfer and declaration). But this intention of the settlor is required to be clearly expressed because, as we have seen, the court will not imply a self-declaration. In any event, the principle involved is that the transfer of the property to the nominated trustee must take effect during the lifetime of the transferor, *Re Ralli*.

KEY CASE ANALYSIS: *Re Ralli's Will Trust* [1964] Ch 288

Background

- In 1899, a testator died, leaving the residue of his estate upon trust for his wife for life with remainder to his two children, Helen and Irene, absolutely.
- In 1924, Helen covenanted in her marriage settlement to settle all her 'existing and after acquired property' upon trusts, which failed, and ultimately on trust for the children of Irene.
- The settlement expressly declared that Helen will hold all of the relevant property upon trust, pending the transfer to the third-party trustee.
- Irene's husband was appointed one of the trustees of this marriage settlement.
- In 1946, Irene's husband was also appointed a trustee of the 1899 settlement.
- In 1956, Helen died and, in 1961, Helen and Irene's mother died.

The question in issue was whether Helen's property that derived from the 1899 settlement was held upon the trusts of Helen's marriage settlement, or subject to Helen's personal estate.

Principle established

The court held that a valid trust had been created. Helen was the initial trustee and, in 1946, Irene's husband (the nominated trustee) acquired Helen's property, as trustee of the 1899 settlement. This was the position even though the vesting of the property in Irene's husband came to him in his other capacity as trustee of the 1899 settlement. The same conclusion may be reached by applying the rule in *Strong v Bird* (1874) LR 18 Eq 315 (see later).

On-the-spot question

How would you reconcile the principle in *Richards v Delbridge* with *Re Ralli*?

LAST ACT THEORY

This principle was laid down in *Milroy v Lord* (above) and involves a relaxation of the strict legal principle requiring a transfer of the legal title to the trustee. The rule is that where the donor has done everything required of him to transfer the property to the intended transferee, but something outside his control is required to be completed by a third party in order to transfer the legal title, the transfer will nevertheless be effective in equity. This involves an interim constructive trust. The principle may be illustrated by reference to the transfer of shares in a private company. The procedure concerning the transfer of such shares is laid down in the Companies Act 2006. This requires the transferor to execute a share transfer form issued under the Stock Transfer Act 1963. The form, along with the share certificates, is required to be sent to the registered office of the company. The company has up to two months to notify the transferor as to whether the transfer had been successful. The legal title will be transferred when the new owner is registered in the company's share register. But the equitable interest will be transferred when the transferor has done everything necessary for him to do in order to complete the transfer. The principle is also known as the *Re Rose* rule.

KEY CASE ANALYSIS: *Re Rose* [1952] Ch 499

Background

- Mr Rose executed two transfers of shares on 30 March 1943.
- He died more than five years after executing the transfers but less than five years (the claw-back period for estate duty at this time) after the transfers were registered in the company's books, on 30 June 1943, the date of the transfer of the legal title.
- The precise date of the transfer was required to be ascertained for estate duty purposes.

Principle established

The court held that the shares were transferred in equity on 30 March 1943. At this time the transferor had done everything in his power to transfer the shares, and all that remained outstanding was for the directors of the company to consent to the transfer and register the new owner.

On the other hand, in *Re Fry* [1946] Ch 312, a gift of shares was not effective in equity. Prior to his death, the donor had failed to obtain Treasury approval before delivering the share transfer form to the company. This approval was required to be obtained before the company became entitled to consider the transfer. The effect was that transfer was not valid during the lifetime of the transferor. In a recent case, *Pennington v Waine*, the Court of Appeal endorsed the *Re Rose* principle, but laid down an alternative formula based on 'unconscionability' on the part of the transferor. The difficulty is that such a vague concept may only be clarified in the future by reference to decided cases.

KEY CASE ANALYSIS: *Pennington v Waine* [2002] All ER (D) 24

Background

* The donor, Ada, intended to transfer 400 shares in a private company to her nephew, Harold, in order to secure his holding of 51% of the shares and appointment as a director.
* She was assured by Mr Pennington, one of the company's auditors, that the transfer of the shares will be made by him.
* The executed transfer form was placed in Mr Pennington's file.
* Mr Pennington assured Harold that he was appointed a director and nothing more was required to be done by him.
* No further action was taken in relation to the transfer.
* Ada died and by her will left her estate to others.

The question in issue was whether a transfer of the shares in equity had been made by Ada before her death in favour of Harold, or whether the shares passed to her heirs under her will.

Principle established

The court decided that a transfer in equity in favour of Harold had been made during Ada's lifetime. The test was whether Ada had done everything required of her to secure the transfer, as distinct from whether she had done everything short of registration. Further, that it would have been unconscionable for Ada and her heirs to deny the interest acquired by Harold.

On-the-spot question

Alvin owns 5,000 shares in Moneyco Ltd, a private company. Alvin wishes to transfer these shares to Bertram and, on 30 July 2011, executes a share transfer form that he sends along with the share certificates to the registered office of Moneyco Ltd. On 10 August 2011 the company pays a dividend of £250 to Alvin in respect of the shares. On 1 September 2011, the company registers Bertram as the new owner of 5,000 shares.

Is Alvin a trustee of the dividend of £250 in favour of Bertram?

MULTIPLE TRUSTEES, INCLUDING THE SETTLOR

Where a settlor clearly intended to create a trust by nominating a number of individuals to become trustees, including himself, the trust will be valid even though he fails to transfer the property to the third-party trustees. The principle is based on the premise that if one trustee acquires the property (the retention of the property by the settlor), this is equivalent to all the trustees acquiring control of the property. For example, Sam, a settlor, agrees to create a trust of £50,000 standing to his credit in Santander Bank plc and appoints Fred, Jones and himself as trustees. The failure to transfer the property to Fred and Jones will not invalidate the trust, for Sam retains the property as a trustee and the trust obligation will attach to the fund. This was decided by the Privy Council in *Choithram v Pagarani*.

KEY CASE ANALYSIS: *Choithram v Pagarani* [2001] 1 WLR 1

Background

- The settlor, Mr Choithram Pagarani (CP), was suffering from a terminal illness but intended to benefit a charitable organisation.
- He executed a trust deed nominating himself and seven other named persons as trustees.
- CP then declared, 'I have given all my wealth to the trust'.
- He then told his accountant to prepare the documents in order to transfer the relevant funds to the trustees.
- At a subsequent meeting with the trustees, CP reported that the trust had been established and all his wealth had been given to the trust, but he refused to sign the documents.
- Evidence was adduced that CP had an aversion to signing such documents and had been advised that it was not necessary to do so.
- CP repeatedly declared that he had given all his wealth to the charity and there was nothing more for him to do.
- In the end, CP had failed to execute the forms that were necessary to carry out the formal transfer of the further assets before his death.

The question in issue was whether the trust was valid, despite the omission to transfer the property to the third-party trustees.

Principle established

The court decided that the trust was valid on the ground that the property was vested in one of the trustees, namely CP himself. Accordingly, there was a duty to transfer the property to the remaining trustees. In principle, there was no distinction between a case where a settlor declared himself to be a sole trustee for a beneficiary and the case where he declared himself to be one of the trustees for that beneficiary. In both cases, the trust was perfect and the beneficiary acquired an equitable proprietary interest in the property.

FUTURE PROPERTY

A clearly established principle is that a trust may only be created in respect of existing property. Accordingly, a trust cannot be created in respect of an 'expectancy' or 'future property' – such as an anticipated interest under a will during the lifetime of the testator – because no property exists that is capable of being subject to the protection of equity. The anticipated property may or may not be acquired by the settlor in the future. In *Re Ellenborough* [1903] 1 Ch 697, an expected legacy under the will of a person who was still alive was incapable of forming the subject matter of a trust.

CHOSES IN ACTION

A 'chose in action' is a right that exists in intangible personal property, such as the right to be paid royalties (copyright), the right to receive dividends (shares), the creditor's right to have a loan repaid, etc. The chose (or right) may be assigned to the trustees in accordance with the intention of the settlor. Thus, a chose is capable of being the subject matter of a trust. In *Don King Productions Inc v Warren* [1998] 2 All ER 608, the court decided that the benefit of promotion and management agreements created by boxing promoters was capable of being the subject matter of a trust.

Likewise, a trust may be created in respect of the 'benefit of a covenant', which is a chose in action. In *Fletcher v Fletcher* (1844) 4 Hare 67, the court decided that a settlor who executed a covenant to transfer £60,000 to the trustees had transferred the benefit of the covenant to the trustees. Thus, the trust was perfect even though the money was not transferred to the trustees. But in *Re Cook's Settlement Trust* [1965] Ch 902, the court restricted the *Fletcher v Fletcher* principle to one type of chose namely, debts enforceable at law (i.e. obligations to transfer money).

On-the-spot question

? Sam executes a deed with Tom and Jerry agreeing to transfer 5,000 shares in Marks and Spencer plc to them to hold upon trust for David absolutely. Sam fails to transfer the shares to Tom and Jerry. Would a trust for David be created under the *Fletcher v Fletcher* rule?

INTER VIVOS DISPOSITIONS OF EQUITABLE INTERESTS

Where the subject matter of the trust is an equitable interest in either real or personal property, the person disposing of such interest (i.e. the beneficiary or equitable owner) is required to express his intention in a signed document. Failure to execute the document means that the intended disposition is void and the intended transferee does not acquire the equitable interest.

Section 53(1)(c) of the Law of Property Act 1925 provides that 'a disposition of an equitable interest or trust subsisting at the time of disposition must be in writing signed by the person disposing of the same or by his agent thereunto lawfully authorised in writing or by his will'.

It should be noted that the subsection is only concerned with 'subsisting equitable interests' (i.e. interests that already exist under a trust).

> ## Example
>
> Tristram and Shirley hold Blackacre upon trust for Blake absolutely. Blake enjoys a subsisting equitable interest. If he wishes to dispose of his interest, he must do so in writing.

The key feature of the subsection is the meaning of the expression 'disposition'. Romer LJ in *Timpson's Executors v Yerbury* [1936] 1 KB 645, classified a disposition by a beneficiary under a trust into the following four categories:

(i)   An assignment to a third party, such as a gift to another by a beneficiary under a trust. In the example above, where Blake makes a gift of his interest to Daphne.

(ii)   A direction to the trustees to hold on trust for a third party. In the example above, where Blake directs Tristram and Shirley to hold his interest upon trust for Daphne absolutely (see *Grey v IRC* [1960] AC 1).

(iii)   A contract for valuable consideration to assign the equitable interest, for example, a sale of an equitable interest. In the example above, Blake agrees to sell his interest to Daphne for £10,000 (see *Oughtred v IRC* [1960] AC 206).

(iv)   A self-declaration by the beneficiary in favour of another, for example, the creation of a trust for another. In the example above, Blake declares himself a trustee for Daphne.

In each of the illustrations above, Blake's disposition of his equitable interest is required to be in writing in order to be effective.

However, in *Vandervell v IRC* [1967] 2 AC 291, the House of Lords decided that s 53(1)(c) has no application where a trust is terminated in favour of a third party by the unification of the legal and equitable interests. For example, if Tom and Fred hold the legal title to property on trust for David absolutely, and David instructs Tom and Fred to transfer the legal title to Frank, and in the same transaction, David transfers his equitable interest to Frank. The effect is that Frank becomes the absolute owner of the property and the trust is terminated.

On-the-spot question

? Harold and Tom hold 50 gold coins upon trust for Charlie. Is s 53(1)(c) of the Law of Property Act 1925 applicable if Charlie:

(i)   orally directs the trustees to hold the coins on trust for Eric?
(ii) orally declares himself a trustee for Eric?

EFFECT OF CREATING A TRUST

When an express trust is created, the beneficiaries are given a recognisable equitable interest in the property. They are entitled to protect their interest against anyone, except the *bona fide* purchaser of the legal estate for value without notice (see Chapter 3). The trustees (as representatives of the trust) are entitled to bring or defend an action on behalf of the trust and, failing this, the beneficiaries have the power to litigate on behalf of the trust. This is the position even if the beneficiary is a 'volunteer' (i.e. has not provided consideration).

Figure 5.2 Illustration of the enforceability of a perfect trust

If the trust is imperfect, the intended beneficiaries may only commence an action if they have provided consideration (i.e. if they are non-volunteers). In other words, a non-volunteer of an imperfect trust is placed in almost the same position as a beneficiary under a trust. In *Pullan v Koe* [1913] 1 Ch 9, a non-volunteer (child of an intended marriage settlement) was entitled to bring a claim in equity to force a settlor to transfer property to the trustees.

On the other hand, where the claimant is a volunteer, he would not be entitled to enforce the imperfect trust, subject to the Contracts (Rights of Third Parties) Act 1999. The imperfect trust is treated as an agreement to create a trust and may only be enforced by a person who has provided consideration. The principle here is that 'equity will not assist a volunteer'. For example, Alvin orally agrees with Bernard to transfer £5,000 to him to hold on trust for Charlie. Alvin fails to transfer the money to Bernard. The trust is therefore imperfect, subject to statutory provisions to the contrary. Charlie cannot sue Alvin to enforce the agreement if he is a volunteer.

A 'volunteer' is one who has not provided valuable consideration. Valuable consideration refers to either money or money's worth or marriage consideration. Money or money's worth (i.e. common law consideration) is the price put on an agreement by each party. Marriage consideration takes the form of an ante-nuptial settlement made in consideration of marriage. The parties to the marriage and their children are deemed to provide marriage consideration and are therefore non-volunteers. For example, on the occasion of Mary's marriage to Douglas, Sam promises to transfer £15,000 to John and Paul to hold upon trust for Mary for life, Douglas for life, with remainder to the children of the marriage absolutely. If Sam fails to transfer the fund to John and Paul, the trust is imperfect and operates as an agreement to create a trust. Mary, Douglas and the children of the marriage are within the marriage consideration and may enforce the agreement as non-volunteers.

The Contracts (Rights of Third Parties) Act 1999 empowers a third party to a contract to bring a claim in his own right to enforce an agreement. This statutory right may assist a volunteer to claim damages (but not an equitable remedy) for a breach of contract to create a trust.

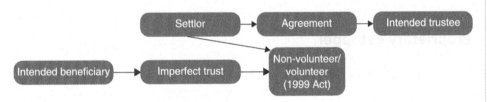

Figure 5.3 Illustration of the enforceability of an imperfect trust

EXCEPTIONS TO THE RULE THAT 'EQUITY WILL NOT ASSIST A VOLUNTEER'

There are a number of occasions when, despite a gift or trust being regarded as imperfect, equity would give assistance to volunteers and force the defendant to complete the intended gift or trust. These are the rules in *Strong v Bird, donatio mortis causa* and proprietary estoppel.

Strong v Bird rule

The rule in *Strong v Bird* (1874) LR 18 Eq 315 is to the effect that where an *inter vivos* gift is imperfect by reason only of the failure to transfer the property to the intended donee, the gift will become perfect if the donee acquires the property in the capacity of executor of the donor's estate. The reason for the rule is that, in probate law, the executor becomes entitled to the estate of the deceased and the ineffective transfer *inter vivos* will be cured by operation of law on the death of the transferor. In *Strong v Bird*, a loan that was granted during the lifetime of a deceased person was effectively discharged without consideration in favour of the debtor/executor.

The donor's intention is of paramount importance. He is required to manifest a present, continuous intention to make an *inter vivos* gift. This is a question of degree.

Donatio mortis causa (DMC)

These are referred to as 'deathbed gifts'. A DMC is an *inter vivos* delivery of property by a person contemplating death, subject to the condition that the gift will take effect only on the donor's death. The effect is that on the donor's death, the conditional transfer becomes complete and the donee (volunteer) is entitled to retain the property. In short, the donee under a DMC takes the property in priority over those beneficiaries named in the will. For example, Thomas made his will appointing Alvin as his executor. By his will, Thomas disposed of all his property to Bret. Feeling unwell, Thomas delivered his Rolex watch to Calvin, telling him that if he were to pass away Calvin could keep the watch. On Thomas's death, the gift of the watch becomes complete.

Proprietary estoppel

Proprietary estoppel is a right given to a volunteer whenever a landowner stands by and permits a volunteer to incur expenditure in order to improve his (the landowner's) property on the promise or assumption that there will be a transfer of an interest to him. The modern tendency of the court is to have regard to all the circumstances of the case and decide whether it would be unconscionable to deny the claimant an interest or right in the land. The key characteristics are assurance, reliance and detriment. In *Greasley v Cooke* [1980] 3 All ER 710, a maid relied on an assurance that she may live in the house as long as she wished, provided she continued to care for the family without payment. The court decided that she was entitled to remain in the property rent free for as long as she wished.

CASE LAW SUMMARY

Milroy v Lord – An intended express trust was imperfect because the transferor had not done everything required of him to transfer the property to the trustees. This case is associated with the requirements for the creation of an express trust and the effects of a perfectly constituted and imperfectly constituted trust.

Richards v Delbridge – The court will not automatically treat an imperfect transfer as a valid self-declaration of trust by the settlor.

Re Ralli – A settlor may expressly declare that, pending a transfer of property to third-party trustees, he or she will become the trustee. If this procedure is adopted, the trust will become perfect when the third-party trustee acquires the property during the settlor's lifetime.

Re Rose – A transfer of the equitable interest in property becomes effective when the transferor has done everything required of him in order to transfer the property.

Re Fry – The transferor had not done everything that was required of him to complete the transfer and, accordingly, the transfer was ineffective in equity.

Pennington v Waine – The Court of Appeal affirmed and applied the *Re Rose* principle (above) and laid down a separate test of unconscionability in order to enforce a transfer in equity

Choithram v Pagarani – The Privy Council decided that where there is evidence that a transferor had a settled and irrevocable intention to create an express trust and appointed multiple trustees including himself, the trust was perfect even though the third-party trustees did not acquire the trust property. The settlor becomes the trustee of the settlement and trustee obligations will be imposed on him.

Fletcher v Fletcher – A transfer of a specified sum of money in a deed (the benefit of a covenant) will be effective where the transferor intended the subject of the transfer to be a chose in action and a debt enforceable at law.

Vandervell v IRC – The House of Lords decided that s 53(1)(c) of the LPA 1925 (dispositions of subsisting equitable interests in writing) was not applicable where the transferor intended to transfer both the legal and equitable interests in property to a third party.

Grey v IRC – The House of Lords decided that an oral direction to the trustees to hold property on trust for beneficiaries was void for non-compliance with s 53(1)(c) of the LPA 1925.

Oughtred v IRC – The Law Lords expressed differences of opinion as to whether s 53(2) (implied resulting and constructive trusts) restricts the application of s 53(1)(c) of the LPA 1925. The preferred view was expressed by Lord Radcliffe to the effect that the resulting or constructive trust limits the effect of s 53(1)(c).

Pullan v Koe – The court decided that a non-volunteer (child within a marriage settlement) was entitled in equity to enforce an agreement to create a trust.

ISSUES TO THINK ABOUT FURTHER

A settlor, Selwyn, executes a deed with an intended trustee, Trevor, to transfer £20,000 to him to hold upon trust for Bernard, a beneficiary, absolutely and Selwyn fails to transfer the sum to Trevor. The question arises as to whether the trust may be treated as perfect. If so, Bernard will be a beneficiary and is capable of enforcing the trust. Since Selwyn has failed to transfer the fund to Trevor, it is arguable that the trust is imperfect (see *Milroy v Lord*) and the court will not imply that Selwyn is the trustee (see *Richards v Delbridge*). But *Fletcher v Fletcher* decided that in such a case the trust may be treated as perfect on the ground that the trust property has been acquired by Trevor. The trust property may be construed as the 'benefit of the covenant' (i.e. a chose in action that had been transferred when the deed was executed).

Critically evaluate the rule in *Fletcher v Fletcher*, indicating what judicial limits have been imposed on the rule.

SUMMARY

- A trust is perfectly created when the settlor declares himself a trustee for the beneficiary or transfers the property to third-party trustees upon trust for the beneficiary.
- In addition, the trust will be perfect where the settlor declares himself a trustee pending the transfer of the property to third-party trustees, provided that they (trustees) acquire the property during the lifetime of the settlor.
- The transfer will be effective in equity where the transferor has done everything required of him to transfer the property, but some action outside the control of the transferor is required to be concluded by a third party to secure the transfer of the legal title.
- If the subject matter of the trust is land, the declaration of trust is required to be evidenced in writing.

- A trust will be created in respect of multiple trustees, including the settlor, even if the third-party trustees do not acquire the trust property during the lifetime of the settlor. In this event, the settlor will become the trustee.
- A trust may only be created in respect of existing property.
- A disposition of a subsisting equitable interest is required to be made in writing.
- The effect of a perfect trust is that the beneficiary acquires an equitable interest that he may enforce, irrespective of whether he is a volunteer or not.
- Subject to the Contracts (Rights of Third Parties) Act 1999, an imperfect trust operates as an agreement to create a trust and may be enforced by those providing consideration.
- In exceptional cases, equity will assist a volunteer. These are the rules in *Strong v Bird, donatio mortis causa* and proprietary estoppel.

FURTHER READING

Battersby G, 'Formalities for the Disposition of Equitable Interests under a Trust' [1979] 43 Conv 17.
[Analyses the leading cases on s 53(1)(c) of the Law of Property Act 1925, *Grey, Vandervell* and *Oughtred*, and considers the various methods by which a beneficiary may deal with his equitable interest and whether his dealings with the interest falls within the ambit of s 53(1)(c).]

Garton J, 'The role of the trust mechanism in *Re Rose*' [2003] Conv 364.
[Considers the application of the *Re Rose* rule in *Pennington v Waine* and examines the point at which the equitable interest passes.]

Green B, 'Grey, Oughtred and Vandervell, a contextual re-appraisal' [1984] 47 MLR 385.
[Analyses the seminal cases, *Grey, Vandervell* and *Oughtred,* which involved the application of s 53(1)(c) of the Law of Property Act 1925. The conclusion is drawn that no distinction exists in the cases between dealings with the equitable interests carrying beneficial rights and dealings with the equitable interests shorn of beneficial rights. Both types of dealings fall within the ambit of s 53(1)(c).]

Jones G, 'The enforcement of settlements in equity by volunteers' [1965] 23 CLJ 46.
[Analyses the principle in *Re Cook* and questions whether Buckley J's conclusion was correct in that the covenant operated only to prevent a sale by the covenantor himself and not a sale by the donee.]

Ramjohn M, 'Text, Cases and Materials on Equity and Trusts', 4th edn (Routledge-Cavendish, 2008).
[A text and casebook that provides a detailed account of the subject.]

Ramjohn M, 'Unlocking Trusts', 4th edn (Routledge, 2013).
[A comprehensive and up to date text written in simple, clear language that de-mystifies complicated concepts in trusts law.]

Rickett C, 'Completely constituting an *inter vivos* trust: property rules?' [2001] Conv 515.
[Critical analysis of the decision in *Choithram v Pagarani* as to the extent of the trust becoming perfect without all the trustees acquiring the property.]

COMPANION WEBSITE

An online glossary compiled by the author is available on the companion website:
www.routledge.com/cw/beginningthelaw

Chapter 6
Private purpose trusts

LEARNING OUTCOMES

At the end of this chapter, you should be able to:

- Define private purpose trusts
- Ascertain the reasons why such trusts are void
- Identify anomalous exceptions to the general rule
- Understand the difficulties created in respect of gifts to unincorporated associations

INTRODUCTION

In Chapter 4 we analysed the 'three certainties' test and, in particular, the test for certainty of beneficiaries, and in Chapter 5 we considered the mechanics of creating an express trust. In this chapter, we will highlight one limitation to the creation of an express trust, namely the 'beneficiary' principle (i.e. the legal requirement that a private trust may only be valid if it is designed to benefit persons who are capable of enforcing the trust). In short, the settlor is required to identify a beneficiary with the capacity to enforce the trust. Thus, a trust that promotes a private purpose is void because a purpose does not have the capacity to enforce the trust. In addition, unincorporated associations (such as many tennis and golf clubs) promote objects that are stated in their constitutions. The status of such associations will be examined and the difficulties posed by making gifts to such bodies will be considered. The courts have adopted a number of approaches in dealing with the validity of such gifts.

PRIVATE PURPOSE TRUSTS

A purpose trust, as the name suggests, is an intended express trust designed to promote a purpose as an end in itself. The settlor intends to create the trust for beneficiaries that are essentially purposes, such as the discovery of an alphabet of 40 letters (*Re Shaw* [1957] 1 WLR 729) or the boarding up of certain rooms in a house (*Brown v Burdett* (1882) 21 Ch D 667). In such cases, the beneficiaries identified by the settlor are *purposes* that are primarily intended to be promoted by the trust, even though individuals may indirectly enjoy benefits from such trusts. The benefit to individuals is regarded as purely incidental to the main purpose of creating the trust. The effect is that such trusts are treated as void and resulting trusts for the settlor or his estate (if he is dead) will arise in default. This rule is subject to a number of exceptions, which are discussed below.

The rationale for invalidating private purpose trusts is that no beneficiary has a sufficient locus standi to enforce the trust. The primary objects of the trust, namely purposes, are incapable of enforcing the trust and incidental beneficiaries, such as individuals, have insufficient interests to be entitled to enforce the trust. But why is it important that the primary beneficiaries are capable of enforcing the trust? The reason is that the trust is required to be subject to the control of the court. In order to ensure that the trust is properly administered by the trustees, there needs to be a beneficiary who is capable of bringing a claim in the court.

Key Definition

Locus standi (a place to stand). The expression signifies a person with an interest in the subject matter of the dispute to such an extent that he may have a right to bring or defend a claim

The general rule was considered in *Morice v Bishop of Durham*.

KEY CASE ANALYSIS: *Morice v Bishop of Durham* (1805) 10 Ves 522.

Background

A bequest was made to the Bishop of Durham on trust for 'such objects of benevolence and liberality as the Bishop shall approve'.

Principle established

The gift was not charitable and failed as a private purpose trust owing to the lack of a beneficiary to enforce the trust. Accordingly, a resulting trust had arisen.

Grant MR said '. . . there can be no trust over the exercise of which this court will not assume control . . . there must be somebody in whose favour the court can decree performance'.

Likewise, the trust failed in *Re Astor's Settlement*.

KEY CASE ANALYSIS: *Re Astor's Settlement* [1952] Ch 534

Background

* An *Observer* newspaper magnate made a gift on trust for 'the maintenance of good understanding between nations and the preservation of the independence and integrity of newspapers'.
* The question in issue was whether the trust was valid.

Principle established

The court decided that the trust was void because of the absence of a beneficiary to enforce the trust and uncertainty regarding the stated aims.

On-the-spot question

 Would the following directions create purpose trusts?

   (a)   A legacy of £5,000 to use the income to maintain my pet cat, Tiddles, for the remainder of her life. Any surplus income and the capital to be shared equally between my nephews and nieces.
   (b)   I declare that the windows and doors of my house, Rose Cottage, be boarded up for a period of 10 years from the date of my death.

PERPETUITY RULE

An additional reason for the failure of such private trusts is the infringement of the rule against perpetuities. The perpetuity rule is based on the principle that property is required to vest in the donee (rule against remote vesting) and be capable of disposal (rule against excessive duration) within a life or lives in being and/or 21 years. Only human lives may be used to measure the perpetuity period. The rule against remote vesting involves the maximum period in which the vesting of the property may be postponed and the rule against excessive duration concerns the maximum period in which the property is incapable of being disposed.

Example

Steven wishes to ensure that a valuable Rembrandt painting is retained within the family for generations. He transfers the painting to Tim and Tom as trustees for himself for life with remainder to his son, Gareth, for life with remainder to Gareth's eldest child for life on condition that the latter enters into a similar arrangement with his or her eldest child. Assuming that Gareth is a toddler of one year, would the property be acquired by Gareth's eldest child? This involves the question of remote vesting. Time starts to run from the date of the creation of the trust. The life in being is Steven and the question arises as to whether the property will vest in Gareth's eldest child within the perpetuity period. This is required to take effect within 21 years from the death of Steven. Since this is unclear, we will have to 'wait and see' until it is clear that the gift will or will not vest. The Perpetuities and Accumulations Act 2009 introduced a perpetuity period of 125 years to replace the uncertain common law period, but this principle does not extend to private purpose trusts that remain subject to the rule at common law.

EXCEPTIONS TO THE BENEFICIARY PRINCIPLE

Over the centuries the courts have regarded a number of purpose trusts as valid and identified certain individuals as having the duty to ensure that the trustees carry out their function. These exceptions are as follows:

(1)   Charitable trusts – the **Attorney General** represents the Crown and one of his responsibilities is to ensure the proper running of such trusts.

Key Definition

Attorney General – The Government's legal advisor. This officer of the Crown has the responsibility for supervising charities.

(2)   Trusts for the maintenance of specific animals such as pet dogs, cats etc. are valid if the trustees express a desire to carry out the testator's wishes. In *Pettingall v Pettingall* (1842) 11 LJ Ch 176, a trust of a legacy was created in order to maintain the testator's black mare. The executor was nominated as the trustee and became entitled to any surplus funds.

(3)   A trust for the building of a memorial or monument for an individual is not charitable, but may exist as a valid purpose trust. In terms of maintaining such a monument, the gift is required to be limited to the perpetuity period. In *Re Hooper* [1932] 1 Ch 38, a gift for the maintenance of a specific grave 'for as long as the law allows' was valid as a private purpose trust.

(4)   Miscellaneous: a trust for the promotion of fox hunting was valid in *Re Thompson* [1934] Ch 342, based on a strained analogy with *Pettingall v Pettingall*, above.

(5)   A trust for the saying of masses in private is not charitable, but may create a valid private trust, see *Bourne v Keane* [1919] AC 815. Moreover, in *Khoo Cheng Teow* [1932] Straits Settlement Reports 226, a trust for the performance of ancestral worship was upheld.

The exceptions as stated above, with the exclusion of charities, were created as concessions to human weakness and the only relaxation of the rule that has been made in these cases is to dispense with a beneficiary with the *locus standi* to enforce the trust. Accordingly, in *Re Endacott* [1960] Ch 232, a trust to provide 'some useful memorial to myself' failed because it clearly did not fall within one of the exceptions and was considered to be too vague and uncertain.

On-the-spot question

Clarence made the following dispositions in his will:

'(a) £2,000 per annum to be used to maintain my grave for as long as the law allows;

(b) £1,000 per annum to maintain my pet dog, Fido'.

Consider the validity of Clarence's dispositions.

DENLEY APPROACH

In *Re Denley's Trust Deed*, the approach adopted by the courts is to ascertain whether a gift or trust is for the promotion of a purpose as an end in itself (within the *Astor* principle), which is void or, alternatively, whether the trust *prima facie* promotes a purpose that benefits identifiable persons who are capable of enforcing the trust. This is a question for the courts to decide on construction of the relevant trust instrument. The promotion of many purposes has a direct or indirect effect on persons. The settlor may, in form, create what appears to be a purpose trust but, in substance, the trust may be considered to be for the benefit of human beneficiaries (e.g. a trust for the planting of trees on an estate owned by an individual, or a gift to provide education for the children of the settlor). In a sense these are purpose trusts but, on reflection, the ultimate objective is to benefit individuals.

The approach of the courts is to draw a distinction between a form of gift remotely in favour of individuals, to such an extent that those individuals do not have a *locus standi* to enforce the trust. Such trusts are void for lack of a beneficiary. On the other hand, a gift may appear to propagate a purpose that is *directly or indirectly* for the benefit of individuals. In this event, if the beneficiaries satisfy the test for certainty of objects, the gift may be valid. The courts are required to consider each gift prior to classification.

KEY CASE ANALYSIS: *Re Denley's Trust Deed* [1969] 1 Ch 373

Background

- A plot of land was conveyed to trustees for use as a sports ground, primarily for the benefit of employees of a company and, secondarily, for the benefit of such other person or persons as the trustees may allow to use the same.
- The gift did not infringe the perpetuity rule.

The question in issue was whether the trust was void as a purpose trust.

Principle established

The court decided that the trust was valid in favour of human beneficiaries; namely, the employees of the company and the beneficiaries under the discretionary trust.

Per Goff J: 'Where the trust, though expressed as a purpose, is directly or indirectly for the benefit of an individual or individuals, it seems to me that it is in general outside the mischief of the beneficiary principle.'

UNINCORPORATED ASSOCIATIONS

An unincorporated association does not have an entity separate from its members. It cannot sue or be sued in its own name. Any claims by the association are required to be made in the names of its officers, chairman, secretary, treasurer and so on, who represent the members collectively. The association was defined by Lawton LJ in *Conservative and Unionist Central Office v Burrell* [1982] 1 WLR 522, as follows:

> two or more persons bound together for one or more common purposes, not being business purposes, by mutual undertakings each having mutual duties and obligations, in an organisation which has rules which identify in whom control of it and its funds rests and on what terms and which can be joined or left at will.

In *Burrell*, the legal status of the Conservative Party was outside the test for unincorporated associations and, by reference to its constitution, involved an amorphous collection of various elements.

Example

A cricket club is formed by the efforts of 50 committed individuals. The club adopts the name Utopia Cricket Club and, at a general meeting, approves a constitution governing the relationship between its members and its powers concerning third parties. Several officers are elected by its members. Subscriptions and donations are paid to the Treasurer. Premises for the use of a cricket ground with a pavilion have been acquired and are held by four members as trustees for the members of the club.

The legal status of this club is an unincorporated association. The name, Utopia Cricket Club, does not have any legal significance but is a means of identifying its members. Contracts with third parties are made with the Club officers or its trustees, as representatives of the members collectively. The constitution creates a contract between the members *inter se* and governs the mutual rights and duties of each member.

The reason for dealing with unincorporated associations in a separate section is because when gifts or trusts are made in favour of such associations, the question arises as to whether the gifts or trusts are made in favour of *persons* or *purposes*. If the gift or trust is construed as promoting a purpose *simpliciter*, the gift or trust is void for lack of a beneficiary. But if the gift or trust is construed as benefiting the members of the association, that gift or trust may be valid. The solution depends on the facts of each case.

In *Neville Estates v Madden* [1962] Ch 832, Cross J in an *obiter* pronouncement summed up the various forms of construction, thus:

> Such a gift may take effect in one or other of three quite different ways. In the first place, it may, on its true construction, be a gift to the members of the

association at the relevant date as joint tenants . . . Secondly, it may be a gift to the existing members not as joint tenants, but subject to their respective contractual rights and liabilities towards one another as members of the association. In such a case a member cannot sever his share . . . Thirdly, the terms or circumstances of the gift or the rules of the association may show that the property in question is not to be at the disposal of the members for the time being, but is to be held in trust for or applied for the purposes of the association as a quasi-corporate entity. In this case the gift will fail unless the association is a charitable body.

These principles may be illustrated by the following cases.

(1)   The transaction may be construed as a gift to the present members as **joint tenants**. The effect is that each member may sever his share of the joint tenancy and claim the property beneficially.

Key Definitions

Joint tenants – This is a form of co-ownership or multiple ownership of property, such as property or an estate being owned by Alfred and Bernard jointly. The key feature of a joint tenancy is the right of survivorship. On the death of one joint tenant, say Alfred, the surviving joint tenant (Bernard) acquires the deceased's interest in the property.

Tenancy in common – If a joint tenancy is severed, another form of co-ownership may be created, namely a **tenancy in common**. In this latter form of co-ownership, each party acquires a separate, quantifiable interest in the property; for example, Charles and David each enjoy an interest in land in equal shares and are regarded as owning 50 percent interest each in the property.

The joint tenancy solution is extremely uncommon but was adopted in *Cocks v Manners*.

KEY CASE ANALYSIS: *Cocks v Manners* (1871) LR 12 Eq 574

Background

- The testatrix left part of her estate to the Dominican Convent at Carisbrooke, 'payable to the supervisor for the time being'.
- The question in issue involved the validity of the gift.

Principle established

The court held that the gift was not charitable, but was valid in favour of the individual members of the stated community as joint tenants.

(2) The donation may be construed as a gift to the existing members of the association but subject to the terms of their contract with each other. The effect is that no member may claim the property beneficially, but his share would accrue to the surviving members of the club, through death or resignation. This is the *prima facie* rule that represents the modern application of the principle by the courts. This solution was laid down in an *obiter* pronouncement in *Re Recher's Will Trust* [1972] Ch 526, per Brightman J:

> In the case of a donation which is not accompanied by any words which purport to impose a trust, it seems that the gift takes effect in favour of the existing members of the association not as joint tenants or tenants-in-common so as to entitle each member to an immediate share, but as an accretion to the funds of the organisation.

Example

In the Utopia Cricket Club illustration above, a donation of £50,000 to the club under the will of a deceased member, Bert, will be received by the Treasurer, Alfred, on behalf of the 50 subsisting members of the club at the time of the donation. The club members individually are not entitled to take the property beneficially, but will be required to deal with the property in accordance with the contract between themselves, as evidenced by the club's constitution.

Recently, in *Re Horley Town Football Club*, the court endorsed the *Recher* principle and construed a gift to the Club as a 'contract-holding' gift to the Club's members.

> **KEY CASE ANALYSIS:** *Re Horley Town Football Club* **[2006] All ER (D) 34**
>
> ### Background
>
> - In 1948, the president of Horley Football Club settled land on trust to secure a permanent sports ground for the Club.
> - In 2002, the land was sold to a developer for £4m.
>
> The question in issue concerned the basis on which the Club assets were held.
>
> ### Principle established
>
> The court decided that the members acquired the assets of the Club subject to the current rules of association. They may, unanimously or by a general meeting, call for the assets to be transferred at their direction.

It follows logically that on the death or resignation of the last but one member of the organisation, the society will cease to exist and the contract between the members will be automatically terminated. Further, any surplus assets of the association will be acquired beneficially by the last surviving member. This was decided in *Hanchett-Stamford v Attorney General*.

> **KEY CASE ANALYSIS:** *Hanchett-Stamford v Attorney General* **[2008] All ER (D) 391 (High Court)**
>
> ### Background
>
> - An unincorporated association called the Performing and Captive Animals Defence League (the League) was formed to introduce legislation to outlaw circus tricks performed by animals.
> - Land valued at £675,000 and a large portfolio of shares valued at £1.77m were acquired on behalf of the League.
> - The League was not regarded as a charitable organisation for it was created to change the law and therefore lacked a public benefit.
> - The claimant, as the sole surviving member, wanted to transfer the assets of the League to an active charity that supported animal welfare. The Born Free Foundation was identified as an appropriate charity to receive the assets.

The question in issue was whether the claimant became entitled to the assets of the association and had the capacity to nominate a charity to receive the funds.

Principle established

The court decided in favour of the claimant and ruled that she was free to devote the funds to the Born Free Foundation if she so wished.

(3)   An alternative solution laid down by the courts is to construe the gift or funds of the association as belonging to the members of the association, both present and future. In coming to this conclusion, the courts are required to consider the rules of the association and its function, in addition to the intention of the donor. However, this approach is restricted by the rule against perpetuities and involves careful consideration of the constitution to determine whether the members collectively have the power to dispose of the capital of the association (i.e. the perpetuity rule). If there is no such power, the gift will be void and a resulting trust will arise (see *Re Grant's Will Trust*).

KEY CASE ANALYSIS: *Re Grant's Will Trust* [1980] 1 WLR 360

Background

- A gift by will was made for the benefit of the Chertsey headquarters of the Chertsey Labour Party.
- The objects of this branch of the party were subject to rules laid down by the National Executive Committee of the Labour Party. The effect was that this branch of the party did not have the power to dispose of its capital.

The question in issue was whether the gift was valid.

Principle established

The court decided that the gift was void for infringing the perpetuity rule (i.e. the rule against excessive duration). The members did not have the power to change the rules of the association. Such control was vested in the National Executive Committee of the Labour Party.

(4)   A benefactor may adopt the institution of a trust in transferring funds to promote the purposes of the association, such as a gift 'on trust' to promote the objectives of the Utopia Cricket Club or 'to the trustees on trust' to erect a new club pavilion. In these circumstances, the gift may be construed as promoting a purpose as an end result and may fall foul of the 'beneficiary' principle. If this construction is adopted, the intended express trust will fail and a resulting trust will arise (see *Leahy v Attorney General for New South Wales*).

KEY CASE ANALYSIS: *Leahy v Attorney General for New South Wales* [1959] AC 457 (Privy Council)

Background

- A testator devised a plot of land of 730 acres on trust for 'such order of nuns of the Catholic church or the Christian brothers as my trustees shall select'.
- This transfer was not wholly charitable as it permitted the trustees to select cloistered nuns.
- Under Australian law the trust was capable of being saved as a charitable donation by confining the gift to non-cloistered orders.
- The trustees, however, wanted to retain the freedom to give to cloistered nuns if possible.

The question in issue was whether the trust in its existing form was valid as a non-charitable trust.

Principle established

The court held that, as a non-charitable gift, the trust failed as the testator's intention was clearly to create an endowment for the order of nuns (both present and future) and not for the benefit of individuals.

---

(5)   A different solution in the context of a trust may be adopted by the court construing the gift on trust for the current members of the association, and not on trust for purposes. In this event, provided that the rules of the association empower the members to liquidate and distribute the assets of the association, the perpetuity rule will not be infringed and the trust will be valid. This is an application of the *Re Denley* principle.

The position remains the same even though the settlor may specify a purpose for which the fund may be used. Such stipulation may be construed as insufficient to prevent the members (beneficiaries) disposing of the property in any way they consider appropriate within the rules of the society (see *Re Lipinski's Will Trust*).

KEY CASE ANALYSIS: *Re Lipinski* [1977] 1 All ER 33

Background

- A testator bequeathed half of his residuary estate on trust for Hull Judeans (Maccabi) Association, a non-charitable association.
- The purpose of the bequest was 'in memory of my late wife' to be used 'solely' in constructing or maintaining the association's buildings.

The question in issue concerned the validity of the gift.

Principle established

The court decided that the transfer was valid as a gift to the subsisting members, subject to a contract between them as members. The reference to the memory of the testator's wife was merely the motive for the gift. Further, the stipulation concerning the use of the funds was not intended to restrict the powers of the members to dispose of the assets in accordance with the rules of the association.

CASE LAW SUMMARY

Re Shaw – The court decided on construction of the terms of the gift that a private trust was intended, which failed for lack of a beneficiary to enforce the intended trust.

Re Astor – An intended private purpose trust failed for want of a beneficiary with a *locus standi* to enforce the same.

Pettingall v Pettingall – Exceptionally, a private purpose trust to benefit the testator's horse was valid as a concession to human weakness.

Re Thompson – The court drew an analogy with *Pettingall* and decided that a trust to promote fox hunting benefited specific, identifiable animals (hounds) and was valid.

Re Endacott – An intended trust in a will to provide some 'suitable memorial to myself' was void as a purpose trust because it was outside the exceptional cases where the courts made concessions to human weakness. The trust purpose was treated as too vague.

Cocks v Manners – A gift to an unincorporated association construed as a gift to the members as joint tenants.

Horley Town FC – A transfer to an unincorporated association regarded as an accretion to the funds of the society.

Hanchett-Stamford v Attorney General – Surplus funds of an unincorporated association on the date of liquidation acquired by sole surviving member beneficially.

Re Grant's Will Trust – A gift to an unincorporated association with no dispositive powers was acquired by the Crown on a *bona vacantia*.

Leahy v AG – A conditional gift to an unincorporated association was construed as a trust for a private purpose and was void under the beneficiary principle.

Re Lipinski – A gift to an unincorporated association purporting to promote a purpose construed as a gift to the members of the association, subject to their obligations under the constitution.

Re Denley's Trust Deed – A disposition of an asset to be used to promote a purpose for the benefit of human beneficiaries was construed as a gift on trust for those beneficiaries

ISSUES TO THINK ABOUT FURTHER

In *Re Denley*, the court construed a gift of an asset (land) to an *incorporated association* to be used by human beneficiaries as a private trust in favour of those beneficiaries and that the test of certainty of objects was satisfied. The difficulty with this principle was that the beneficiaries did not have an equitable interest in the asset and they were not capable of terminating the trust under the *Saunders v Vautier* principle. In effect, the beneficiaries' interests were suspended during the continuance of the trust. However, this principle was extended in *Re Lipinski* to a gift to the members of an *unincorporated association* who were entitled to claim the property beneficially, subject to the limitations laid down in the constitution of the association.

To what extent would you regard the construction of the residuary gift by will in *Re Lipinski* as similar to the *Re Denley* principle?

SUMMARY

- We can see that the rationale underlying the 'beneficiary' principle is that a person on whose behalf the trust is created is identified to ensure that the trustees perform their duties.
- There are a number of well-established exceptions to this requirement that have been developed by the courts over the centuries to benefit charities and specific animals, to erect and maintain monuments and to say masses in private.
- An additional hurdle to overcome is the rule against perpetuities.
- In *Re Denley* the court decided that the issue involved a question of construction to determine whether the gift was intended to benefit persons or to promote purposes.
- The status of unincorporated associations creates a special problem because such societies do not have separate legal entities.
- Gifts to such associations may be construed in favour of the subsisting members as joint tenants, or subject to the contract between the members, or to the present and future members, or on trust for purposes or, alternatively, the current members.

FURTHER READING

Brown J, 'What are we to do with testamentary trusts of imperfect obligations?' [2007] Conv 148.
[Identifies the types of testamentary private purpose trusts that have been recognised as valid and suggests statutory reform that would facilitate such trusts.]

Gardner S, 'A detail in the construction of gifts to unincorporated associations' [1998] Conv 8.
[A reply to an article written by Paul Matthews on the relevance of the donor's intention when considering gifts to unincorporated associations.]

Gravells N, 'Gifts to unincorporated associations: where there is a will there is a way' (1977) 40 MLR 231.
[Gifts to unincorporated associations cause difficulty for testamentary draftsmen. If the gift is made in favour of a non-public association, its validity will depend on the construction of the will as to whether the gift is made in favour of individual members of the association or not. The difficulty stems from the anomalous rules relating to private purpose trusts.]

Lovell P, 'Non-charitable purpose trusts – further reflections' [1970] Conv 77.
[Analyses the *Denley* case and concludes that the 'beneficiary' principle that justified the existence of the trust meant those who were entitled to the actual or prospective enjoyment and advantage, and not an equitable interest in the traditional sense.]

Luxton P, 'Gifts to clubs: contract holding is trumps' [2007] Conv 274.
[Considers the *Horley Town Football Club* case and examines the effect of changes in membership rules on entitlement to beneficial interests.]

Matthews P, 'A problem in the construction of gifts to unincorporated associations' [1995] Conv 302.
[Considers the implications between gifts to the members of an unincorporated association for their benefit and gifts to members as an accretion to the funds of the association.]

McKay L, 'Trusts for purposes: another view' [1973] Conv 420.
[Considers the rationale behind the 'beneficiary' principle and suggests that where the general rule is not satisfied, the arrangement amounts to the conferment on the 'trustee' of a power of ownership, not a trust.]

Ramjohn M, 'Text, Cases and Materials on Equity and Trusts', 4th edn (Routledge-Cavendish, 2008).
[Detailed consideration of equity and trusts principles.]

[Ramjohn M, 'Unlocking Trusts', 4th edn (Routledge, 2013).
[A comprehensive and up to date text written in simple, clear language that de-mystifies complicated concepts in trusts law.]

Rickett C, 'Unincorporated associations and their dissolution' [1980] CLJ 88.
[Considers the destination of funds on the liquidation of an unincorporated association.]

COMPANION WEBSITE

An online glossary compiled by the author is available on the companion website:
www.routledge.com/cw/beginningthelaw

Chapter 7
Charitable trusts

LEARNING OUTCOMES

At the end of this chapter, you should be able to:

- Identify the privileges that are available to charities
- Understand the requirement of public benefit
- Recognise charitable purposes within the Charities Act 2011
- Appreciate the need for the High Court to retain jurisdiction over charities with a foreign element
- Understand the *cy-près* doctrine

INTRODUCTION

The law of charities involves another form of express trust, namely a purpose trust for the benefit of the public but enforceable by the Attorney General. As a public trust, a number of privileges are enjoyed by such organisations.

The law of charities has been a feature of the law of trusts for over four centuries, as evidenced by a wealth of case law. What constitutes a charitable purpose has now been enacted for the first time in the Charities Act 2006, which has been repealed and replaced by the Charities Act 2011. The definition incorporates a list of some 13 purposes as well as satisfying the public benefit requirement. Charities registered in the United Kingdom regularly conduct activities abroad and the legal issues raised by such activities involve the scope of the jurisdiction of the High Court. Finally, on the winding-up of a charitable body, the question of the destination of its funds will be considered under the *cy-près* doctrine.

PRIVILEGES ENJOYED BY CHARITABLE STATUS

Charitable institutions have long been endowed with special privileges not accorded to private trusts. These privileges are recognition of the admirable work that is conducted by charities, and are in respect of (a) certainty of objects, (b) the perpetuity rule, (c) taxation and (d) the *cy-près* doctrine.

(a)   *Certainty of objects*: Reference was made in Chapter 6 to the 'beneficiary' principle (i.e. the requirement that a beneficiary needs to have the capacity to enforce the trust). This principle is restricted to private trusts. A public or charitable trust is subject to a unique test for certainty of objects. First, the Attorney General has the *locus standi* to ensure the performance of the trustee's duties. Secondly, charitable trusts are subject to a broad test for certainty of objects. This test is whether the objects are *exclusively* charitable. Section 1(1)(a) of the Charities Act 2011 endorses this principle by enacting that a 'charity means an institution that is established for charitable purposes only.' Thus, if funds are capable of being devoted for both charitable and non-charitable purposes, the gift may be construed as being void as a charity. This involves a question of construction to ascertain whether the non-charitable purpose is an integral part of the organisation, in which case the gift will fail. Alternatively, if the non-charitable purpose is merely incidental to the main charitable purpose, the gift will be valid as a charity (see *IRC* v *City of Glasgow Police Athletic Association*).

KEY CASE ANALYSIS: *IRC v City of Glasgow Police Athletic Association* [1953] 1 All ER 747

Background

*   The primary object of the association was the provision of recreation and sport for its members.
*   The question in issue was whether the association was charitable.

Principle established

The House of Lords decided that the association promoted both a charitable purpose (efficiency of the police force) and a non-charitable purpose (promotion of sport) and therefore failed as a charity.

Lord Normand: 'The private advantage of members is a purpose for which the association is established and it therefore cannot be said that this is an association established for a public charitable purpose only.'

Similarly, where the draftsman of the objects clause uses words such as 'charitable *or* benevolent purposes', the court may, on construction of the clause, decide that the word 'or' ought to be interpreted disjunctively with the effect that benevolent purposes that are not charitable are capable of taking and the gift will therefore fail as a charity. On the other hand, the conjunction, 'and' in the phrase 'charitable *and* benevolent objects' is generally construed conjunctively, but exceptionally may be construed disjunctively, see *Attorney*

General of the Bahamas v Royal Trust Co [1986] I WLR 1001, where a bequest to provide education *and* welfare for Bahamian children failed as a charity.

In addition, the test for certainty of charitable objects will be satisfied if funds are devoted solely or mainly for charitable purposes without specifying the objects. Thus, a gift 'on trust for charitable purposes' *simpliciter* will satisfy this test. The Charity Commission and the court have the jurisdiction to establish a scheme for application of the funds. In other words, the court will make an order indicating the specific charitable objects that will benefit. In *Moggridge v Thackwell* (1807) 13 Ves 416, a bequest to such charities as the trustee sees fit was valid as a gift for charitable purposes.

In two circumstances, an objects clause that seeks to benefit both charitable and non-charitable purposes will not fail as a charity if:

- The non-charitable purpose is construed as being incidental to the main charitable purpose. This involves a question of construction for the courts to evaluate the importance of each class of objects, see *Re Coxen.*

KEY CASE ANALYSIS: *Re Coxen* [1948] Ch 747

Background

- A testator bequeathed £200,000 on trust to pay £100 per annum for a dinner for the trustees and the remainder of the fund to benefit orthopaedic hospitals.

The question in issue was whether the gifts were charitable.

Principle established

The court decided that the gifts as a whole were charitable. The private purpose was purely incidental to the main charitable purpose.

- The court is able to apportion the fund and devote the charitable portion of the fund for charitable purposes. An apportionment will be ordered where only part of the fund is payable for charitable purposes and the other part for non-charitable purposes. In the absence of circumstances requiring a different division, the court will apply the maxim 'equality is equity' and order an equal division of the fund (see *Salusbury v Denton*).

KEY CASE ANALYSIS: *Salusbury v Denton* (1857) 3 K&J 529

Background

- A testator's widow was under a duty by will to devote part of a fund to a charity for the benefit of the poor.
- The remainder was to be disposed of in favour of the testator's relatives.
- The widow failed to apportion the funds by her will.

The question in issue concerned the validity of the testator's bequest

Principle established

The court decided that the fund will be divided into two equal parts and a portion of the fund was payable for charitable purposes (the relief of poverty).

(b)   *Perpetuity*: This principle was considered in outline in Chapter 6. Charities are not subject to the rule against excessive duration. Indeed, many charities (schools and universities) continue indefinitely and rely heavily on donations. But charitable gifts, like private gifts, are subject to the rule against remote vesting (i.e. the subject matter of the gift is required to vest in the charity within the perpetuity period of 125 years). But even in this respect the courts have introduced a concession for charities, namely charitable unity. Once a gift has vested in a specific charity, then, subject to any express declarations to the contrary, it vests forever for charitable purposes. This principle has now been endorsed in s 2(2) of the Perpetuities and Accumulations Act 2009. Accordingly, a gift that vests in one charity (A) with a gift over in favour of another charity (B) on the occurrence of an event will be valid even if the event occurs outside the perpetuity period.

(c)   *Taxation*: A variety of tax reliefs are enjoyed by both charitable bodies and members of the public (including companies) who donate funds for charitable purposes. A detailed analysis of such concessions is outside the scope of this book.

(d)   *Cy-près*: The advantage over private trusts is that when a gift vests in a charity, then, subject to express provisions to the contrary, the gift vests for charitable purposes. Accordingly, the settlor (and his estate) is excluded from any implied reversionary interests by way of a resulting trust in the event of a failure of the charitable trust. Thus, the *cy-près* doctrine is an alternative to the resulting trust principle. This will be examined later.

Key Definition

Cy-près – As near as possible to the original charitable purpose.

PUBLIC BENEFIT

Section 2(1)(b) of the Charities Act 2011 states that a charitable purpose (as defined) is required to satisfy the public benefit test. This test has always been a requirement of the law of charities and distinguishes such institutions from private trusts. Prior to the passing of the Charities Act 2011, certain purposes were presumed to satisfy the test but s 4(2) of the 2011 Act abolishes the presumption. The effect is that all charitable purposes are treated in the same way and, in the event of a dispute, the proponent is required to establish that the purpose satisfies the public benefit test. However, in *Independent Schools Council v Charity Commission* [2011] UKUT 421, the Upper Tribunal analysed the case law on the subject and decided that there was no evidence of the existence of a presumption in favour of public benefit for some charitable purposes, and that s 4(2) will have no impact on the law of charities.

Section 4(3) of the Charities Act 2011 consolidates the definition of the public benefit test as laid down by case law over the centuries. Section 17 of the Act requires the Charity Commission to issue guidelines in order to promote public awareness and understanding as to the operation of this requirement. The Commission guidelines (published in January 2008) indicate that this requirement of public benefit will be construed in the context of modern conditions; requires clarity in terms of the organisation's aims, with the provision of benefits being restricted to the aims; may provide a direct or indirect benefit to the public; and does not exclude the less well-off members of our society.

The approach of the courts incorporates two elements, namely:

- whether the purpose involves any useful activity to society (merits objective), and
- whether the benefit is available to the public at large or an appreciable section of society (identification of the community).

The 2011 Act lays down 13 purposes that are capable of amounting to charitable purposes. These will be considered in the next section. The second requirement concerns the identification of the community and a value judgment as to whether the community is large enough to justify the use of public funds. In essence, the test will be satisfied if the potential beneficiaries under the trust are:

- not numerically negligible, and
- there is no personal nexus between the donor and the intended beneficiaries.

This is a question of degree that varies with the facts of each case and the charitable purpose. On the one hand, a benefit may be available to the entire community but, owing to limited resources, may be enjoyed by some members of society, such as a public bridge. On the other hand, where the gift is to be enjoyed by a limited number of individuals to the exclusion of the rest of the public, the test may not be satisfied, such as a private bridge.

The existence of a personal nexus in contract or in 'blood' may not satisfy the public benefit test (see *Oppenheim v Tobacco Securities Trust*).

KEY CASE ANALYSIS: *Oppenheim v Tobacco Securities Trust* [1951] AC 297

Background

- The tobacco company created a gift for the education of the children of employees and ex-employees of the company.
- The employees and ex-employees numbered 110,000.

The issue was whether the gift satisfied the public benefit test.

Principle established

The House of Lords decided that the gift failed as a charity and a resulting trust was created.

Likewise, in *Re Compton* [1945] 1 All ER 198, the Court of Appeal decided that a gift to educate the children of three named relatives of the donor failed as a charity. By parity of reasoning, where the gift is made in favour of a 'class within a class', the test will not be satisfied. In *IRC v Baddeley* [1955] AC 572, a trust to provide recreational facilities for Methodists of West Ham and Leyton failed for this reason. Likewise, in *Williams v IRC* [1947] AC 447, an institute in London for the promotion of Welsh culture for Welsh people living in London was not charitable. In contrast, in *Re Lewis* [1954] 3 All ER 257, the court decided that a gift to benefit 10 blind boys and 10 blind girls in Tottenham was charitable.

CHARITABLE PURPOSES

Most charitable bodies are required to be registered with the Charity Commission under s 30 of the Charities Act 2011. The effect of registration creates a conclusive presumption of charitable status – see s 37 of the Charities Act 2011. It is at this stage that the Commission may refuse to register an organisation on its own accord or based on objections from interested parties such as Revenue and Customs. An appeal from the decision of the Commission lies to the newly created Charity Tribunal and thereafter to the High Court on a point of law.

Prior to the Charities Act 2006, the predecessor of the Charities Act 2011, the classification of charitable purposes was construed by reference to the **Preamble** to the Charities Act 1601.

Key Definition

Preamble – The recital at the beginning of some Acts of Parliament to explain the aims of the statute.

The Preamble to the Act contained a limited catalogue of charitable purposes that were classified by Lord McNaghten in *IRC v Pemsel* [1891] AC 531 into four categories:

- trusts for the relief of poverty
- trusts for the advancement of education
- trusts for the advancement of religion, and
- trusts for other purposes beneficial to the community.

The approach of the courts over four centuries was to consider whether a purpose fell within the preamble or was based on a precedent, or based on an analogy with a precedent or within the 'spirit and intendment' of the preamble. The effect has been that a large body of case law has been created concerning the meaning of charitable purposes.

Section 3(1) of the Charities Act 2011 now enacts a statutory definition of charitable purposes by reference to 13 purposes – see s 3(1)(a) to (m) of the 2011 Act. This is the first occasion that a definition of a charitable purpose has been attempted. Further, s 3(3) incorporates the case law definition of the purposes referred to in s 3(1)(a) to (l), and s 3(1)(m)(i) does the same for the purposes within s 3(1)(m). The effect is that the wealth of case law compiled over the centuries concerning the definition of charitable purposes may still be relevant and we will now outline these purposes.

Section 3(1)(a) of the Charities Act 2011 refers to the 'prevention or relief of poverty'.

Poverty connotes that the beneficiaries are in straitened circumstances and unable to maintain a modest standard of living (determined objectively). The beneficiaries need not be destitute but suffer from a standard of living lower than that generally enjoyed in the community. The section refers to the 'prevention' or 'relief' of poverty. Prevention involves a scheme of arrangements designed to avoid poverty, whereas relief concerns the means of alleviating the misery associated with poverty. Relief may take many forms such as, for example, direct payments to the poor (see *Pemsel's case*), the funding of soup kitchens (see *Biscoe v Jackson* (1887) 35 Ch D 460), and the provision of rest homes or flats let out at below commercial rents (*Re Cottam* [1955] 1 WLR 1299).

Trusts for the relief of poverty are required to satisfy the public benefit test even though the approach of the courts has been fairly relaxed in this context. The test has been satisfied even though the beneficiaries are linked *inter se* or with an individual or small group of individuals. The courts have drawn a subtle distinction between private trusts for the relief of poverty and public trusts for the same purpose. It appears that the distinction lies in the degree of precision in which the objects have been identified. The more precise the language used by the settlor in identifying the poor relations, the stronger the risk of failure as a charitable trust. This is a question of degree. In *Re Scarisbrick* [1951] Ch 622, a bequest was made on trust 'for such relations of my said son and daughters as in the opinion of the survivor shall be in needy circumstances'. The court held that the gift was charitable – see also *Dingle v Turner*.

KEY CASE ANALYSIS: *Dingle v Turner* [1972] AC 601

Background

- The testator by his will transferred property to his trustees and directed them to apply the income in paying pensions to poor employees of Dingle Ltd.
- There were 705 full-time employees and 189 part-time employees of the company.

The question in issue was whether the gift was charitable.

Principle established

The House of Lords decided that the gift was charitable for the relief of poverty and, in particular, the public benefit test was satisfied.

In *AG v Charity Commission* [2012] WTLR 977, the Upper Tribunal endorsed the pre-Charities Act approach to the public benefit test for trusts that are designed to prevent or relieve poverty. This approach was to the effect that a personal nexus between the donor and the beneficiaries of a charity was not inconsistent with the public benefit test. This concession existed only for trusts for the relief of poverty.

On-the-spot question

 How would you reconcile *Dingle v Turner* with *Oppenheim v Tobacco Securities Trust* on the issue of the public benefit?

Section 3(1)(b) of the Charities Act 2011 deals with the advancement of education as a charitable purpose.

At common law, education has been interpreted generously and is not restricted to the classroom mode of disseminating knowledge but requires some element of instruction or supervision. Research is also capable of being construed as the provision of education. Per Wilberforce J in *Re Hopkins*:

> I think that the word, 'education' . . . must certainly be used in the wide sense, certainly extending beyond teaching and that . . . research must either be of educational value to the researcher or must be so directed as to lead to something which will pass into the store of educational material, or so as to improve the sum of communicable knowledge.

Examples of the provision of education are a gift to the Francis Bacon Society, which existed to encourage the study of Bacon's works and investigate the possibility that Bacon had written plays attributed to Shakespeare, *Re Hopkins* [1965] Ch 669; the advancement of education and learning in every part of the world, *Whicker v Hume* (1858) 7 HL Cases 124; donations to specific educational institutions such as universities or museums, *Baldry v Feintuck* [1972] 2 All ER 81; the publication of law reports that record the development of judge-made law, *ICLR v AG* [1971] 3 All ER 1029; the promotion of artistic and cultural activities of value to the community and the promotion of concerts and choral works of renowned composers, *Re Delius' Will Trusts* [1957] 1 All ER 854; the furtherance of a conference centre for discussion of matters of international importance, *Re Koeppler's Will Trust* [1986] Ch 423; trusts for choral singing in London, *Royal Choral Society v IRC* [1943] 2 All ER 101.

In disputed cases, expert evidence is admissible to determine the value to the public of the relevant activity – see *Re Pinion*.

KEY CASE ANALYSIS: *Re Pinion* [1965] 1 Ch 85

Background

- A studio and contents were donated by will to the National Trust.
- The items were to be exhibited as a collection without the possibility of separating any of the items.
- There were only a few items of intrinsic value to the public.
- The National Trust refused to accept the gift.

The question in issue was whether the collection as a whole was of any value to the public.

Principle established

The court decided that, by reference to expert evidence on the subject, the collection as a whole lacked any artistic merit and was not charitable. The court could conceive of no useful purpose of 'foisting upon the public this mass of junk'.

Section 3(1)(c) of the 2011 Act enacts the advancement of religion: section 3(2)(a) defines religion as 'including belief in more than one god' (such as Hinduism) and a faith 'which does not involve belief in god' (such as Buddhism). Thus, the broadest definition of religion has been enacted in the 2011 Act.

The meaning of advancement of religion was described by Donovan J in *United Grand Lodge of Freemasons in England and Wales v Holborn Borough Council* [1957] 1 WLR 1090, thus:

> To advance religion means to promote it, to spread its message ever wider among mankind; to take some positive steps to sustain and increase religious belief; and these things are done in a variety of ways which may be comprehensively described as pastoral and missionary. It should include religious instruction, a programme for the persuasion of unbelievers, religious supervision to see that its members remain active and constant in the various religions they may profess.

Accordingly, the Freemasons society did not constitute a religious organisation. Similarly, in *Re South Place Ethical Society* [1980] 1 WLR 1565, it was decided that the study and dissemination of ethical principles, which did not involve faith in a deity, could not constitute religion. Per Dillon J:

> 'Religion', as I see it, is concerned with man's relations with God and 'ethics' is concerned with man's relation with man. The two are not the same and are not made the same by sincere inquiry into the question: What is God?

Religion may be advanced in a variety of ways such as the maintenance of places of worship including the upkeep of churchyards, gifts for the clergy, the provision of a church organ or maintenance of a choir and the active spread of religion at home and abroad, although a gift for 'parish work' will be void as including many objects that are not charitable – see *Farley v Westminster Bank* [1939] 3 All ER 491.

Unlike trusts for the advancement of education, the courts do not evaluate the merit of one religion as opposed to another or, indeed, the benefit to the public of religious instruction. Provided that the religious gift is not subversive of all morality, the gift will be charitable. A gift for the saying of masses in public is charitable for the gift promotes an integral part of religion, namely the saying of prayers. Such prayers, although incapable *per se* of proving to be beneficial to mankind, are assumed to provide a sufficient element of public benefit. The *prima facie* assumption is that prayers stipulated by a settlor in a will or *inter vivos* instrument are assumed to be said in public and therefore charitable, until the contrary is established (see *Re Hetherington* [1989] 2 All ER 129).

Section 3(1)(d) of the 2011 Act lays down that the advancement of health or the saving of lives is a charitable purpose. Section 3(2)(b) enacts that this head includes 'the prevention or relief of sickness, disease or human suffering'.

The promotion of health has always been treated as a charitable purpose and includes the establishment and maintenance of hospitals, see *Re Resch's Will Trust* [1969] 1 AC 514; the supply of contraceptives, see *Family Planning Association* (1969) Ch Comm. Rep 111; the provision of a 'home of rest' for nurses in a hospital, see *Re White's Will Trust* [1951] 1 All ER 528; and the provision of emergency services, see *Re Wokingham Fire Brigade Trusts* [1951] Ch 373. The Charity Commission in August 2009 declared that this head of charitable activity includes:

> conventional methods as well as complementary, alternative or holistic methods which are concerned with healing the mind, body and spirit in the alleviation of symptoms and the cure of illness.

The charging of fees for the services is not *per se* a ground for disqualification under this or any other head of charitable purposes. The public benefit test will be satisfied provided that the less well-off members of society are not excluded by the level of the fee. This is a question of degree.

Section 3(1)(e) of the Charities Act 2011 enacts that the advancement of citizenship or community development amounts to a charitable activity. This head includes 'rural and urban regeneration and the promotion of civic responsibility . . . the voluntary sector or the effectiveness or efficiency of charities'.

Under this head the Charity Commission refers to 'the improvement of the social and economic infrastructure and by assisting people who are at a disadvantage because of their social and economic circumstances'. Thus, voluntary organisations responsible for giving free or discounted legal advice or advice on business or employment opportunities may satisfy this test.

Section 3(1)(f) of the 2011 Act refers to the 'advancement of the arts, culture, heritage or science' as a charitable purpose. There may be an element of overlap between this purpose and the advancement of education, but s 3(1)(f) has been established as a separate purpose in its own right. Museums, art galleries, exhibition centres, public monuments, National Trust buildings and areas of historic or natural beauty will clearly be allocated under this head. In *Re Cranstoun* [1949] 1 Ch 523, a charitable gift was created for the preservation of places of historical importance or beauty.

Section 3(1)(g) of the Charities Act 2011 refers to 'the advancement of amateur sport' as a charitable head. Section 3(2)(d) defines sport as 'sports or games which promote health by involving physical or mental skill or exertion'.

At common law the advancement of sport as an end in itself was not considered a charitable purpose – see *IRC v City of Glasgow Police Athletic Association* (see above, under the heading 'Privileges enjoyed by charitable status'), sport within the police force. But in appropriate cases, such gifts may be included under the heading 'advancement of education'. To achieve this status the sport is required to be provided within a school or as part of the educational curriculum. It is well recognised that adequate recreational activities (physical and mental development) are an integral part of the educational process – see *IRC v McMullen* [1981] AC 1, the encouragement of football within schools. Section 3(1)(g) of the Act modifies this principle.

In addition, the Recreational Charities Act 1958 was passed in order to clarify the law in respect of charitable recreational facilities. This Act has been repealed and replaced by s 5 of the Charities Act 2011. Section 5(1) of the 2011 Act stipulates that the provision of recreational facilities shall be charitable if 'the facilities are provided in the interests of "social welfare"'.

Section 5(3) of the 2011 Act specifies the 'basic conditions' when facilities are provided in the interests of social welfare. These are:

(a) they are provided with the object of improving the conditions of life of those for whom they are primarily intended, and

(b) either (i) those persons have need for such facilities by reason of their youth, age, infirmity or disablement, poverty or social and economic circumstances; or

(ii) the facilities are available to the male members or female members of the public at large.

The House of Lords in *Guild v IRC* [1992] 2 All ER 10 construed the requirements under the predecessor to s 5(3) liberally and rejected the view that it is necessary to prove that the beneficiaries were deprived of such facilities in the first place. The test today is whether the facilities are provided with the purpose of improving the conditions of life of the beneficiaries, irrespective of whether the participating members of society are disadvantaged or not. In short, the material issue concerns the nature of the facilities rather than the status of the participants. In this case the devise of land by will for use as a sports centre in North Berwick was considered to be charitable.

Section 3(1)(h) of the Charities Act 2011 deals with 'the advancement of human rights, conflict resolution or reconciliation or the promotion of religious or racial harmony or equality and diversity'.

Section 3(1)(h) provides a statutory basis for the promotion and preservation of human rights. This may be achieved in a variety of ways such as education and providing redress for victims of human rights abuses. In addition, mediation services for conflict resolution are included as charitable activities. Finally, the provision of harmony amongst diverse groups based on race, religion, gender or sexual orientation has always been treated as a charitable activity.

Section 3(1)(i) of the 2011 Act provides that 'the advancement of environmental protection or improvement' is within the definition of charitable purposes. This subsection enacts the fundamental principle of conservation of the environment, which includes areas of natural beauty, as well as particular species of flora and fauna.

Section 3(1)(j) of the 2011 Act declares as a charitable purpose 'the relief of those in need by reason of youth, age, ill-health, disability, financial hardship or other disadvantage'. Section 3(2)(e) of the Act declares that relief may be provided by the provision of accommodation or care for the relevant persons.

The common law regarded such purposes as charitable and interpreted the expression 'relief' as requiring individuals to establish a need for such facilities in the first place. In *Joseph Rowntree Memorial Trust Housing Association v AG* [1983] Ch 159, the court decided that the provision of housing for the elderly was a charitable activity. The approach of the courts may be summarised by Vaisey J in *Re Hillier* [1944] 1 All ER 480, in deciding that a trust for the sick and wounded was charitable:

> the charitable element in a purpose is to be found . . . in the notion of rendering assistance to those persons who are in dire want of it, or to meet some form of human need – need which would appeal to the benevolent feelings of mankind and not necessarily that which has its origin in the lack of money.

Accordingly, the provision of medical care including rehabilitation programmes for addicts, accommodation, meals and advice and guidance for the vulnerable members of society may satisfy the requirement.

Section 3(1)(k) of the Charities Act 2011 enacts that 'the advancement of animal welfare' is a charitable purpose. This purpose is a reflection of the common law principles.

A trust that promotes the welfare of animals in general, or even a species of animal, is a valid charitable trust. Such trust is calculated to promote public morality by checking an inborn tendency in humans towards cruelty. Illustrations include *Re Wedgewood* [1915] 1 Ch 113, a trust for the protection and benefit of animals; *University of London v Yarrow* (1857) 1 De G & J 72, a hospital for sick animals; and *Re Moss* [1949] 1 All ER 495, a home for unwanted or stray cats.

It is essential to establish that the welfare of the animals provides some benefit to mankind, albeit indirect. Failure to establish such benefit was fatal in *Re Grove-Grady* [1929] 1 Ch 557, which concerned an animal sanctuary free from human intervention. Moreover, when there is a conflict of interests between the welfare of animals (anti-vivisection) and the interests of humans (scientific research), the latter prevails and the animal welfare body will not be charitable. Such an organisation does not promote a public benefit owing to its detrimental effect on medical science and research. In *National Anti-Vivisection Society v IRC* [1948] AC 31, the society was not a charitable body.

Section 3(1)(l) of the Charities Act 2011 declares that the 'efficiency of the armed forces of the Crown, or the efficiency of the police, fire and rescue services or ambulance services' are charitable purposes.

This subsection reflects the undisputed policy that the efficiency of the emergency services has always been treated as a charitable purpose. Examples include the training of officers of the Royal Navy, *Re Corbyn* [1941] Ch 400; the protection of the UK from hostile attack, *Re Driffill* [1950] Ch 92; the promotion of the defence of the UK, *Re Good* [1950] 2 All ER 653; and the provision of a local fire brigade, *Re Wokingham Fire Brigade Trusts* [1951] 1 All ER 454.

Section 3(1)(m) of the Charities Act 2011 enacts 'any other purposes' that have been recognised as charitable under existing charity law.

This is a residual category of charitable purposes that not only consolidates the diverse multitude of charitable purposes that existed before the Charities Act, but allows the law to be maintained as new purposes arise. Section 3(1)(m)(i) to (iii) lays down the broad approach that is envisaged by this provision, including the 'spirit' of any purposes falling within s 3(1)(a) to (l). Illustrations include the general improvement of agriculture, *IRC v Yorkshire Agricultural Society* [1928] 1 KB 611; the promotion of inexpensive and sanitary methods of disposal of the dead, *Scottish Burial Reform and Cremation Society v Glasgow City Corporation* [1968] AC 138; the study and dissemination of ethical principles, *Re South Place Ethical Society* [1980] 1 WLR 1565; a gift to the inhabitants of a town or village, *Goodman v Saltash Corporation* [1882] 7 App Cas 633; a gift unto my country, England, *Re Smith* [1932] 1 Ch 153; a bequest to the Chancellor of the Exchequer for the benefit of Great Britain, *Nightingale v Goulbourn* (1849) 5 Hare 484; a gift to benefit the 'black' community, *Re Harding* [2007] EWHC 3; a gift to the schoolchildren of Turton, *Re Mellody* [1918] 1 Ch 228; a gift for the relief of the National Debt, *Newland v AG* (1809) 3 Mer 684, and many more.

POLITICAL PURPOSES

A gift to promote a political purpose is incapable of being charitable. The reason is that such trusts are designed to change the law and do not satisfy the test of usefulness to the public. The court cannot stultify itself by deciding that it is in the public interest that the law be changed. Whether a trust promotes a political purpose as an integral part of its constitution involves a question of construction. Illustrations include a gift to promote the interests of the Labour Party, *Re Hopkinson* [1949] 1 All ER 346; anti-vivisection, *National Anti-Vivisection Society v IRC* [1948] AC 31; Amnesty International, *McGovern v AG* [1981] 3 All ER 493; and the promotion of military disarmament, *Southwood v AG* [2000] WTLR 1199.

However, charities are entitled to mount political campaigns as incidental objectives that promote awareness on social issues within their field of activity. The Charity Commission published guidelines that do not discourage charities from campaigning or voicing their concerns on social issues, provided that this is done in the context of supporting the delivery of the charitable purpose.

ACTIVITIES OUTSIDE THE UK

The approach of the courts is that no distinction is drawn between the nature of charitable activities conducted within or outside the UK. Once the charity has been registered with the Charity Commission, the status of the organisation's activities is measured by reference to the law in the UK.

KEY CASE ANALYSIS: *Keren Kayemeth Le Jisroel v IRC* [1932] AC 650

Background

- A company was formed with the main object of purchasing land in Palestine, Syria and parts of Turkey for the purpose of settling Jews in such lands.

The question in issue was whether the company was a charity.

Principle established

The House of Lords held that the company was not charitable because of the lack of evidence of charitable purposes based on English law.

Conversely, in *Re Jacobs* [1970] 114 SJ 515, a trust for the planting of a clump of trees in Israel was held to be charitable because soil conservation in arid parts of Israel is of essential importance to the Israeli community. The court relied on the principle laid down in *IRC v Yorkshire Agricultural Society* [1928] 1 KB 611.

In addition, s 1(1)(b) of the Charities Act 2011 defines a charity as an institution that 'falls to be subject to the control of the High Court'. This provision clarifies the status of a charity in English law. It would be impractical for the High Court to seek to extend its supervisory jurisdiction to control an overseas-based charity. The territorial limits of the legislation and practical considerations of enforceability are decisive factors in determining the connecting factors with the UK – see *Gaudiya Mission v Brahmachary* (1997).

KEY CASE ANALYSIS: *Gaudiya Mission v Brahmachary* [1997] 4 All ER 957

Background

- The claimants (the Mission) were an Indian-registered religious charity.
- The defendants were a rival religious faction (the Society) registered in England with the Charity Commission.
- The claimants contended that the assets held by the Society belonged to them and that the Society was passing itself off as the Mission.

The question in issue was whether the Mission was an English charity.

Principle established

The Court of Appeal decided the Mission was not an English charity and thus the court had no jurisdiction to entertain the claim.

On-the-spot question

Consider whether the following dispositions under the will of Alfred create charitable trusts:

(1) £10,000 to my executors to distribute amongst such persons or charitable objects as they shall decide in their discretion;
(2) £500,000 to Birmingham City Council upon trust to purchase a suitable site in Birmingham for a football field for the use of all inhabitants of Birmingham;
(3) £100,000 to the University of London upon trust to establish and maintain in perpetuity a School of Law Reform.

CY-PRÈS DOCTRINE

Where a donation for charitable purposes is made but the specified purposes cannot be achieved, the trust objectives will not necessarily fail. Those funds may be applied *cy-près* or for a purpose as close as possible to the specified charitable purpose. The *cy-près* doctrine enables the Charity Commission and the court to make a scheme for the application of the funds. For example, David, a donor, bequeaths £20,000 by his will to set up a dog's home in South London. The fund is insufficient to achieve the charitable purpose but a scheme may be drawn up to utilise the fund for a similar venture. The effect is that no resulting trust arises in favour of the residuary beneficiaries under the will or the next of kin.

There are only two conditions to be satisfied for a *cy-près* application, namely:

• the impossibility or impracticality of carrying out the original charitable purpose or the existence of a surplus of funds after the charitable purpose has been fulfilled, and
• the manifestation of a general charitable intention by the donor as opposed to a specific charitable intention.

Impossibility or impracticality

The impossibility or impracticality in carrying out the original charitable purpose, as opposed to mere inconvenience in doing so, was the subject of intense analysis by the courts over the centuries. Today, the modern law on impossibility has been consolidated in s 62 of the Charities Act 2011, repealing and replacing s 13(1)(a) to (e) of the Charities Act 1993. This involves questions as to whether the original purposes have been fulfilled in whole or in part, or where there is a surplus fund left over, or whether the purposes may be merged with other charities or have subsequently ceased to be charitable.

KEY CASE ANALYSIS: *Biscoe v Jackson* (1887) 35 ChD 460

Background

- A fund was donated by will to provide for a soup kitchen and cottage hospital in the parish of Shoreditch.
- No suitable site could be found to carry out the testator's wishes.

Principle established

The court decided that a general charitable intention to benefit the poor and sick in the parish was manifested and the fund was applied *cy-près*.

KEY CASE ANALYSIS: *Re Lepton's Charity* [1972] Ch 276

Background

- A testator who died in 1716 devised specific property to trustees on trust to pay an annual sum of £3 to the Protestant Minister in Pudsey and the surplus income to the poor and aged people of Pudsey.
- In 1716, the total income was £5.
- On the date of the application to the court, the income was £790 per annum.

Two questions arose for the determination of the court, namely:

(i) whether on a true construction of the will the minister ought to be paid a fixed sum of £3 or 3/5 of the annual income, and

(ii) whether the court would approve a *cy-près* scheme increasing the minister's entitlement to £100 per annum.

Principle established

The court decided that a *cy-près* scheme would be approved, entitling the minister to £100 per annum.

General charitable intention

The second requirement in the context of the *cy-près* doctrine is to ascertain whether the donor had manifested a general charitable intention, despite identifying a specific charity to benefit from his funds. This involves a question of construction of the trust instrument and the surrounding circumstances of each case. A number of leading cases have established the following guidelines:

- Initial or subsequent failure: The issue here is that in the case of an initial failure of the gift to vest in the relevant charitable organisation, a general or paramount charitable intention must be established as a pre-condition for the *cy-près* doctrine.

KEY CASE ANALYSIS: *Biscoe v Jackson* (1887) 35 ChD 460

Background

- A legacy was donated to establish a soup kitchen and a cottage hospital in the parish of Shoreditch.
- A suitable site could not be found.

Principle established

The court decided that the gift will be applied *cy-près* for a general charitable intention to benefit the poor in Shoreditch was established.

Whereas, in the case of subsequent failure of the charitable gift, a general charitable intention is not required. A subsequent failure occurs where the gift has vested in a charity but the charitable body subsequently ceases to exist.

- Form and substance: The approach here is to determine whether, in appearance, a gift provides for a particular purpose but, on construction, the court decides that the paramount intention of the donor, in substance, is to promote a general charitable purpose.

KEY CASE ANALYSIS: *Re Lysaght* [1966] Ch 191

Background

- A bequest was made to the Royal College of Surgeons but subject to a religious bar.
- The College declined to accept the gift owing to the religious bar.

Principle established

The court decided that a general charitable intention was manifested in order to make the College the trustee of the gift. This was the position despite the appearance to benefit a specific charity. Accordingly, a *cy-près* scheme of deleting the religious bar was adopted.

- Incorporated and unincorporated associations: A gift to an incorporated body is *prima facie* a gift to that named institution. But a gift to an unincorporated association is *prima facie* a gift for the objectives of the relevant association. In the latter case, the purpose(s) may continue despite the liquidation of the association and, for this reason, it may be easier to find a general charitable intention.
- In addition, ss 63–66 of the Charities Act 2011, repealing and replacing s 14 of the Charities Act 1993, enact that property given for specific charitable purposes that fail shall be applicable *cy-près* as if given for charitable purposes generally. This is the case where the property belongs to a donor who cannot be identified or found after reasonable inquiries and advertisements have been made, or who disclaims his right to the property in writing.

CASE LAW SUMMARY

IRC v City of Glasgow Police Athletic Association – A purported charitable gift failed on the ground that non-charitable purposes were entitled to benefit.

IRC v Baddeley – A gift for an intended charitable purpose failed because the objects were not exclusively charitable.

Re Coxen – A gift for a charitable purpose succeeded because the non-charitable purpose was incidental to the main charitable purpose.

Salusbury v Denton – A non-charitable purpose was capable of being severed from the main charitable purpose, thus validating the charitable gift.

Oppenheim v Imperial Tobacco Co – The public benefit test was not satisfied owing to a contractual link between the donor and donees.

Re Compton – The test of public benefit was not satisfied because of a personal nexus in blood between the donor and the donees.

Williams v IRC – Failure to satisfy the public benefit test because the gift favoured a class within a class.

Biscoe v Jackson – A trust for the relief of poverty was manifested by the provision of soup kitchens for the local community.

Re Cottam – The provision of flats for those in need satisfied the test for the relief of poverty.

Dingle v Turner – Trusts for the relief of poverty are not subject to the strict public benefit test.

Re Hopkins – Trusts for the advancement of education include research, provided that a number of conditions are complied with.

Re Koeppler – The advancement of education includes a conference centre for the discussion of international issues of importance.

Re Delius – The promotion of the works of a famous composer was charitable for the advancement of education.

Re South Place Ethical Society – The advancement of ethical principles did not advance religion but was charitable under the residual head of charities.

Re Hetherington – The saying of public masses is a charitable purpose for the advancement of religion.

Re Resch – The promotion of fee-paying hospitals was a charitable purpose for the advancement of health.

IRC v McMullen – The promotion of football in schools was a charitable purpose for the advancement of education.

Guild v IRC – Land devoted to a local community for use as a sports centre was construed as charitable for recreational purposes.

National Anti-Vivisection Society v IRC – The discouragement of scientific research on animals was not a charitable purpose.

Scottish Burial Reform Society v IRC – The promotion of cremation was a charitable purpose as a means of disposal of the dead.

McGovern v AG – The organisation, Amnesty International, was not recognised as charitable because it promoted political purposes.

Re Lepton – The test of impracticality was satisfied for the purpose of the *cy-près* doctrine.

Re Lysaght – A general charitable intention was manifested and a religious bar deleted where the testator's dominant intention was to benefit the Royal College of Surgeons.

ISSUES TO THINK ABOUT FURTHER

Prior to the enactment of the Charities Act 2006 (the forerunner to the Charities Act 2011), the application of the test of public benefit not only varied with the nature of the charitable purpose but an exception was recognised for trusts for the prevention or relief of poverty. The Charities Act introduced a requirement that all charitable purposes are required to satisfy the test of public benefit and abolished any presumption in favour of public benefit. At the same time, the Act consolidated the common law relating to public benefit that existed before the passing of the Act

To what extent has the Charities Act 2011 (the successor to the Charities Act 2006) created clarity in the interpretation of public benefit test?

SUMMARY

- A charitable trust enjoys privileges in relation the test of certainty of objects, perpetuities, taxation and the *cy-près* doctrine.
- The public benefit test is definitive in respect of public trusts.
- The test for charitable purposes is laid down in s 3(1) of the Charities Act 2011, by reference to 13 purposes.
- A charity is required to be subject to the jurisdiction of the High Court.
- The *cy-près* doctrine operates when a charitable gift fails to vest in a charitable institution and the donor manifests a general charitable intention.

FURTHER READING

Buckley C, 'The Charities Act 2006: consolidation or reform?' (2008) 11(1) CL & PR 1.

[Provides a clear analysis of the Charities Act 2006, highlighting the definitions of 'charity', 'charitable purposes' and the 'public benefit' test.]

Chesterman M, 'Foundations of charity law in the new welfare state' (1999) 62 MLR 333.
[Argues that the principle that political activities by charitable organisations may invalidate the charitable purpose ought not to be followed rigidly. Participation in public debate about changes in the law or policy in an area of charitable activity ought to be recognised as beneficial to the community within a democratic society and should not deprive the organisation of its charitable status.]

Charity Commission website: http://www.charity-commission.gov.uk
[Contains practical and legal commentary on charities.]

Garton J, 'Justifying the *cy-près* doctrine' (2007) 21 Trust Law International 134.
[Discusses the legal justification of the *cy-près* doctrine and how it operates.]

Nobles R, 'Politics, public benefit and charity' (1982) 45 MLR 704.
[Analyses *McGovern v Attorney General*, and concludes that the decision is incompatible with the duty to consider the question of public benefit.]

Quint F, 'Recent developments in the *cy-près* principle' (2009) 11(2) CL & PR 49.
[Discusses the development of the *cy-près* doctrine and focuses on changes introduced by the Charities Act 2006.]

Ramjohn M, 'Text, Cases and Materials on Equity and Trusts', 4th edn (Routledge-Cavendish, 2008).
[Detailed analysis of the law on charities.]

Ramjohn, M, 'Unlocking Trusts', 4th edn (Routledge, 2013).
[A comprehensive and up to date text written in simple, clear language that de-mystifies complicated concepts in trusts law.]

COMPANION WEBSITE

An online glossary compiled by the author is available on the companion website:
www.routledge.com/cw/beginningthelaw

Chapter 8
Resulting trusts

INTRODUCTION

A resulting trust is an implied trust that arises in favour of the settlor or donor during his lifetime or his estate on his death. The occasions when this event may take place are extremely limited but involve a failure of the trust or gift. These trusts are classified as **automatic** and **presumed** resulting trusts. The latter type of trusts may be rebutted by evidence to support a contrary intention. An attempted fraudulent transfer on the part of the transferor may not constitute a disentitlement in his favour in respect of a resulting trust. Finally, the resulting trust concept may be an inappropriate vehicle to apply with regard to the liquidation of an unincorporated association.

WHAT IS A RESULTING TRUST?

A resulting trust, as distinct from an express trust, is implied by the court in favour of the settlor/transferor, or his estate if he is dead. Such trusts arise by virtue of the unexpressed or implied intention of the settlor or testator and the need is created invariably as a result of defective drafting. The settlor or his estate becomes the beneficial owner under the resulting trust. It is as if the settlor had reserved a residual or default interest in the property, albeit declared by the courts, in the event of the failure of the transfer or the transfer of the bare legal title to another. The expression 'resulting trust' derives from the Latin verb, *resultare*, meaning 'to spring back' (in effect to the original owner). Examples are the transfer of property subject to a condition precedent that cannot be achieved, see *Barclays Bank v Quistclose*; or the creation of an express trust that becomes void, see *Re Ames*.

KEY CASE ANALYSIS: *Barclays Bank v Quistclose* [1970] AC 567

Background

- A loan was provided by Quistclose Ltd to Rolls Razor Ltd for the specific purpose of paying a dividend.
- Before the dividend could be declared, Rolls Ltd went into liquidation.

The question in issue was whether Quistclose may recover its funds.

Principle established

The House of Lords decided that a resulting trust in favour of Quistclose had arisen.

It must be stressed that the *Quistclose* solution was based on a loan for a clearly expressed purpose (to pay a dividend) that did not materialise. The loan therefore did not form part of the general property of Rolls Razor. The court controversially decided that a primary trust to pay a dividend (purpose) was created and when this failed, a resulting trust had arisen in favour of Quistclose.

KEY CASE ANALYSIS: *Re Ames* [1946] Ch 217

Background

- The settlor transferred funds to trustees subject to a marriage settlement.
- The settlement was void because the bridegroom had earlier contracted a valid marriage.

Principle established

The court decided that a resulting trust had arisen in favour of the settlor.

In *Re Vandervell's Trusts (No. 2)* [1974] 1 All ER 47, Megarry J classified resulting trusts into two categories, namely **automatic** and **presumed** (see above). Automatic resulting trusts arise where, following a transfer of property upon trust or subject to a specific purpose, the beneficial interest remains undisposed. Such trusts are created in order to fill a gap in ownership. The equitable or beneficial interest cannot exist 'in the air' and ought to remain with the settlor/transferor. The presumed resulting trust arises when property is purchased in the name of another, or property is voluntarily transferred to another, without the destination of the equitable interest being specified. For example, Alfred purchases property and directs that the legal title be conveyed in the name of Bernard; or Charles voluntarily transfers the bare legal title to property in the name of Derek. In these circumstances Bernard and Derek *prima facie* hold the property on trust for Alfred and Charles respectively.

Automatic resulting trusts

The rationale behind this type of resulting trust is that following a transfer of property on trust or subject to a specified condition, an event arises that was not foreseen by the settlor or transferor. In these circumstances, the courts decide that the equitable interest be returned to the settlor or transferor. This type of resulting trust arises in a variety of situations as follows:

- The failure of an express trust, see *Re Ames* (see above), where a purported marriage settlement was void.
- The transfer of property to trustees without specifying the terms of the trust, see *Vandervell v IRC* [1967] 2 AC 291 (see above), vagueness as to the destination of the equitable interest in a share option scheme.
- The transfer of property subject to a condition precedent that was not achieved, see *Barclays Bank v Quistclose* (see above), a loan created for a specific purpose which that was not fulfilled.
- Where the trust object had been achieved with the use of some of the trust property, the surplus may be held on resulting trust, see *Re Abbott*.

KEY CASE ANALYSIS: *Re Abbott* [1900] 2 Ch 326.

Background

- An appeal was launched to provide funds for two ladies who had very limited means.
- There was a surplus of funds left over after both beneficiaries had died.

The issue arose as to the destination of the funds.

Principle established

The court decided that the remainder of the fund was required to be returned to the contributors.

By way of contrast, the court may decide that, on construction of the instrument, the ulterior purpose of the settlor may be achieved by permitting the transferee to retain the property beneficially. In these circumstances there is no room for a resulting trust.

KEY CASE ANALYSIS: *Re Osoba* [1979] 1 WLR 247

Background

- A testator bequeathed his residuary estate to his widow 'for her maintenance and training of my daughter up to University grade'.
- The widow died and the daughter completed her formal education with use of only part of the fund.

Principle established

The court decided that references to maintenance and education in the will expressed the testator's motives for the gifts. But the testator's intention was to benefit his daughter out and out. Accordingly, the daughter took the surplus fund beneficially.

On-the-spot question

Read the judgment of Lord Wilberforce in *Barclays Bank v Quistclose* and consider the following questions:

- What conditions are required to be satisfied in order to trigger the so-called *Quistclose* trust?
- Critically consider Lord Wilberforce's analysis of a 'primary trust' for the creditors.

Presumed resulting trusts

A presumed resulting trust is a *prima facie* rule of evidence that creates a rebuttable presumption of law. It is a starting point that is required to be drawn until the contrary is proved. Where there is a purchase of property in the name of another or the voluntary transfer of property to another, and there is no definitive evidence concerning the transferor's real intention, equity *prima facie* considers that the transferee is a trustee for the transferor. In short, the transferor is presumed to have retained the equitable title and the transferee acquires the bare legal title. The rule is arbitrary but the presumption has the advantage of clarifying the ownership of the beneficial interest, subject to evidence to the contrary.

There are two occasions when the presumption arises, namely:

- a purchase of property in the name of another, and
- a voluntary conveyance of property in the name of another.

Purchase in the name of another

The rule is that where a purchaser contracts with a vendor to acquire real or personal property, but directs the vendor to transfer the property in the name of another, the transferee (with the legal title) is presumed to hold the property on trust for the purchaser. **Parol** evidence is admissible in order to identify the purchaser.

Key Definition

Parol – Evidence of oral statements and conduct.

For example, if Ambrose purchases shares in the name of Beatrice (i.e. Beatrice becomes the legal owner), the latter is presumed to hold the shares on trust for Ambrose.

The same rule applies where the property was jointly purchased by more than one purchaser and the property is conveyed in the name of one person (legal owner). The legal owner is presumed to hold the property on resulting trust for the purchasers in proportion to the contribution made by each party.

Voluntary transfer in the name of another

Another transaction that gives rise to a presumed resulting trust is the occasion where a **voluntary** transfer of personal property is made in the name of another.

Key Definition

Voluntary – Without consideration.

For example, David transfers the legal title to shares in the name of Erica and a resulting trust is presumed in favour of David, see *Re Vinogradoff* [1935] WN 68.

With regard to real property, s 60(3) of the Law of Property Act 1925 enacts that a resulting trust will not be implied. However, *Hodgson v Marks* decided that a resulting trust may still be implied in respect of transfers of realty.

ABOLITION OF THE PRESUMPTION OF ADVANCEMENT

At common law there used to be a presumption of advancement (gift) where there was a special relationship between the transferor and transferee. The categories of special relationships were fixed and arose where the transferee was the wife of the transferor, or where a father transferred property in favour of his legitimate child or stood *in loco parentis patris* to the child. The effect of the presumption was that it reversed the legal burden of proof and required the purchaser or transferor to prove that no gift was intended in favour of the transferee.

Section 199 of the Equality Act 2010 abolishes the presumption of advancement on the grounds that it was discriminatory against husbands and fathers, it was outdated and was possibly incompatible with rights under the European Convention on Human Rights.

REBUTTAL OF THE PRESUMPTION

The presumption of a resulting trust is, in a sense, an artificial rule for deciding the possible intention of the transferor or purchaser, and may give way to the real intentions of the parties. Although the weight of the presumption depends on the circumstances of each case, the courts will consider all the surrounding facts and decide whether the presumption has been rebutted or not. The quality of the rebutting evidence varies from case to case. Much depends on the relationship between the parties, their conduct and any statements made by them. For example, strong evidence will be needed to rebut the presumption of a resulting trust where a transfer of the legal title to property is made by a client to his solicitor. On the other hand, less evidence will be needed to rebut the presumption where a transfer is made by an uncle to his favourite nephew.

INTENDED UNLAWFUL TRANSACTIONS

Before the definitive case of *Tinsley v Milligan*, the maxim 'he who comes to equity must come with clean hands' was applied rigidly by the courts as though it was a fixed and immutable principle of equity. The effect was that the status of a transaction was determined conclusively by reference to the original intention of the transferor. For example, assume that a voluntary transfer was made (by Tom) in favour of a nominee (Norman) in an attempt to promote some unlawful activity that makes the transaction voidable (such as avoiding creditors). Before the unlawful purpose is completed, the transferor (Tom) repents and wishes to recover his property from the transferee (Norman). In *Tinker v Tinker* the court applied the maxim.

KEY CASE ANALYSIS: *Tinker v Tinker* [1970] 1 All ER 540

Background

- A husband transferred the matrimonial home to his wife in order to defeat his creditors if his business failed.
- His business flourished so that the unlawful activity was not achieved.
- His marriage failed and he wished to recover the house from his wife.
- The wife refused to re-transfer the house and claimed it as her own.

Principle established

The Court of Appeal decided against the husband on the ground that the transfer was tainted with impropriety and the husband was not entitled to adduce such evidence in order to establish his genuine intention.

The House of Lords in *Tinsley v Milligan* reviewed this principle and decided that if the transferor does not rely on the intended illegal transaction in order to establish a claim to an equitable interest, the intended unlawful nature of the transaction would be too remote to prevent a successful claim. In other words, if the claimant enjoys an equitable interest by way of a resulting trust, his subsequent intended unlawful transaction would not be a bar to a successful claim.

KEY CASE ANALYSIS: *Tinsley v Milligan* [1994] 1 AC 340

Background

- The defendant and claimant jointly purchased a property that was conveyed in the name of the claimant.
- Having the property in the name of the claimant assisted the defendant in committing a fraud on the Department of Health and Social Security (DHSS).
- A small amount of the proceeds of the fraud was used to purchase the house.
- The parties' relationship came to an end and the claimant sought to evict the defendant from the house.
- The defendant defended on the ground that she had an interest in the property based on her contribution to the purchase price.
- The claimant relied on *Tinker v Tinker* and contended that the defendant was not entitled to prove her contribution to the purchase price owing to the proceeds of fraud, albeit a small amount, being used in the purchase.

Principle established

The House of Lords decided in favour of the defendant on the ground that she based her claim on her contributions and therefore a resulting trust and was not relying on her impropriety to acquire an interest in the property.

On-the-spot question

To what extent may the maxim 'he who comes to equity must come with clean hands', which was applied in *Tinker v Tinker*, be reconciled with the principle adopted by the House of Lords in *Tinsley v Milligan*?

WINDING-UP OF UNINCORPORATED ASSOCIATIONS

An unincorporated association was considered in Chapter 6 and the point was made that such a body does not have a separate legal existence from its members. The issue here concerns the ownership of assets of the association on liquidation, in the absence of any definitive rules in the constitution of the association. A solution that is now outdated involved the resulting trust in favour of the subsisting members of the association on the date of liquidation – see *Re Printers and Transfers Society* [1899] 2 Ch 84.

The modern view is that membership of the association is based on contractual principles between the members. Equally, the winding-up of the association ought to be based on contractual principles. If the association was created to benefit its members, then only subsisting members on the date of liquidation are entitled to participate, see *Re Bucks Constabulary Society (No 2)* [1979] 1 WLR 936. If, on the other hand, the society was created to benefit third parties who are not members, then the members are not entitled to partake in a distribution of the assets, see *Re West Sussex Constabulary Fund* [1971] Ch 1. By the same reasoning, where the society is liquidated on the death of the penultimate member of the association, the assets will be held on trust for the last surviving member, see *Hanchett-Stamford v Attorney General* [2008] All ER (D) 391.

Occupational pension schemes

A pension is an annual payment made to an employee on his retirement. In some instances, the employee may be entitled to a lump sum in addition to the annuity. Contributions may be subject to tax relief but the pension is treated as income for the individual and may be subject to income tax. The quantification of the pension may be based on his final salary, referred to as a 'final salary' scheme. The costs of providing the annual sum cannot be accurately predicted and the employer may undertake to contribute to the scheme in order to maintain the value of the fund needed to pay the pension. The effect is that any surplus funds will benefit the employer. On the other hand, a 'money purchase' scheme is one where contributions are invested for the benefit of the individual. The individual is allocated a notional account or a 'pot of money', which is credited with contributions and investment growth of the fund. In contrast to the final salary scheme, the level of the 'pot' and therefore the benefit is not guaranteed and the investor takes the risk of a shortfall. In addition, a hybrid scheme may be operated involving a combination of final salary and money purchase.

The law on pension schemes involves a combination of contract law, trust law and statute law. The employer, as well as the employee, may be required to contribute to pension schemes. This manifests itself in a contract between the employer and employee specifying the amount of contributions each party is required to make and the entitlement to benefits. In addition, the trust institution may be extended to pension schemes. This would entail the advantages of separating the funds from the employer's assets in the event of insolvency and also allocating an equitable proprietary interest in the fund in the hands of the employee. However, the employee would have provided consideration (his services) for the trust relationship and occasionally the employer may be the settlor, one of the trustees and possibly a beneficiary. To that extent it is arguable that a special trust relationship will be created in connection with pension funds. In *Mettoy Pension Trustees v Evans*, the court decided that a power of appointment was required to be exercised in a fiduciary manner. The fact that the employees were non-volunteers was influential in coming to this conclusion.

KEY CASE ANALYSIS: *Mettoy Pension Trustees v Evans* [1990] 1 WLR 1587

Background

Mettoy Co plc launched an occupational pension scheme in 1968. The claimant became the sole trustee of the scheme. In 1980, new scheme rules were made that empowered the trustees to apply surpluses at their discretion. In 1983 the company was wound up and the issue concerned the exercise of the power to distribute surplus funds.

Principle established

The court decided that the exercise of the power was subject to fiduciary obligations imposed on the trustee company and could not be released in favour of the creditors of the company.

In *Davis v Richards and Wallington Industries Ltd*, the court relied on trust principles in deciding on the destination of surplus funds on the liquidation of an occupational pension scheme.

KEY CASE ANALYSIS: *Davis v Richards and Wallington Industries Ltd* [1990] 1 WLR 1511

Background

A group of companies had set up a pension scheme. The contributions were derived from three sources, namely employers' contributions, employees' contributions and funds transferred from companies that were taken over. Owing to financial difficulties, the company terminated the scheme, creating a surplus of funds.

Principle established

The court decided on trust principles that the employers' contributions were held on resulting trust. The employees' contributions and the transferred funds were taken by the Crown on a *bona vacantia*.

However, in *Air Jamaica v Charlton* [1999] 1 WLR 1399, the Privy Council criticised the solution adopted in the *Davis* case and decided that a resulting trust in favour of the employer and employees in proportion to their respective contributions was appropriate to reflect their implied intention.

Owing to the scandal involving Robert Maxwell's group of newspaper publishing companies, in which the pension funds of the Mirror Group Newspapers were unlawfully appropriated, a Pension Law Review Committee was set up under the Chairmanship of Professor Roy Goode. His report led to the passing of the Pensions Act 1995. This Act, together with the Pensions Act 2004, has increased the protection available to beneficiaries from fraud, maladministration and insolvency by tightening up on the regulation of such activities. The post of a Pensions Regulator has been created to police the proper running of pension schemes. In addition, a Pensions Ombudsman has been appointed to investigate complaints regarding maladministration. Hopefully these measures go a long way to avoid a repetition of the outrageous events that were orchestrated by Robert Maxwell and his accomplices.

CASE LAW SUMMARY

Barclays Bank v Quistclose – A loan for an identified purpose, which did not form part of the general assets of the debtor, was held on resulting trust for the creditor when the purpose was not achieved.

Re Ames – The creation of an express trust that failed triggered an automatic resulting trust for the settlor.

Re Vandervell Trusts (No 2) – Significant *obiter* pronouncement by Megarry J classifying resulting trusts into two categories – automatic and presumed.
The case involved the application of the formal requirements under s 53(1)(c) of the LPA 1925.

Re Abbott – The creation of an automatic resulting trust of surplus funds for contributors when the trust purpose came to an end.

Re Osoba – The resulting trust was not applicable where the trust purpose was still capable of being satisfied.

Tinsley v Milligan – A presumed resulting trust was capable of subsistence despite the existence of an element of illegality in purchasing an asset.

Tinker v Tinker – Application of the maxim 'he who comes to equity must come with clean hands' to a transaction entered into with a fraudulent intention. There was no room for equitable assistance by way of a resulting trust.

Re West Sussex Constabulary Fund – Principles of contract law, as distinct from trusts law, were applicable in respect of surplus funds of a defunct society.

Re Bucks Constabulary – Return of surplus funds to the members of a liquidated organisation by way of contractual principles.

ISSUES TO THINK ABOUT FURTHER

In *Vandervell Trusts (No 2)*, Megarry J classified resulting trusts into two categories – automatic and presumed. Professor Birks advocated a theory that the resulting trust is created in order to reverse the unjust enrichment of the legal owner of property. Lord Browne-Wilkinson in *Westdeutsche Landesbank* rejected this idea and decided that the resulting trust arose in order to give effect to the intentions of the parties. In *Air Jamaica v Charlton*, Lord Millett decided that the resulting trust is imposed on the basis of an absence of an intention on the part of the transferor to pass a beneficial interest to the transferee.

Do you think that the classification of resulting trusts by Megarry J in *Re Vandervell Trust (No 2)* into 'automatic' and 'presumed' is comprehensive enough to deal with the variety of events that create resulting trusts?

SUMMARY

- A resulting trust is a default mechanism that arises where a transfer in favour of a stated objective fails in whole or in part and the property is required to be returned to the transferor or settlor (automatic); see *Barclays Bank v Quistclose*.
- In addition, a resulting trust is presumed to arise in favour of a purchaser or transferor where property is purchased or transferred in the name of another (presumed). In this event, evidence may be admitted to establish the intention of the transferor and rebut the existence of the trust; see *Re Vinogradoff*.
- Where the transferor wishes to rely on evidence of an unlawful transaction in order to support the existence of a beneficial interest, the court may refuse to admit such evidence of illegality in accordance with the maxim 'he who comes to equity must come with clean hands'; see *Tinker v Tinker*.
- Exceptionally, where the transferor attempts to procure an unlawful transaction by transferring property to another, but repents and does not carry out the transaction, he may still be entitled to secure his interest in the property by relying on the principle of the resulting trust; see *Tinsley v Milligan*.
- The destination of assets on the winding-up of an unincorporated association is based on the 'contract holding' principle. Accordingly, only subsisting members of the association are entitled to participate in the winding-up of the body; see *Re Bucks Constabulary*.
- The last surviving member of the association is entitled to claim any surplus funds beneficially; see *Hanchett-Stamford v Attorney General*.
- Pension schemes are subject to the traditional trust principles but with special adaptations.

FURTHER READING

Creighton P, 'The recovery of property transferred for illegal purposes' (1997) 60 MLR 102.
[Examines Australian and English cases and notes a change in the courts' approach to proprietary claims based on unlawful purposes.]

Green G, 'The dissolution of unincorporated non-profit associations' (1980) 45 MLR 626.
[Considers alternative bases of distributing surplus funds on the liquidation of unincorporated associations to its members as tenants in common and by way of a resulting trust.]

Hayton D, 'Trust law and occupational pension schemes' [1993] Conv 283.
[Analyses and compares the key elements of occupational pension schemes with traditional trusts.]

Hayton D, 'Pension trusts and traditional Trust: dramatically different species of trusts' (2006) Conv 229.
[Considers the extent to which trust principles may be extended to pension fund trusts.]

Millett P, 'The *Quistclose* Trust: Who can Enforce It?' (1985) 101 LQR 269.
[Detailed analysis of the decision in *Quistclose* trust, concluding that the result in *Quistclose* does not involve the recognition of a new kind of enforceable private trust. It involves a different analysis of the issues posed in *Quistclose.*]

Ramjohn M, 'Cases and Materials on Equity and Trusts', 4th edn (Routledge-Cavendish, 2008).
[Detailed analysis of the law relating to equitable and trust principles.]

Ramjohn M, 'Unlocking Trusts', 4th edn (Routledge, 2013.
[A comprehensive and up to date text written in simple, clear language that de-mystifies complicated concepts in trusts law.]

Swadling W, 'A new role for resulting trusts' (1996) 16 LS 110.
[Analysis of the law relating to the relationship between restitution and resulting trusts.]

Swadling W, 'Explaining resulting trusts' (2008) 124 LQR 72.
[Examines the rationale behind the resulting trust and considers Lord Browne-Wilkinson's notion of failed resulting trusts.]

COMPANION WEBSITE

An online glossary compiled by the author is available on the companion website:
www.routledge.com/cw/beginningthelaw

Chapter 9
Constructive trusts

LEARNING OUTCOMES

At the end of this chapter, you should be able to:

- Define constructive trusts and appreciate the rationale for the creation of such trusts
- Distinguish between 'institutional' and 'remedial' constructive trusts
- Identify the categories of constructive trusts
- Comprehend the declaratory rules in respect of proprietary rights in the family home
- Appreciate the occasions when a stranger to a trust may become a constructive trustee or accountable for any profits received

INTRODUCTION

A constructive trust is an institution that has been created by the courts in order to promote justice and fairness between the parties. The effect of the trust is that the defendant holds the relevant property upon trust for the claimant whenever it would be **unconscionable** for the defendant to deny the claimant an interest in the property. Generally, constructive trusts are institutional in that they operate in accordance with established principles and may affect the interests of third parties. An alternative approach, which has found favour in North America, is that the trust is remedial in the sense that the court in its discretion declares the trust, which then operates prospectively. The categories of constructive trusts have been deliberately left vague by the court so as not to restrict its discretion. The Supreme Court has recently re-stated in *Jones v Kernott* that proprietary rights in the family home are subject to the constructive trust, provided that there is no evidence of a contrary intention. Finally, there are a number of occasions when a stranger to a trust may become a constructive trustee or may be accountable to the beneficiaries without becoming a constructive trustee.

Key Definition

Unconscionable – A broad concept in equity that seeks to maintain a balance between parties of unequal standing. The overriding requirement here is fairness between the parties.

CONSTRUCTIVE TRUSTS

A constructive trust is a residual category of trust that comes into play whenever the court decides that it would be unconscionable for the defendant to deny an interest in the property in favour of the claimant. The defendant is required to hold the property upon trust for the claimant. This type of trust is fundamentally different from an express or resulting trust. The constructive trust is not created in accordance with the express or implied intention of the settlor or transferor. It is a device created by the courts in the interests of justice and good conscience. The rationale for the creation of such a trust is to maintain a balance between a fiduciary and the innocent beneficiary. The courts reserve to themselves the power to interpret a transaction as giving rise to a constructive trust. All the circumstances surrounding a transaction will be taken into account, including the conduct of the relevant parties. The issue is whether, in the interests of justice, a trust ought to be imposed on the defendant.

For example, Tom and Terry hold property on trust but, in breach of trust, purport to sell the property to Charles, a third party, who has knowledge of the breach of trust. Although Tom and Terry are already express trustees and liable to the beneficiaries for breach of trust, they will become constructive trustees of any unauthorised profit made from their office as trustees, such as the proceeds of sale received from Charles. By virtue of Charles's participation in the breach with knowledge of the facts, he will be treated as a constructive trustee of the property acquired by him. The effect is that Tom and Terry, as fiduciaries, will be accountable to the trust for the profits they unfairly made, and Charles, a stranger to the trust, will be required to hold the trust property on behalf of the beneficiaries.

Institutional and remedial constructive trusts

An institutional constructive trust is a traditional trust that arises from the date of misconduct by the trustees. In appropriate cases the court merely declares the trust and imposes an order on the defendant in favour of the claimant. To this extent, the trust is retrospective from the date of the misconduct and affects the interests of parties who subsequently intermeddle with the trust property.

A remedial constructive trust is essentially a judicial remedy that gives rise to an equitable obligation whenever the court decides in its discretion to impose such a duty on the defendant. This type of trust operates prospectively from the date of the court order and is based on the principle of preventing unjust enrichment of the defendant at the expense of the innocent party.

The traditional view is that English law does not countenance the existence of the remedial constructive trust, see *Halifax Building Society v Thomas*.

KEY CASE ANALYSIS: *Halifax Building Society v Thomas* **[1996] 2 WLR 63**

Background

- The defendant obtained a mortgage by a fraudulent misrepresentation to the building society.
- He fell into arrears and the property was repossessed by the building society.
- The property was sold and the society was repaid the sum loaned, leaving a surplus of funds.
- The society claimed the surplus funds based on a remedial constructive trust of preventing an unjust enrichment of the defendant.

Principle established

The court rejected the claim by the society. There was no universal principle that required restitution of a benefit derived from wrongdoing. The defendant was merely a debtor as opposed to being a fiduciary for the society. Thus, the surplus belonged to the defendant although it could be confiscated as the proceeds of crime in separate criminal proceedings under the Criminal Justice Act 1988.

In the same vein, the expression 'constructive trust' has been confusingly used in a different sense, namely to refer to the duty to account. In this regard a trust and, in particular, a constructive trust attaches to specific property that is not received by the defendant in his own right, but by virtue of a transaction intended from the outset to create a trust in the hands of the defendant. Accordingly, an appropriation by the defendant for his own use will amount to a breach of trust.

On the other hand, the expression 'constructive trust' has been used and misconstrued as extending to cases that involve only a personal right to account to the claimant. These are occasions where it is alleged that the constructive trust obligation arises as a direct consequence of the unlawful transaction. In other words, the claimant obtains a remedial mechanism designed to give equitable relief for fraud. These are cases where the term has been inaccurately used as it amounts to upgrading a personal claim into a proprietary action.

The importance of the distinction concerns the limitation periods and obtaining priority when the defendant becomes bankrupt. By virtue of the Limitation Act 1980, there is no limitation period in respect of claims against trustees for the recovery of trust property.

Thus, if the defendant already holds property upon trust, a breach of trust by him will not involve the limitation periods if the purpose is to recover the property from the defendant. Likewise, if the trustee becomes insolvent, the rights of the beneficiaries will not be affected and their claims will be given priority over the claims of the creditors, see Lord Millet in *Paragon Finance v DB Thakerar & Co* [1999] 1 All ER 400.

On-the-spot question

 Distinguish a constructive trust from an express and resulting trust. Explain the justification for the constructive trust and identify the various meanings of such trusts.

RECOGNISED CATEGORIES OF CONSTRUCTIVE TRUSTS

Trustee or fiduciary making unauthorised profits

The rule is that a person occupying the position of a **fiduciary** (such as a trustee or agent) is prohibited from deriving any personal benefit by availing himself of his position, in the absence of authority from the settlor in the trust instrument, the consent of all of the beneficiaries or the permission of the court.

Key Definition

Fiduciary – A person who has contracted a relationship of confidence with another, such as a trustee or an agent. The relationship gives rise to an overriding duty of loyalty in favour of the innocent party – see the definition laid down by Millett LJ in *Bristol and West Building Society v Mothew* [1996] 4 All ER 698.

In other words, the trustee or fiduciary should not place himself in position where his duty may conflict with his personal interest. If such a conflict occurs and the trustee obtains a benefit or profit, the advantage is held on constructive trust for the beneficiary. In short, the trustee is accountable to the beneficiaries for the unauthorised profit. In particular, a trustee, without specific authority to the contrary is not entitled to purchase trust property for his own benefit. The position remains the same even if the purchase appears to be fair. If such a purchase takes place, the transaction is treated as **voidable** at the instance of the innocent party – see *Keech v Sandford* (1726) Sel Cas Ch 61, unauthorised renewal of a lease (trust property) by a trustee for his own benefit.

Key Definition

Voidable – A transaction that is valid until it is avoided by the innocent party.

The principle in *Keech v Sandford* has been extended to other fiduciary relationships including agents acting on behalf of their principals, directors in respect of companies, partners *vis-à-vis* co-partners and solicitors who act on behalf of their clients. A leading case on the point is *Boardman v Phipps*.

KEY CASE ANALYSIS: *Boardman v Phipps* [1967] 2 AC 46

Background

- Mr Boardman, a solicitor acting on behalf of a trust, became entitled to attend board meetings of the company.
- He became disgruntled with the way the company's business was organised.
- Acting on information he obtained from attending board meetings, Mr Boardman made a bid to take over the company.
- Mr Boardman incorrectly believed that he had the authority of all the beneficiaries to mount the takeover bid.
- The takeover bid was successful and the company, trust and Mr Boardman made huge profits.
- One of the beneficiaries (John Phipps), who did not give his consent, brought a claim against Mr Boardman to obtain the profits.

Principle established

The House of Lords decided that:

- Mr Boardman, as solicitor acting on behalf of the trust, became a fiduciary.
- He obtained confidential information as a representative of the trust.
- This special information was treated as an extension of the trust property.
- He utilised the information to reorganise the company and received huge profits.
- Since not all of the beneficiaries consented to the transaction, the defendant was accountable for the profits.
- Exceptionally, the court awarded generous remuneration to Mr Boardman for his unique skill, ability and determination.

In effect, the claimant is required to establish each of the following elements in order to succeed in a claim against the fiduciary:

(i)   the defendant owes fiduciary duties to the claimant (question of law); and
(ii) the defendant obtained a benefit (question of fact); and
(iii) there is a causal connection between the fiduciary relationship and the benefit (question of fact).

In *Holder v Holder* [1968] Ch 353, the claim failed in respect of the purchase of a farm by the defendant, the reason being that there was no causal connection between the benefit and the fiduciary relationship (executorship).

Bribes or secret profits received by fiduciaries

When a bribe is received in money or in kind, the money or property constituting the bribe at law belongs to the recipient or fiduciary. In other words, the property in the bribe passes to the recipient of the bribe in accordance with the intentions of the parties. The relationship between the parties is one of creditor and debtor only. These are not cases of the proprietary constructive trusts, but are merely occasions involving the duty to account for the bribe to the person to whom the duty was owed, see *Lister v Stubbs*.

KEY CASE ANALYSIS: *Lister v Stubbs* (1890) 45 Ch D 1

Background

• An employee received a bribe from a third party who supplied goods to the employer.
• The employer claimed the fund as the owner of trust property.

Principle established

The Court of Appeal decided that the bribe could not be considered as the property of the employer.

> Lindley LJ: 'Then comes the question, as between [employer] and [employee], whether [the employee] can keep the money he has received without accounting for it? Obviously not. I apprehend that he is liable to account for it the moment that he gets it. It is an obligation to pay and account to [the employer]. But the relation between them is that of debtor and creditor; it is not that of trustee and *cestui que trust*.'

An alternative approach was to treat the receipt of the bribe as trust property due to the person to whom the fiduciary duties are owed, namely the beneficiaries. Thus, the bribe is treated as payable on behalf of the beneficiaries. The maxim 'equity considers as done that which ought to be done' applies to the defendant and the fiduciary becomes a trustee of the bribe for the claimant. This approach was adopted by the Privy Council in *Attorney General for Hong Kong v Reid*.

KEY CASE ANALYSIS: *Attorney General for Hong Kong v Reid* **[1994] 1 All ER 1**

Background

- The DPP of Hong Kong received bribes from individuals for not maintaining certain prosecutions.
- The amount of the bribes was invested in several properties in New Zealand.
- The Attorney General of Hong Kong brought proceedings against the ex-DPP and claimed the houses bought with the proceeds of the bribes.
- The value of the houses had declined.

Principle established

- The Privy Council distinguished *Lister v Stubbs* and decided that the bribes were received by the DPP as a constructive trustee on behalf of the Government of Hong Kong.
- The bribes were traced to the properties that were bought and were subject to charges in favour of the Government of Hong Kong.
- Since the value of the properties had declined, the defendant was accountable for the difference between the bribes and the undervalue.

In *Reid*, the Privy Council refused to follow *Lister* and was influenced by the principle that the fiduciary ought not to be unjustly enriched at the expense of another. It felt that the imposition of the constructive trust had the effect of disentitling the defendant from any benefit received as a result of the bribe. Academics and textbook writers criticised the *Reid* decision and it was felt that depriving the fiduciary of the benefit may be achieved without resort to the constructive trust. The unjust enrichment by the defendant may be dealt with by adjusting or extending the rules relating to equitable compensation. This approach would be a more sensible course to take compared with the modification of the principles relating to proprietary interests as laid down in *Reid*.

In *Sinclair Investments Ltd v Versailles Ltd*, the Court of Appeal decided that unauthorised profits obtained in breach of fiduciary duties impose only a personal liability to account, as distinct from a proprietary right over the property.

KEY CASE ANALYSIS: *Sinclair Investments Ltd v Versailles Ltd* [2011] EWCA Civ 347

Background

- The defendant company acquired funds from investors and loans made by banks.
- The defendant was required to purchase stock with the funds but failed to do so.
- Instead, the company used the funds to inflate the value of its shares.
- A fraudulent director of the company sold a proportion of his shares in the company for £29m, which was then distributed to various parties.
- The claimants who lost out on substantial sums asserted a proprietary claim in respect of the proceeds of sale of the shares that it alleged were held on constructive trust on its behalf.

Principle established

The court decided against the claimant on the ground that no proprietary interest was acquired in the proceeds of sale of the shares. Instead, the claimant was entitled to an equitable account in respect of the money and other assets acquired by the fiduciary in breach of his duties.

On-the-spot question

 Should the receipt of a bribe or secret commission by a fiduciary be subject to the broad notion of a constructive trust?

Contracts for the sale of land

Once a specifically enforceable contract for the sale of land is made, the purchaser (who does not acquire the legal title to the property at this time) becomes the equitable owner of the property. Thus, on the date of the exchange of contracts, the vendor becomes a constructive trustee for the purchaser until the date of the completion of the sale.

KEY CASE ANALYSIS: *Lysaght v Edwards* (1876) 2 Ch D 499

Background

- Edwards agreed in writing to sell real property to the claimant.
- Edwards died before completion.
- By his will, Edwards transferred his property to trustees to sell and invest the proceeds of sale.
- The claimant applied to the court for an order requiring the executors to complete the sale.

Principle established

The court decided that on the creation of the contract, the equitable interest in the property was transferred to the purchaser by operation of law.

Equity will not allow a statute to be used as an engine of fraud

Acts of Parliament are binding on all courts, even courts of equity. But courts of equity are entitled to adopt a pragmatic approach in considering the validity of claims in equity with an overriding objective to achieve justice. Accordingly, if strict compliance with a statutory provision (such as the formalities) has the incidental effect of perpetrating a fraud, the court is entitled to suspend the operation of such provision. This compromise solution has the effect of preventing unjust enrichment, see *Rochefoucauld v Boustead* [1897] 1 Ch 196, considered in Chapter 1.

The family home

The current principles concerning the interest of the parties in the family home may be summarised as follows:

(1) The family home is regarded in the majority of families as the most valuable asset. The legal title may be vested in the joint names of the partners or, as is sometimes the case, only one partner acquires the legal title.

(2) The presumption of the resulting trust (and before its abolition, the presumption of advancement) were regarded as outmoded principles better suited to a different society, see *Pettit v Pettit* [1970] AC 777.

(3) The interest in the home is based on settled principles of property law.

(4) The same common law principles are applicable to married and unmarried partners.

(5)   If the parties have expressly declared their beneficial interests in writing, then, in the absence of fraud or mistake, this will be conclusive as to their interests, see *Goodman v Gallant* [1986] 2 WLR 236.

(6)   If the express intention of the parties is not declared in writing, the intention becomes unenforceable for non-compliance with s 53(1)(b) of the Law of Property Act 1925 (see *ante*).

(7)   The court may **infer** the intention of the parties based on all the circumstances of the case under s 53(2) of the Law of Property Act 1925 (i.e. resulting and constructive trusts). The overriding objective of creating such trusts is not primarily to achieve justice between the parties, but to give effect to their intentions.

(8)   Where the legal title to the property is vested in the name of one party, the other party without the legal title has the burden of proving that a constructive trust under s 53(2) of the Law of Property Act 1925 operates.

(9)   Where the property is taken in the joint names of the parties who are jointly responsible for the payment of the mortgage (subject to any express agreement between the parties), the presumption is that equity follows the law. The effect is that the parties are treated as joint tenants at law and in equity, see *Stack v Dowden* [2007] 2 AC 432.

(10)   The presumption could be rebutted by a party proving a different common intention, reliance and detriment, either at the time they acquired the property or that they later formed a common intention that their respective shares have changed. This common intention is based on objective evidence, see *Jones v Kernott* (2011) Times LR 10 November, Supreme Court.

(11)   Where the parties have an interest in the property but it is not possible to ascertain their interest by direct evidence or by inference, the court may **impute** an intention to the parties that is considered to be fair. The entire course of dealing with the property between the parties will be taken into consideration, see *Oxley v Hiscock* [2005] Fam 211.

(12)   Domestic services such as looking after the children, without more, will be insufficient to create an interest in the home, see *Burns v Burns* [1984] 2 WLR 582.

(13)   In commercial cases, such as 'buy-to-let' transactions, where the property is bought in joint names, the presumption that equity follows the law does not apply. Instead, the presumption of a purchase money resulting trust will operate, see *Laskar v Laskar* [2008] 1 WLR 2695.

(14)   In the case of married couples, the same principles as outlined above will apply in order to ascertain the interests of the parties in family assets. In addition, under ss 23 to 25 of the Matrimonial Causes Act 1973 the court is given wide discretionary powers to declare or vary the interests of spouses in family assets on a divorce, decree of nullity or judicial separation.

(15)   Under s 37 of the Matrimonial Proceedings and Property Act 1970, spouses – including registered civil partners (but not unmarried couples) – who

contribute in a substantial way in money or money's worth to the improvement of real or personal property in which either or both of them have a beneficial interest, may enjoy a share or an enlarged share in the asset. The court decides whether a contribution is substantial or not by having regard to all the circumstances of the case.

(16)   Once the claimant has established an interest in the house, the value of that interest is ascertained at the time the property is sold. Accordingly, any increases or decreases in the value of the property are taken into consideration. If a party remains in occupation paying the mortgage, rates and other outgoings, he or she is credited with these expenses. Conversely, the party in occupation is debited with occupation rent for using the premises partly owned by the other, see *Oxley v Hiscock*.

(17)   The claimant is entitled to apply to the court under s 14 of the Trusts of Land and Appointment of Trustees Act 1996 for an order of sale.

Key Definitions

Inferred intention – An inferred intention is one that is objectively deduced to be the subjective actual intention of the parties in the light of their actions and statements.

Imputed intention – An imputed intention is one that is attributed to the parties even though no such actual intention can be deduced from the parties' actions and statements. The imputed intention involves deciding what the parties would have intended and is based on fairness.

KEY CASE ANALYSIS: *Jones v Kernott* **(2011) Times LR 10 November, Supreme Court.**

Background

- In 1985 the claimant and defendant co-habited with each other and bought a property in their joint names.
- The claimant paid the deposit and the balance was raised by a joint mortgage.
- The parties paid the joint mortgage and other household expenses out of their joint resources.
- In 1993 the defendant moved out of the house.
- The claimant continued living in the house with their two children and paid all outgoings.

- In 1996 the defendant purchased another property with the aid of a mortgage.
- In 2007 the claimant commenced proceedings claiming a declaration as to her interest under s 14 of the Trusts of Land and Appointment of Trustees Act 1996.

Principle established

The Supreme Court decided that the claimant was entitled to a 90 percent interest in the property by way of a constructive trust based on the inferred intentions of the parties.

On-the-spot question

? The definitive principles laid down by the House of Lords in *Stack v Dowden* (2007) have the potential to create a high degree of uncertainty for they are tantamount to the creation of the remedial constructive trust.

Discuss.

Secret trusts

A secret trust is an equitable obligation communicated to an intended trustee during the testator's lifetime, but which is intended to attach to a gift arising under the testator's **will**.

Key Definition

Will – A will is a formal document created by a testator under the Wills Act 1837 (as amended) that represents his wishes as to the distribution of his property after his death.

On a testator's death his will is **probated** and becomes open to public scrutiny.

Key Definition

Probate – A formal document in which an executor appointed under the testator's will becomes empowered to deal with the estate of the deceased.

But the testator may wish to make provision, after his death, for what he considers to be some embarrassing object, such as to benefit a mistress or an illegitimate child. To avoid adverse publicity, he may make an apparent gift by will to an intended trustee, subject to an understanding that he (the trustee) will hold the property for the benefit of the secret beneficiary.

In enforcing such trusts, equity does not contradict s 9 of the Wills Act 1837 (as amended) because the trust operates outside (*dehors*) the Wills Act. Indeed, the secret trust complements the will in that a valid will is assumed, but it is recognised that the will, on its own, does not reflect the true intention of the testator.

The bare minimum requirements to constitute a secret trust are a validly executed will that transfers property to the trustees, whether named as such under the will or not; and the acceptance by the donees or trustees *inter vivos* of an equitable obligation. It is immaterial that one of the intended beneficiaries under the trust, as distinct from the will, witnesses the will. Section 15 of the Wills Act 1837, which deprives a donee under the will or his spouse (or registered civil partner) from inheriting the property, is not applicable in this context. The beneficiary under the secret trust takes the property not under the will, but by virtue of the trust.

KEY CASE ANALYSIS: *Re Young* [1951] Ch 344

Background

- A testator made a bequest to his wife.
- Prior to his death the testator made an agreement with his wife to transfer property to specific beneficiaries, including his chauffeur.
- The chauffeur had witnessed the testator's will.

Principle established

The court decided that the chauffeur's interest did not lapse because he acquired his interest in the property under the trust and not under the will

There are two types of secret trusts: fully secret and half-secret trusts.

Fully secret trusts

These trusts are fully concealed on the face of the will. The testator transfers property by will to the trustees, apparently beneficially, but subject to an understanding that they will hold on trust for beneficiaries when they acquire the property. For example, Thomas, a testator, transfers 50,000 BT plc shares by will to his legatee, Len. Prior to his death, Thomas informs Len that he wishes Len to hold the shares on trust for Bertie absolutely, the secret beneficiary. Len becomes a trustee for Bertie on Thomas's death and is not allowed to take the property beneficially.

The following conditions are required to be fulfilled in order to create a fully secret trust.

(1)   It is essential that during his lifetime the testator communicate the terms of the intended trust to the trustee (**legatee** or **devisee**). This requirement reflects the distinction between a gift on trust and an absolute gift to the legatee.

> ### Key Definitions
>
> **Legatee** – A person who inherits personal property under a will.
>
> **Devisee** – A person who inherits real property under a will.

It follows that if the legatee or devisee only hears of the trust after the testator's death, no secret trust is created and the legatee or devisee may take beneficially. Accordingly, s 9 of the Wills Act 1837 may be used as a defence by the legatee or devisee who did not give such an undertaking, see *Wallgrave v Tebbs* (1855) 2 K & J 313.

(2)   If the testator communicates to the legatee the fact that he is to hold the legacy on trust, but fails to disclose the terms of the trust before his death, the intended secret trust fails. But the legatee will not take the property beneficially; instead, he will hold the property on resulting trust for the testator's estate or **next of kin**, see *Re Boyes*.

> ### Key Definition
>
> **Next of kin** – The nearest blood relation of the deceased. The next of kin inherits property on an intestacy.

KEY CASE ANALYSIS: *Re Boyes* (1884) 26 Ch D 531

Background

- A testator, by his will, transferred property to a legatee.
- Prior to executing the will, he secured an agreement from the legatee to hold the property upon trust with the terms to be supplied later.
- The testator died before communicating the terms to the legatee.

Principle established

The court decided that the intended secret trust failed and a resulting trust was created.

---

(3)   The communication of the terms of the trust may be made before or after the execution of the will, provided that it is made during the lifetime of the testator. Communication may be made directly with the legatee or may be effected constructively (i.e. the testator delivers a sealed envelope to the legatee subject to a direction, 'Not to be opened before my death'). Once the legatee is aware that the contents of the envelope are connected with a transfer of property by will, communication to the intended trustee is effective, see *Re Keen* [1937] Ch 236.

(4)   The legatee may 'expressly' or 'impliedly' accept the obligation imposed by the testator. An 'implied' acceptance is signified by silence on the part of the legatee or acquiescence after the communication of the terms of the trust. Thus, it is incumbent upon the legatee to inform the testator during his lifetime that he does not wish to undertake the onus of holding property on trust for the secret beneficiary. Failure to achieve this amounts to an acceptance of the obligation by the legatee.

(5)   The fully secret trust obligation may take the form of the trustee holding the property on trust for the secret beneficiary. Alternatively, the obligation may involve the legatee executing a will in favour of the secret beneficiary. In this event, the legatee may enjoy the property beneficially during his lifetime, see *Ottoway v Norman*.

KEY CASE ANALYSIS: *Ottoway v Norman* [1972] Ch 698

Background

- The testator, Harry Ottoway, by his will devised his bungalow and a legacy of £15,000 to his housekeeper, Miss Hodges.

- He orally agreed with Miss Hodges that she would leave the bungalow and 'the money' to his son, William Ottoway.
- Miss Hodges died leaving her estate to another.

Principle established

The court decided that a fully secret trust was created with regard to the bungalow only but not the 'money' because of uncertainty as to the subject matter in the latter case.

(6)   Where a testator leaves property to two or more legatees but informs one or some of them (but not all of them) of the terms of the trust, the issue arises as to whether the uninformed legatees are bound by the communication to the informed legatees. The solution here depends on the timing of the communication and the status of the legatees. If (a) the communication was made to the legatees before or at the time of the execution of the will and (b) they take as joint tenants, the uninformed legatees are bound to hold for the purposes communicated to the informed legatees. The reason commonly ascribed to this principle is that no one is allowed to take property beneficially under a fraud committed by another. If any one of the above conditions is not satisfied, the uninformed legatees are entitled to take the property beneficially, see *Re Stead* [1900] 1 Ch 237.

Half-secret trusts

This classification arises where the legatee or devisee takes as trustee on the face of the will but the terms of the trust are not specified in the will. For example, Tom, a testator, transfers property to Linden, a legatee, to 'hold upon trust for purposes that have been communicated to him'. The will acknowledges the existence of the trust but the terms have been concealed.

The following points are relevant in order to establish a half-secret trust.

(1)   The will is irrevocable on the death of the testator. It has been laid down that evidence is not admissible to contradict the terms of the will. To adduce such evidence would be tantamount to perpetrating a fraud; for example, where the will points to a past communication (i.e. a communication of the terms of the trust before the will was made), evidence is not admissible to prove a future communication. Similarly, since the will names the legatee as trustee, evidence is not admissible to prove that he is a beneficiary, see *Re Rees* [1950] Ch 204.

(2)   Where the communication of the terms of the trust is made before or at the time of the execution of the will, evidence may be adduced to prove the terms of the trust, see *Blackwell v Blackwell*.

KEY CASE ANALYSIS: *Blackwell v Blackwell* [1929] AC 318

Background

- A testator by a codicil (an amendment to a will executed in accordance with the Wills Act 1837) bequeathed a fund of £12,000 to legatees 'to apply for the purposes communicated to them'.
- Before the execution of the codicil, the terms of the trust were communicated to and accepted by them.
- The claimant asked the court to declare that the trust was invalid on the ground that the evidence did not satisfy s 9 of the Wills Act 1837.

Principle established

The court decided that the evidence was admissible and the half-secret trust was valid.

---

(3)   If the communication of the terms of the trust is made after the execution of the will but during the lifetime of the testator, the courts have decided that such communication is inadmissible. The justification commonly given for this principle is that a testator is prohibited from making a future unattested disposition by naming a trustee in the will and supplying the purposes subsequently. This principle was stated in an *obiter* pronouncement by Viscount Sumner in *Blackwell v Blackwell* (it must be said that this rule is not without its critics):

> A testator cannot reserve to himself a power of making future unwitnessed dispositions by merely naming a trustee and leaving the purposes of the trust to be supplied afterwards . . . To hold otherwise would be to enable the testator to 'give the go-by' to the requirements of the Wills Act.

(4)   The persons named as trustees on the face of the will are not entitled to take any part of the property beneficially, even if this is consistent with the intention of the testator. Likewise, on a failure, wholly or partly, of the half-secret trust, the trustee will hold the property on resulting trust for the testator's estate or next of kin.

On-the-spot question

The principles requiring communication of the terms of a half-secret trust to be made before or at the time of the execution of the will cannot be justified. Do you agree?

Strangers as constructive trustees or accountable to the innocent party

The general rule is that third parties or persons who have not been appointed trustees (agents of trustees such as accountants, bankers and solicitors) are not constructive trustees if they act in breach of their duties. They may be personally liable in damages for breach of contract or tort and are answerable to their principals, the trustees who appointed them. Provided that the agent acts within the course of his authority, does not receive the trust property for his own benefit and does not have knowledge that he is acting in a manner inconsistent with the terms of the trust, he does not become a constructive trustee.

KEY CASE ANALYSIS: *Barnes v Addy* (1874) LR 9 Ch App 244

Background

- A firm of solicitors was approached by the trustee for advice on whether a beneficiary ought to be appointed a sole trustee of part of the trust fund.
- The firm gave the trustee sound advice as to the risks of such appointment.
- The trustee disregarded such advice and instructed the firm to proceed with the appointment.
- This ultimately resulted in loss to the trust.
- A claim was brought against the firm of solicitors as constructive trustees.

Principle established

The court rejected the claim as the firm acted honestly, reasonably and within the course of its authority.

However, there are three occasions when a stranger to a trust may become liable as a constructive trustee or accountable for the loss suffered:

(i)   A stranger who becomes a trustee *de son tort* (i.e. a trustee of his own wrong).
       To fall within this category, the stranger is required to undertake acts
       characteristic of trusteeship and act on behalf of the trust and not for his own
       benefit. In short, this type of constructive trustee is one who, by mistake,
       believes that he was properly appointed to act on behalf of the trust, see
       Boardman v Phipps (earlier).

(ii)   The stranger knowingly receives trust property for his benefit. The rationale for
       liability under this head is that a stranger who knows that a fund is trust
       property transferred to him in breach of trust cannot take possession of the
       property for his own benefit, but is subject to the claims of the trust. He is not a
       bona fide transferee of the legal estate for value without notice. Thus, liability
       may arise where the stranger:

       •   receives trust property knowing that his possession is in breach of trust, or
       •   receives trust property initially without knowledge that his acquisition is in
            breach of trust, but subsequently becomes aware of the existence of the
            trust and acts in a manner inconsistent with the trust.

       The contest in this context is based on the assertion of proprietary rights. The trust
       sues the stranger claiming that it has better title to the property. Equity is entitled to
       adopt the most strenuous efforts in order to protect the beneficiary's interest under
       the trust and, in the majority of cases, has declared that any form of knowledge on
       the part of the trustee, subjective or objective, will be sufficient to make him liable
       under this head, see *Belmont Finance Corp v Williams Furniture (No. 2)* [1980] 1 All
       ER 393. On the other hand, in *Re Montagu* [1987] Ch 264, the court advocated that
       only subjective knowledge is relevant to make the stranger liable under this head.

       Recently, the Court of Appeal in *BCCI v Akindele* [2000] 3 WLR 1423 decided that
       the element of knowledge may be abandoned in favour of a broad test as to
       whether the defendant has so conducted himself that it would be
       unconscionable for him to retain the benefit of the profit received by him.

       It should be noted that this broad test of liability is likely to cause more
       confusion rather than clarity in the law.

(iii) Dishonest assistance in a fraudulent design in respect of trust property. Under
       this head of liability, a stranger to a trust becomes personally liable to account
       to the trust (as distinct from a constructive trustee) if he dishonestly assists in a
       fraudulent scheme conducted by another (perhaps the settlement trustee). This
       is the position even though the stranger does not receive the trust property. The
       basis of liability is the stranger's dishonesty and assistance in procuring the
       fraudulent transaction. In short, the stranger acts as an accomplice in a
       fraudulent design and his liability is not dependent on the principal being shown
       to be fraudulent, see *Royal Brunei Airlines v Tan*.

KEY CASE ANALYSIS: *Royal Brunei Airlines v Tan* [1995] 2 AC 378

Background

- The claimant appointed the defendant to act as a travel agent.
- The defendant acted through his company and defrauded the claimant.
- The company, controlled by the defendant, became insolvent and was liquidated.

The question in issue was whether the defendant was accountable to the claimant for the sums fraudulently received.

Principle established

The defendant was liable to the claimant and it was immaterial that it was not proved that the defendant's company acted dishonestly.

The following four elements are required to be established in order to attach liability on the stranger. They are (a) the existence of the trust (or a fiduciary relationship); (b) the existence of a dishonest or fraudulent design on the part of the trustees (or fiduciary); (c) the assistance by the stranger in that design; (d) dishonesty on the part of the accomplice (defendant). Since the benchmark of liability is dishonesty, the type of knowledge involved is subjective but based on an objective analysis. The test of dishonesty in criminal law is not appropriate in this context, see *Barlow Clowes v Eurotrust*.

KEY CASE ANALYSIS: *Barlow Clowes v Eurotrust* [2006] 1 All ER 333, Privy Council

Background

- The claimant was the liquidator of a company that operated a fraudulent investment scheme.
- The defendants were a company and its principal director who assisted in the misappropriation of investors' funds.
- The trial judge found that the director acted dishonestly by reference to an objective standard.

Principle established

The court decided in favour of the claimant. The principal director had suspicions that the relevant funds were tainted with fraud and failed to make inquiries. The standard of dishonesty was objective and no honest person would have assisted in the disposal of the funds.

CASE LAW SUMMARY

Halifax v Thomas – The court rejected the notion that a surplus of funds derived from a fraudulent transaction may be subject to a remedial constructive trust. Instead, the relationship of debtor and creditor had been created between the parties.

Keech v Sandford – A trustee who purchases trust property without the informed consent of the beneficiaries is subject to the sale being set aside.

Boardman v Phipps – A fiduciary who obtained unauthorised profits from his position as trustee is under a duty to account for those benefits.

Holder v Holder – In the absence of evidence that the defendant is a fiduciary, there was no basis to invalidate a purchase of trust property by the defendant.

Lister v Stubbs – A debtor/creditor relationship arises when a defendant receives a bribe or secret profit.

Attorney General for Hong Kong v Reid – A proprietary claim exists to recover the traceable proceeds of a bribe on the ground that the receipt of the bribe was made on behalf of the claimant.

Sinclair v Versailles – A personal liability to account arises where the defendant receives a bribe for abusing his position.

Stack v Dowden – Where the family home has been conveyed in the joint names of co-habiting parties, the maxim 'equity follows the law' is applicable and the equitable interest follows the legal title, in the absence of evidence to the contrary.

Jones v Kernott – A common intention constructive trust of the family home may arise for the benefit of both parties where the property has been conveyed in the joint names of the parties.

Oxley v Hiscock – The quantification of the interests of the parties in the family home is based on fairness, in the absence of evidence of the actual intentions of the parties.

Re Young – A secret trust arises outside the confines of the will. Thus, s 15 of the Wills Act 1837, which forfeits the interests of attesting witness, does not operate to deprive the witness of an interest under the trust.

Wallgrave v Tebbs – In the absence of evidence that, during the lifetime of the testator, the legatee had agreed to hold property upon trust, the legatee will be entitled beneficially to the property transferred by will.

Ottoway v Norman – A fully secret trust may be created where the secret trustee is required to execute a will transferring property to nominated beneficiaries.

Blackwell v Blackwell – To constitute admissible evidence, the terms of a half-secret trust are required to be communicated to the secret trustee before or at the time of the execution of the will.

Barnes v Addy – Strangers to a trust may become accountable for any benefits received, provided that they fall within the exceptional principles stated by Lord Selborne.

BCCI v Akindele – The test for the liability of a stranger to a trust was modified to accommodate the test of whether it is unconscionable for the stranger to retain the unauthorised benefit.

Re Montagu – Liability based on 'knowingly' receiving trust property involves a subjective test of knowledge equivalent to 'want of probity'.

Royal Brunei Airlines v Tan – The Privy Council decided that liability for dishonest assistance in a fraudulent transaction is not dependent on the liability of the fraudulent trustee.

Barlow Clowes v Eurotrust – The scope of the test of dishonesty is not dependent on the realisation of the defendant that the scheme is dishonest. The test for dishonesty involves an objective analysis by the courts.

ISSUES TO THINK ABOUT FURTHER

There has been a great deal of confusion as to the scope of the element of dishonesty in order to support a claim against a third party for dishonest assistance in a fraudulent transaction. In *Tan*, Lord Nicholls advocated an objective test, but with a subjective element, in evaluating whether the defendant was dishonest. In *Twinsectra v Yardley* [2002] UKHL 12,

Lord Hutton interpreted *Tan* to mean the combined objective and subjective test of dishonesty as exists in the criminal law, see *R v Ghosh* [1982] 2 All ER 689. In *Barlow Clowes v Eurotrust*, the Privy Council rejected the notion of the criminal law test and decided that the issue concerns an objective analysis to be decided by the judge. In *Abou Ramah v Abacha* [2006] EWCA Civ 1492, the Court of Appeal affirmed the approach in *Barlow Clowes* and decided that the test is objective, but in deciding this question the court is entitled to consider the knowledge and experience of the defendant. In *Bryant v Law Society* [2009] 1 WLR 163, in cases concerning disciplinary proceedings involving solicitors, the court decided that the test of dishonesty is the criminal law, combined objective and subjective standards test.

To what extent do you consider the law regarding dishonesty to be settled in a claim for dishonestly assisting another in a fraudulent transaction?

SUMMARY

- A constructive trust constitutes a residual category of trusts created by the courts whenever it would be inequitable for the defendant to deny the claimant an interest in the property.
- The traditional view of this type of trust is that the interest of the claimant does not arise for the first time when the court declares the trust to exist (institutional trust). A minority view is that the trust is remedial in the sense that the court creates a remedy to prevent the unjust enrichment of the defendant.
- Although the courts jealously guard their discretion to impose such trust whenever the occasion demands it, there are a number of traditional categories of constructive trusts.
- An illustration of the broad discretionary power of the court is the rule in *Keech v Sandford*, applicable whenever a trustee or fiduciary abuses his position and receives an unauthorised profit.
- With regard to bribes and secret profits, the courts have recently repositioned themselves by treating such occasions as giving rise to a personal liability to account, as distinct from a constructive trust.
- Specifically enforceable contracts for the sale of land give rise to constructive trusts.
- In appropriate cases, the maxim 'equity will not allow a statute to be used as an engine for fraud' may be adopted in order to suppress fraudulent conduct in the interests of justice.
- The constructive trust may be deployed in order to ascertain the interest of a party in the family home.
- Secret trusts, whether fully or half-secret, may be enforced by the courts in order to give effect to the intention of the testator, expressed outside the will.
- A stranger to a trust may exceptionally become a constructive trustee or accountable for any unauthorised benefits received by him.

FURTHER READING

Battersby G, 'Ownership of the family home; *Stack v Dowden* in the House of Lords' (2008) CFLQ 255.
[Analyses the impact of the House of Lords judgments in *Stack v Dowden* on the principles concerning ownership of interests in the family home.]

Lord Clarke MR, 'Claims against professionals: Negligence, dishonesty and fraud' (2006) 22 Professional Negligence 70.
[Discusses the nature of the test for dishonest assistance and the defendant's objective knowledge that his conduct is dishonest.]

Etherton T, 'Constructive trusts: A new model for equity and unjust enrichment' (2008) Cambridge Law Journal 265.
[Analyses the role of the constructive trust and considers whether it satisfies claims for unjust enrichment.]

Ferris G, 'The Advice of the Privy Council in *Royal Brunei Airlines v Tan* (1996) 30 Law Teacher 111.
[Examines the elements of liability of third parties for dishonest assistance in a fraudulent scheme.]

Hibbert T, 'Dishonesty and knowledge of accessories and recipients' (2000) JIBL 138.
[This article focuses on the mental state of the defendant on a claim for knowingly receiving trust property and dishonest assistance in a fraudulent scheme.]

Kincaid D, 'The tangled web: The relationship between a secret trust and the will' (2000) 64 Conv 421.
[Discusses a variety of controversial issues concerning secret trusts.]

Ramjohn M, 'Text, Cases and Materials on Equity and Trusts', 4th edn (Routledge-Cavendish, 2008).
[Standard text providing detailed treatment of equity and trust issues.]

Ramjohn M, 'Unlocking Trusts' 4th edn (Routledge, 2013).
[A comprehensive and up to date text written in simple, clear language that de-mystifies complicated concepts in trusts law.]

Tattersall M, '*Stack v Dowden*; Imputing an intention' (2008) Fam Law 424.
[Considers whether the principles concerning an imputed intention could be applied to family homes in the sole name of one of the parties as it is applied to homes in joint names.]

Wilde D, 'Secret and semi-secret trusts: Justifying distinctions between the two' (1995) Conv 366.
[Considers whether the tests for the validity of fully and half-secret trusts may be justified.]

COMPANION WEBSITE

An online glossary compiled by the author is available on the companion website:
www.routledge.com/cw/beginningthelaw

Chapter 10
Breach of trust

LEARNING OUTCOMES

At the end of this chapter, you should be able to:

- Ascertain the occasions that give rise to the appointment, retirement and removal of trustees
- Understand why it is necessary to impose a number of onerous duties on the trustees
- Identify the various duties that are imposed on trustees
- Understand the scope of the powers that may be vested in trustees
- Recognise when and how the terms of a trust may be modified
- Analyse the occasions when a breach of trust may take place
- Appreciate whether the trustee may enlist a defence to a claim for breach of trust
- Comprehend the process of tracing and proprietary remedies

INTRODUCTION

Trustees play an essential role in the administration of a trust. There are a number of occasions that create a need to appoint trustees. In addition, there are both statutory and common law provisions to facilitate the retirement and removal of trustees during the continuance of the trust. Trustees are regarded as occupying a fiduciary position and are required to comply with a number of duties in order to maintain the proper administration of the trust. By the same token, trustees are vested with additional powers in order to facilitate their dealings with the trust property. Where the trustees neglect their duties or misconduct themselves in exercising their powers, they may become liable to the beneficiaries for breach of trust. In exceptional circumstances, the trustees may be relieved from liability by reference to a clause contained in the trust instrument or by relying on a statutory provision. Finally, the beneficiaries may use personal or proprietary remedies against the trustees or defaulting third parties in order to alleviate their losses.

APPOINTMENT, RETIREMENT AND REMOVAL OF TRUSTEES

There are only two occasions when it is necessary to appoint trustees: on the creation of a new trust and during the continuance of an existing trust. Where a settlor attempts to create an *inter vivos* trust but fails to appoint trustees, the intended express trust will fail because the intended trustees do not acquire the trust property. But where a testator leaves property upon trust set out in the will but fails to appoint a trustee, the executors will become the trustees and the trust will be constituted by the will.

Where the trust is created and the property has become vested in more than one trustee, they acquire the property as joint tenants. Accordingly, on the death of a trustee the property automatically accrues to the survivors, see s 18(1) of the Trustee Act 1925. The authority to appoint trustees (replacement or additional) may be derived from three sources – express power, statutory and the court.

Express power

The trust instrument may confer authority to appoint trustees generally or in specific circumstances. The latter would be unusual as the statutory powers, referred to below, are regarded as adequate. A general, unrestricted authority to appoint trustees will be treated as conclusive of the authority to appoint trustees. A special authority to appoint trustees will be construed strictly and the occasion is required to fall squarely within the circumstances laid down in the trust instrument. In *Re Wheeler and De Rochow* [1896] 1 Ch 315, the authority was exercisable where a trustee became 'incapable' of acting. One of the trustees became bankrupt. It was decided that this made him 'unfit' but not 'incapable' of acting. Thus, there was no express authority.

Statutory powers

The most popular source of authority to appoint trustees is derived from the Trustee Act 1925. Section 36(1) of the Trustee Act 1925 lists the circumstances when replacement trustees may be appointed. These include the occasions when a trustee is dead, remains outside the UK for a continuous period of 12 months or more, desires to be discharged, refuses to act, is unfit or incapable of acting or the trustee is an infant. The persons who may exercise this power, in chronological order, are those nominated in the trust instrument, the surviving trustees if willing, and the personal representatives of the last surviving trustee. Section 36(6) of the 1925 Act outlines the circumstances when additional trustees (up to a maximum of four) may be appointed. Sections 19–21 of the Trusts of Land and Appointment of Trustees Act 1996 (TOLATA) enact powers authorising beneficiaries to direct the retirement of trustees and/or the appointment of trustees, if the beneficiaries are of full age and capacity and, collectively, are absolutely entitled to the trust property.

Appointment by the court

Section 41 of the Trustee Act 1925 outlines the sweeping provisions when the court may appoint replacement or additional trustees where it is 'expedient, difficult or impracticable to do so without the assistance of the court'. In exercising its discretion, the court will have regard to the interests of the beneficiaries and the efficient administration of the trust, see *Re Tempest* (1866) 1 Ch App 485, where the court exercised its power to avoid family dissension.

Retirement

A trustee may retire from the trust in one of five ways:

- By taking advantage of a power in the trust instrument.
- By taking advantage of a statutory power under:

  - section 36(1) of the Trustee Act 1925 when a new trustee is appointed, or
  - section 39 of the Trustee Act 1925 where no new trustee is appointed.

- By obtaining the consent of all the beneficiaries who are *sui juris* (full age and sound mind) and absolutely entitled to the trust property under the *Saunders v Vautier* principle.
- By direction from the relevant beneficiaries under s 19 of TOLATA 1996.
- By obtaining the authority of the court.

Removal

A trustee may be removed from office in one of the following four ways:

- By virtue of a power contained in the trust instrument. This is highly unusual but, if the circumstances are clear, authority may exist.
- Under s 36(1) of the Trustee Act 1925. This involves the removal of a trustee and appointment of a replacement trustee in circumstances laid down within the statutory provision.
- In the circumstances specified in ss 19 and 20 of TOLATA 1996.
- Under a court order under s 41 of the Trustee Act 1925 or the inherent jurisdiction of the court. In *Letterstedt v Broers* (1884) 9 AC 371, the Privy Council decided that hostility between the trustees and beneficiaries that was likely to prejudice the proper administration of the trust may be a ground for the removal of a trustee in accordance with the inherent jurisdiction of the court.

On-the-spot question

 In what circumstances, and by whom, may a trustee be appointed to, or removed from, office?

DUTIES OF TRUSTEES

The office of trusteeship is restricted by a number of wide-ranging duties created by the courts and statute law over the centuries. The rationale for these duties is based on the fiduciary position of trustees or the inequality of the position of the parties. Equity principles were designed to protect beneficiaries from the possibility of a trustee or other fiduciary abusing his position. Thus, in Chapter 9 when dealing with the constructive trust, we highlighted the rule that prevented a trustee from putting himself in a position where his duty conflicted with his personal interest. This includes the 'self-dealing' rule to the effect that a trustee who purchases trust property without authority will be liable to have the sale set aside at the instance of the beneficiaries, see *Boardman v Phipps* (*ante*). By the same reasoning, the rule prohibits the trustee from purchasing the beneficiary's interest – also known as the 'fair-dealing' rule, see *Keech v Sandford* (*ante*). In addition, trustees are required to conform to a number of non-fiduciary duties. These are the duty of care, the duties to act unanimously, impartially and personally in the administration of the trust, and the duty to provide information and accounts to the beneficiaries. The failure on the part of the trustees to comply with these duties may amount to a breach of trust.

Duty of care

The trustee's general duty of care has been created by the courts and recently this duty has been broadened by the Trustee Act 2000 with regard to the investment powers of the trustees.

Throughout the administration of the trust, the common law duty of care imposed on trustees is to exhibit an objective standard of skill as would be expected from an ordinary prudent man of business. This test was stated by Lord Watson in *Learoyd v Whiteley* (1887) 12 AC 727, thus:

> As a general rule the law requires of a trustee no higher degree of diligence in the execution of his office than a man of ordinary prudence would exercise in the management of his own private affairs.

The trustee's duty of care concerning the investment of trust property and associated activities has been laid down in the Trustee Act 2000. Section 1(1) of the Act lays down that the trustees have a duty of care to act reasonably, having regard to any special knowledge and experience possessed or held out by them personally or in the course of their business or profession. Thus, solicitors and bankers may be under a more stringent duty of care than a layperson. This test is subject to any contrary intention expressed in the trust instrument.

In accordance with Schedule 1 of the 2000 Act, the statutory duty of care arises in respect of investment powers as well as arrangements to delegate functions to agents, nominees and custodians and the review of their actions. In addition the duty arises in respect of the power to insure the trust property.

Duty to act unanimously

Trustees have control of the trust property and are given the joint responsibility to act on behalf of the trust. Trustees are jointly and severally liable for their actions. Thus, subject to provisions to the contrary in the trust instrument, the acts and decisions of the trustees (even a majority of the trustees) are not binding on others. The issue is whether one or more trustees ought to stand firm and oppose the decision of others. Accordingly, a 'passive' or 'sleeping' trustee may be liable to the beneficiaries for breach of trust along with the 'active' trustees – see *Bahin v Hughes* (1886) 31 Ch D 390.

Duty to act impartially

In performing their duties, trustees are required to act honestly, diligently and in the best interests of the beneficiaries. Accordingly, trustees are not entitled to show favour to any beneficiary to the detriment of others. This duty to deal with the beneficiaries even-handedly is part and parcel of the trustees' fiduciary duty owed to all the beneficiaries. Thus, the trustees must not favour those beneficiaries entitled to the capital of the fund to the detriment of the income beneficiaries, but must maintain a balance between the beneficiaries.

Duty to act personally

Generally, the trustees were appointed by the settlor because of their personal qualities and it is expected that they will act personally in executing their duties. However, in the modern commercial climate it is unrealistic to expect trustees to perform all the activities of the trust personally. Sections 11–23 of the Trustee Act 2000 deal with the trustees' power to appoint agents, nominees and custodians to perform '**delegable functions**' subject to a power to review their actions.

Key Definition

Delegable functions – These are defined in s 11(2) of the Trustee Act 2000 as any function of the trustees. Excluded are dispositive discretions and powers to allocate fees and other payments to capital or income.

Duty to provide information and accounts

Trustees are required to keep proper accounts for the benefit of the trust and may employ an agent to do so. The beneficiaries are entitled to inspect the accounts. In *O'Rourke v Darbishire* [1920] AC 581, the House of Lords decided that the beneficiary's right of disclosure of trust documents is proprietary in the sense that the documents are owned by the beneficiaries who therefore have access to the documents. But in *Schmidt v Rosewood Trust Ltd* [2003] 3 All ER 76, the Privy Council questioned this principle and decided that the beneficiary's right to disclosure is based on the trustees' fiduciary duty to inform the beneficiary and to render accounts, not on a proprietary right to trust documents.

POWERS OF TRUSTEES

To assist the trustees in managing the trust property in the best interests of the beneficiaries, a number of default powers have been vested in the trustees. These include the power of investment, the powers of maintenance and advancement, the power to give receipts and the power to insure the trust property.

Power of investment

Trustees are obliged to maintain the value of the trust fund in the interests of the beneficiaries and may be given wide powers of investment by the settlor in the trust instrument. However, a default power of investment has been created by ss 1–10 of the Trustee Act 2000. The wide power of investment has been laid down in s 3(1) of the Act to the effect that the trustee may make such investments as if 'he were absolutely entitled to the assets of the trust'. Of course, trustees are required to comply with the duty of care (see earlier) not only in selecting but in reviewing the investments.

When investing the trust fund, trustees are required to have regard to the 'standard investment criteria'. This requires the trustees to decide on the suitability of the investment, the need for diversification and to obtain and consider proper advice before investing. This test varies from trust to trust. In addition, trustees are entitled to purchase land as an investment or for the occupation by a beneficiary.

Power of maintenance

A power of maintenance is a discretion granted to the trustees to pay or apply income for the benefit of an infant beneficiary at a time prior to the beneficiary acquiring a right to the income or capital of the trust. Maintenance payments are expenditure incurred out of the income of a fund for routine recurring purposes such as food, clothing, rent and education. The power of maintenance may be derived from the trust instrument but in default may be created under s 31 of the Trustee Act 1925. The statutory power is exercisable during the infancy of the beneficiary and until he becomes of full age or acquires a vested interest in the capital. The factors that are required to be taken into account are the age of the infant, his requirements, the general circumstances of the case and whether other income is available for his maintenance. For example, a trust of £100,000 has been created by Sam for the benefit of his grandson, Charles, provided he attains the age of 25. Charles is 12 years old and his parents, Mary and Michael, are in need of funds to provide for his education. The trustees are required to decide whether to exercise their discretion to pay or apply part or all of the fund for Charles's education.

Power of advancement

The power of advancement may be created expressly or by s 32 of the Trustee Act 1925. An advancement is a payment from the capital funds of a trust to, or on behalf of, a beneficiary in respect of some long-term commitment, such as the purchase of a house or establishment of a business. A potential beneficiary may be in need of capital from the trust fund before becoming entitled, as of right, to the capital from the fund. In such a case the trustees may be entitled to accelerate the enjoyment of his interest by an advance payment of capital. The policy behind s 32 is to invest trustees with discretion to appoint up to half of the presumptive share of the capital of the beneficiary for his advancement or benefit. The value of the presumptive share of the beneficiary is measured on the date of the advancement. If the ceiling concerning the statutory power of advancement has been reached (i.e. half the presumptive share of capital), the statutory power of advancement would be exhausted even if the value of the capital subsequently increases – see *Marquess of Abergavenny v Ram* [1981] 2 All ER 643. The settlor, of course, may modify the ceiling of advancement payments.

Power to give receipts

Section 14(1) of the Trustee Act 1925 enacts that a receipt in writing will be a sufficient discharge of the trustee's duty of payment, except that a sole trustee is not exonerated in respect of the proceeds of sale arising from the sale of land.

Power to insure

Section 19 of the Trustee Act 1925 creates a power to insure the trust property against loss or damage and the trustees are allowed to pay the premiums out of the income. Section 20 of the 1925 Act enacts that the proceeds of insurance money received by the trustees will be treated as capital.

VARIATION OF THE TERMS OF A TRUST

Trustees are under an obligation to comply with the terms of the trust. A failure to obey these trust requirements may result in breach of trust claims. However, there are processes by the beneficiaries and the courts that authorise the modification of the trusts terms.

- Rule in *Saunders v Vautier* (1841) 4 Beav 115: The principle in this case is that a beneficiary who is sui juris and absolutely entitled to the trust property is entitled to terminate the trust even against the wishes of the settlor or trustee. Thus, the beneficiary is entitled to rewrite the terms of the trust. The same principle applies where there are multiple beneficiaries.

Key Definition

Sui juris – A phrase denoting that a person has the mental and legal capacity to transfer property.

The court has the power to approve arrangements amounting to a departure from the terms of a trust. These are as follows:

- Emergencies: The court has an inherent power to depart from the terms of a trust where some unforeseen emergency arises concerning the management and administration of the trust. In *Re New* [1910] 2 Ch 524, the court authorised the trustees to exchange trust shares for more realisable shares in a different company.
- Section 57(1) of the Trustee Act 1925: The court may authorise the trustees to enter into a transaction where it is 'expedient' to do so in the administration and management of the trust. Expediency refers to occasions where there is no emergency as such, but the court decides that the specific transaction will be

advantageous to the trust. The section has been used to extend the trustees' power of investment – see *Mason v Farbrother* [1983] 2 All ER 1078.

- Section 53 of the Trustee Act 1925: The court may authorise dealings with an infant beneficiary's property for his maintenance, education or benefit.
- Section 64(1) of the Settled Land Act 1925: This section empowers the court to sanction departures from the trust that are for the benefit of the settled land or beneficiaries provided that they could be effected by an absolute owner. This section authorises the alteration of beneficial interests. In *Raikes v Lygon* [1988] 1 WLR 281, the court authorised the re-moulding of the interests of the beneficiaries under a settlement.
- Section 24 of the Matrimonial Causes Act 1973: The court is empowered to vary settlements for the benefit of the parties to a marriage and children.
- Section 1 of the Variation of Trusts Act 1958: Under this Act the court may approve variations of interests under a trust on behalf of persons who cannot assent because of incapacity, persons not yet born or those who may become entitled directly or indirectly to an interest at a future date. The proposed variation is required to be for the 'benefit' of the persons concerned. 'Benefit' is not restricted to financial advantage but may extend to moral or social benefit. In *Re Remnant's Settlement Trust* [1970] Ch 560, the court sanctioned the removal of a religious limitation in order to avoid family dissension.

On-the-spot question

 How broadly has the expression 'benefit' under the Variation of Trusts Act 1958 been interpreted by the courts?

BREACH OF TRUST

A trustee is liable for a breach of trust if he fails to perform his duties either by omitting to do any act that he ought to have done, or doing an act that he ought not to have done. The beneficiary is required to establish a causal connection between the breach of trust and the loss suffered either directly or indirectly by the trust. Indeed, even if the trust suffers no loss, the beneficiary is entitled to claim any profit that accrues to the trustees as a result of a breach. Once a breach of trust has been committed, the trustees become liable to place the trust estate in the same position as it would have been if no breach had been committed. This is based on equitable principles of restitution. In *Target Holdings v Redfern* [1995] 3 All ER 785, Lord Browne-Wilkinson summarised the test thus:

> ... the basic rule is that a trustee in breach of trust must restore or pay to the trust estate either the assets which have been lost ... or compensation for such loss ... the common law rules of remoteness and causation do not apply.

In assessing the compensation, the nature of the breach of duty and whether the trust is 'traditional' or 'commercial' are factors to be considered. In the case of commercial transactions, the basis of compensation is that applied in the case of common law damages. But in the case where the breach occurs in a traditional type of family trust, the trustee is required to account for and restore all that had been lost by the trust. In *Target Holdings v Redfern*, the court rejected the claim of the claimants to the effect that in the case of a commercial transaction the loss was to be measured at the time of the breach. This would have entitled the claimants to obtain compensation of an amount that exceeded its loss and would not have reflected the basic principles of equitable compensation.

Contribution and indemnity between trustees

In principle, the liability of the trustees is joint and several. The innocent beneficiary may sue one or more or all of the trustees. If a successful action is brought against one of several trustees, he has a right of contribution from his co-trustees. The effect is that each trustee will contribute equally to the damages awarded in favour of the claimant, unless the court decides otherwise. The position today is that the right of contribution is governed by the Civil Liability (Contribution) Act 1978. The court has a discretion concerning the amount of the contribution that may be recoverable from any other person liable in respect of the same damage.

The Act does not apply to an indemnity that is governed entirely by case law. There are three circumstances when a trustee is required to indemnify his co-trustees in respect of their liability to the beneficiaries.

(i)   Where one trustee has fraudulently obtained a benefit from a breach of trust, see *Bahin v Hughes* (1886) 31 Ch D 390.
(ii)   Where the breach of trust was committed on the advice of a solicitor-trustee, see *Re Partington* (1887) 57 LT 654.
(iii) The rule in *Chillingworth v Chambers* [1896] 1 Ch 385. The rule is that where a trustee is also a beneficiary (whether he receives a benefit or not is immaterial) and the trustees are liable for breach of trust, the beneficiary/trustee is required to indemnify his co-trustee to the extent of his beneficial interest. If the loss exceeds the beneficial interest, the trustees will share the surplus loss equally, insofar as it exceeds the beneficial interest.

Defences to actions for breach of trust

If the trustees have been sued for breach of trust, there are a number of defences that they are entitled to raise. These are outlined below:

Consent of the beneficiary

A beneficiary who has freely consented to or concurred in a breach of trust is not entitled to renege on his promise and sue the trustees. The beneficiary is required to be of full age and sound mind, with full knowledge of all the relevant facts and to exercise an independent judgment. The burden of proof will be on the trustees to establish these elements, see *Nail v Punter* (1832) 5 Sim 555.

Impounding the interest of the beneficiary

Under the inherent jurisdiction of the court, a beneficiary who instigated the breach of trust may be required to indemnify the trustees. The rule of equity was extended in s 62 of the Trustee Act 1925. Under this section the court has a discretion that it will not exercise if the beneficiary was not aware of the full facts. Section 62 is applicable irrespective of any intention, on the part of the beneficiary, to receive a personal benefit or not. The consent of the beneficiary is required to be executed in writing.

Relief under s 61 of the Trustee Act 1925

Section 61 of the Trustee Act 1925 provides three main ingredients for granting relief, namely:

(a)   the trustee acted honestly, and
(b)   reasonably, and
(c)   he ought fairly to be excused in respect of the breach.

These ingredients are cumulative and the trustee has the burden of proof. The expression 'honestly' means that the trustee acted in good faith. This is a question of fact. The word 'reasonably' indicates that the trustee acted prudently. If these two criteria are satisfied, the court has discretion as to whether to excuse the trustee or not. The test in exercising the discretion is to have regard to both the interests of the trustees and the beneficiaries, and deciding whether the breach of trust ought to be forgiven in whole or in part. In the absence of special circumstances, a trustee who has acted honestly and reasonably ought to be relieved.

KEY CASE ANALYSIS: *Perrins v Bellamy* **[1899] 1 Ch 797**

Background

- Trustees of a settlement sought the advice of solicitors in respect of an asset of the trust.
- Acting on such advice, the trustees executed a sale of leasehold properties.
- The advice proved to be incorrect, thereby diminishing the income of the claimant.

Principle established

On a claim for breach of trust, the trustees successfully claimed relief under the predecessor to s 61 of the Trustee Act 1925.

Limitation and laches

In order to pursue a claim for breach of trust, the action is required to be commenced within the limitation period. The limitation period is six years from the date of the breach of trust, see s 21(3) of the Limitation Act 1980. For these purposes a cause of action does not accrue in respect of future interests (remainders and reversions) until the interest falls into possession. In addition, time does not begin to run against a beneficiary suffering from a disability (infancy or mental incapacity) until the disability ends.

By way of exception, s 21(1) of the 1980 Act declares that no limitation period operates in respect of a claim against the trustee for a fraud or to recover the trust property from the trustee. In these cases, the doctrine of laches operates.

The doctrine of laches consists of a substantial lapse of time coupled with the existence of circumstances that make it inequitable to enforce the claim of the claimant. The doctrine is summarised in the maxim 'equity aids the vigilant and not the indolent'. It may be treated as inequitable to enforce the claim where the delay has led the defendant to change his position to his detriment in the reasonable belief that the claimant's cause of action has been abandoned, or the delay has led to the loss of evidence that might assist the defence. The defendant bears the burden of proving that his position has changed to his detriment because of the delay of the claimant in pursuing the action.

KEY CASE ANALYSIS: *Fisher v Brooker* (2009), The Times, 12 August

Background

- A claim for a share of the copyright was brought in respect of the music for the song 'A Whiter Shade of Pale'.
- The claim was brought more than 40 years after the song was recorded.
- The defendant pleaded laches.

Principle established

The House of Lords decided in favour of the claimant on the ground that the defendants failed to prove that they had suffered detriment and in any event had derived a financial advantage from the claimant's delay.

Exclusion clauses

A trustee may escape liability by relying on an exclusion clause validly inserted into the trust instrument. Such clauses are not, without more, void on public policy grounds. Moreover, provided that the clause does not purport to exclude the basic minimum duties ordinarily imposed on trustees, it may be valid. Some of the minimum duties that cannot be excluded are the duties of honesty, good faith and acting for the benefit of the beneficiaries, see *Armitage v Nurse*.

KEY CASE ANALYSIS: *Armitage v Nurse* [1997] 3 WLR 1046

Background

- The claimant sued the trustees for breach of trust.
- The trust settlement contained an exclusion clause to the effect that the trustees were not liable for any loss or damage 'unless caused by their own actual fraud'.

Principle established

The court decided that the clause protected the trustees from the claim. 'Actual fraud' was equivalent to dishonesty or deceit.

On-the-spot question

To what extent may exclusion clauses protect trustees who act in breach of trust?

PROPRIETARY REMEDIES

A proprietary remedy is one that attaches to property subject to the trust and the claimant contends that the defendant is required to concede that the property is subject to his interest. This is a claim '*in rem*' (to recover the property or its traceable proceeds) as opposed to claims against the defendant personally, referred to as claims '*in personam*', such as damages. The proprietary remedy requires the claimant to be able to trace his property in the hands of the trustees or third parties, not being *bona fide* transferees of the legal estate for value without notice, and recover such property or obtain a charging order in priority over the trustees' creditors.

The proprietary remedy has a number of advantages over the claim *in personam*, such as:

- the success of the claim does not rest on the solvency of the defendant
- the claimant will be able to benefit from increases in the value of the property
- the claimant is entitled to interest from the date that the property came into the defendant's hands and not only from the date of the judgment, and
- the limitation period of six years does not operate in respect of the recovery of the trust property.

The common law had recognised the right to trace to a limited extent (i.e. provided that the property had remained unmixed). For example, a painting belonging to a trust had been acquired in breach of trust by Thomas, a purchaser in bad faith. The beneficiaries have traced their asset in the hands of Thomas and will be entitled to recover the same by a court order. Indeed, the right to trace at law may subsist even though the original property has changed in form. In the example above, Thomas has sold the painting to a *bona fide* purchaser of the legal estate for value without notice. The painting cannot be recovered but Thomas may be liable to pay over the proceeds of sale to the claimant.

KEY CASE ANALYSIS: *Taylor v Plumer* (1815) 3 M&S 562

Background

- The defendant transferred a fund to a stockbroker, Walsh, to purchase specified bonds.
- Walsh purchased different investments and attempted to abscond to America.
- Walsh handed over the investments to the defendant's agent and was later adjudicated bankrupt.
- His assignee in bankruptcy claimed to recover the property from the defendant.

Principle established

The court decided in favour of the defendant because the property belonged to him.

Equity adopted a broader approach as opposed to the common law. Once property was identifiable, the claimant's right was given effect by attaching a court order:

- to specific property, or
- by charging the asset for the amount of the claim.

Where the trustee or fiduciary mixes his funds with that of the beneficiary or purchases further property with the mixed fund, the beneficiary would be entitled to have the property charged for the amount of the trust money.

KEY CASE ANALYSIS: *Re Hallett's Estate* (1880) 13 Ch D 696

Background

- Mr Hallett was a solicitor and trustee and paid trust monies into his personal bank account.
- He also paid funds belonging to a client, Mrs Cotterill, into his personal account.
- At the time of his death, his funds were insufficient to pay the claims of the trust, the client and his general creditors.

Principle established

The court decided that funds in the account belonged to the innocent beneficiaries and Mrs Cotterill.

The rule in *Re Hallett's Estate* is to the effect that where a trustee or fiduciary mixes trust monies with his own:

- the beneficiary is entitled in the first place to a charge on the amalgam of the fund in order to satisfy his claim; and
- if the trustee or fiduciary withdraws monies for his own purposes, he is deemed to draw out his own monies so that the beneficiary may claim the balance of the fund as against the trustee's general creditors.

In addition, where the beneficiaries are entitled to trace their property (including a charge) into a mixed fund, it follows that that right (to trace) may extend to property (assets) acquired with the mixed fund. Accordingly, if a part of the fund has been used to purchase an asset that is identifiable and the remainder of the fund has been exhausted (the right to trace against the fund becoming otiose), the beneficiary may claim to trace against the asset acquired by the trustees – see *Re Oatway*.

KEY CASE ANALYSIS: *Re Oatway* [1903] 2 Ch 356

Background

- Mr Oatway, the trustee, mixed their funds with trust monies and bought shares in Oceana Ltd with part of the fund.
- The remaining funds in the account became exhausted.
- Oceana shares were sold and the proceeds paid into Mr Oatway's account.
- Mr Oatway died insolvent.
- His personal representatives claimed the value of the shares.

Principle established

The court held that the beneficiaries were entitled to claim the proceeds of sale of the shares.

The right to trace into a mixed-fund bank account in equity is limited to the 'lowest intermediate balance' (i.e. the lowest fund that exists in the bank account from the date of the mixture), the reason being that funds in the bank account falling below the amount of the funds originally paid into it are presumed to be spent – see *Roscoe v Winder*.

KEY CASE ANALYSIS: *Roscoe v Winder* **[1915] 1 Ch 62**

Background

- A trustee had agreed to collect a debt (£623) but paid £455 into his personal bank account.
- The rest of the debt had remained unaccounted for.
- The trustee drew out funds from his account, which were dissipated.
- The remaining balance in the account at this time stood at £25.
- He subsequently paid in further funds belonging to others into the account, leaving a balance of £358 at the time of his death.

Principle established

The court decided that the original beneficiaries were entitled to a charge of the lowest intermediate balance of £25 on the account.

Sargant J: '. . . you must for the purpose of tracing put your finger on some definite fund which either remains in its original state or can be found in another shape. That is tracing and tracing seems to be excluded except as to £25'.

It follows that where funds had become mixed in a bank account and the account becomes overdrawn, the right to trace ceases even if funds are subsequently paid in, see *Bishopsgate Investment Management Ltd v Homan* [1994] 3 WLR 1270.

On the other hand, where a trustee mixes trust funds subsisting in an active current bank account belonging to two innocent beneficiaries, the amount of the balance in the account is determined by attributing withdrawals in the order of sums paid into the account: first in, first out (FIFO). This is a rule of banking law and one of convenience. It must be stressed that this is an exceptional rule applied as between the two innocent beneficiaries only, see *Clayton's* case (1816) 1 Mer 529.

However, *Clayton* was distinguished in *Barlow Clowes International Ltd (in liquidation) and others v Vaughan and others* [1992] 4 All ER 22, where the court decided that innocent beneficiaries were entitled to share the fund rateably. The rule in *Clayton* was considered to be impractical, or unjust, or contrary to the intention of the investors. Accordingly, the court was entitled to refuse to apply it, provided that an alternative method of distribution is available.

The right to trace in equity is subject to the following limitations:

- Tracing cannot affect rights acquired by a *bona fide* purchaser of the legal estate for value without notice (i.e. equity's darling).
- Tracing is extinguished where property cannot be identified (e.g. the fund has been spent on a holiday).
- Tracing is not allowed where it would lead to inequitable consequences, now called a 'change of position' defence, such as where the innocent volunteer adjusts his position by selling the property.
- It is essential for the claimant to establish that the property was held by a trustee or fiduciary, even though the mixing need not be effected by the fiduciary.

CASE LAW SUMMARY

Letterstedt v Broers – The court has an inherent jurisdiction to remove a trustee if this will enhance the administration of the trust.

Bahin v Hughes – A 'passive' trustee may be liable along with his co-trustees for a breach of trust. The liability of trustees for breach of trust is joint and several. The passive trustee is not entitled to an indemnity from the other trustees.

O'Rourke v Darbishire – The beneficiary is entitled to force trustees to disclose trust documents.

Schmidt v Rosewood – The Privy Council decided that the right to disclosure stems from the trustee's duty to account to the beneficiaries and doubted the concept of trust documents.

Target Holdings v Redfern – The measure of the trustee's liability for breach of trust is based on the principle of compensating the trust for the loss suffered.

Perrins v Bellamy – Trustees who are in breach of trust are entitled to relief under s 61 of the Trustee Act 1925, provided that they discharge a burden of proving that they acted honestly and reasonably and ought fairly to be excused.

Fisher v Brooker – The doctrine of laches, which is equivalent to the claimant acquiescing in a breach of trust because of a substantial delay in bringing an action for breach of trust, is subject to the discretion of the court. The discretion may be exercised in favour of the claimant if the defendant fails to prove that he had suffered a detriment.

Armitage v Nurse – An exclusion clause is effective to protect trustees from a claim for breach of trust, except in cases of dishonesty.

Taylor v Plumer – A tracing claim exists at common law, provided that the trust property does not become mixed with other property.

Re Hallett – A tracing claim exists in equity where the trustee mixes trust property with his property. Any withdrawal from a mixed fund is presumed to be the trustee's funds.

Re Oatway – Withdrawals by a trustee to purchase an asset from a fund mixed with his property and the beneficiary's may be claimed by the beneficiary or the asset may be charged with the *pro rata* amount of the beneficiary's funds.

Roscoe v Winder – The right to trace into a bank account mixed with the trustee's and beneficiary's funds is subject to the limitation of the lowest intermediate balance.

Clayton's case – Where the claim to funds in a mixed, active, current bank account is between two innocent beneficiaries, the identification of ownership of the funds remaining in the account is based on the principle of first in, first out.

Barlow Clowes v Vaughan – Where the claim is between two innocent beneficiaries to a common fund, the court will apportion the loss proportionately between the beneficiaries, who will accordingly be entitled to share in the fund proportionately.

ISSUES TO THINK ABOUT FURTHER

The rule in *Re Hallett* is to the effect that where the trustee mixes funds with his own in a single bank account, the beneficiaries have a first charge on the resulting mixed fund. Where he withdraws funds from the account and uses them for his own purposes, he is presumed to have withdrawn his own funds first. But where the trustee withdraws an amount from the mixed fund and purchases an asset for his own benefit, the presumption is that the beneficiaries are entitled to claim the asset or charge the same with the amount of the trust fund, *Re Oatway*. These principles appear to be contradictory.

How would you reconcile the rule in *Re Hallett* with the rule in *Re Oatway*?

SUMMARY

- There are a variety of provisions created under express authority in the trust instrument, by statute, by the beneficiaries and by the court in order to effect the appointment, retirement and removal of trustees.
- Owing to the confidential and representative nature of trusteeship, a collection of fiduciary and non-fiduciary duties are imposed on trustees to provide for equality in the treatment of the beneficiaries.

- As an integral part of the trustees' duties, the courts and Parliament have created a number of discretionary powers that trustees are required to exercise in order to ensure the proper administration of the trust.
- A breach of trust occurs where the trustees exercise their duties inappropriately and cause loss to the trust estate.
- Trustees may be liable to compensate the trust for the loss from their personal funds, subject to defences available to the trustees laid down in the trust instrument, created by Parliament or the courts.
- Finally, the beneficiaries may avail themselves of a proprietary claim in order to recover or charge the property with the scope of their interest.

FURTHER READING

Bell C, 'Some reflections on choosing trustees' (1988) Trust Law and Practice 86.
[Research project on trustees' powers of appointment of new trustees.]

Capper D, 'Compensation for breach of trust' (1997) 61 Conv 14.
[Considers the extent to which the principles for compensation for breach of trust are based on the test of causation.]

Cotterrell R, 'The requirement of "benefit" under the Variation of Trusts Act' [1971] 34 MLR 96.
[Each case under the Variation of Trusts Act 1958 involving proof of 'benefit' is required to be determined on its own facts. This article concludes that it would be regrettable if judges underestimate the importance of precedent, wisely used as an aid to uniformity of treatment and coherence, in their interpretation of 'benefit'.]

Hayton D, 'Rights of creditors against trustees and trust funds' (1997) 11 Tru LI 58.
[Considers proposals for determining the duties of trustees and the rights of creditors to trust funds.]

Hochberg D and Norris W, 'The rights of beneficiaries to information concerning a trust' (1999) PCB 5, 292.
[Considers proposals for law reform in Jersey where beneficiaries sought disclosure of the identity of trustees.]

Lord Nicholls of Birkenhead, 'Trustees and their broader community: Where duty, morality and ethics converge' (1995) 9 Tru LI 71.
[Considers the extent to which non-financial factors may guide trustees when investing the trust funds.]

O'Hagan P, 'Trustees' duty to disclose' (1995) 145 NLJ 1414.
[Considers whether beneficiaries under a pension scheme are entitled to inspect trust documents disclosing confidential decisions of the trustees.]

Panesar S, 'The Trustee Act' (2001) ICCLR 151.
[Assesses a number of duties imposed on trustees under the Trustee Act 2000.]

Pawlowski M, 'The demise of the rule in *Clayton's Case*' (2003) Conv 339.
[Considers the diminishing application of the rule in *Clayton's* case.]

Ramjohn M, 'Text, Cases and Materials on Equity and Trusts', 4th edn (Routledge-Cavendish, 2008).
[Detailed commentary on equitable and trusts principles.]

Ramjohn M, 'Unlocking Trusts' 4th edn (Routledge, 2013).
[A comprehensive and up to date text written in simple, clear language that de-mystifies complicated concepts in trusts law.]

Sheridan L, 'Excusable breaches of trust' (1955) 19 Conv (NS) 420.
[Considers the extent to which trustees may be excused from liability for breaches of trust.]

COMPANION WEBSITE

An online glossary compiled by the author is available on the companion website:
www.routledge.com/cw/beginningthelaw

Chapter 11
Specific performance and injunctions

LEARNING OUTCOMES

At the end of this chapter, you should be able to:

- Understand the reasons for the creation and development of the equitable remedies of specific performance and injunctions
- Appreciate the nature of these equitable remedies
- Identify the main equitable principles underlying these remedies
- Ascertain the limits of these remedies

INTRODUCTION

In Chapter 1, we considered the origin of the trust as a unique facet of English law. Allied to this notion is the feature that, before the Judicature Acts 1873–75, English law was administered in the courts as two streams of law: the common law and rules of equity. In this chapter, we will focus on another major contribution of equity, namely the equitable remedies of specific performance and injunctions. These remedies were created exclusively in accordance with the 'concurrent' jurisdiction of equity. This jurisdiction followed the common law in recognising the rights of claimants but improved on the legal rules by creating of a variety of unique remedies. For example, a vendor of land may be liable to the claimant for breach of contract but the common law remedy of damages may be inadequate to compensate the claimant. In these circumstances the claimant may be successful in obtaining an order for **specific performance** of the contract. Before the Judicature Acts, the claimant was required to bring his suit in the Chancery Court in order to obtain specific performance. Today, the rules of equity have been integrated with the rules of law and any civil court may award an equitable remedy.

There are two striking features that underpin equitable remedies. First, they are only available where the common law remedy of damages is inadequate by reference to all the circumstances of the case. Second, equitable remedies are discretionary in the sense that they would not be available as of right and would not be available to a claimant where a decree would create disproportionate hardship to the defendant. However, the discretion of the court is now exercised in accordance with settled principles.

SPECIFIC PERFORMANCE

A decree of specific performance is an order of the court that directs a party to perform his obligations under a contract or trust. Failure to comply with the order without reasonable justification is a **contempt of court** and may involve criminal sanctions.

Key Definition

Contempt of court – Unlawful conduct that amounts to a disregard of the authority of the court, punishable with imprisonment.

A claimant who petitions the court for an order of specific performance is required to establish: first, that the defendant has acted in breach of his duty under a contract or trust, and second, that damages for the breach would not adequately compensate him for the loss he has suffered. Accordingly, specific performance will not be granted where the defendant acts in breach of his contract to sell shares in a public company as the claimant may obtain the same property on the open market. But where the subject matter of the breach of contract involves land or some other unique asset, specific performance may be ordered by the court. In the exceptional case of *Beswick v Beswick*, the House of Lords made a decree of specific performance in respect of a breach of an obligation to pay an annuity, the reason being that only nominal damages were available to the claimant.

KEY CASE ANALYSIS: *Beswick v Beswick* [1968] AC 58, HL

Background

Peter Beswick assigned his coal merchant's business to his nephew, the defendant, in consideration of the defendant paying him an annuity for the remainder of his life and, after his death, paying the claimant's (Peter's) wife an annuity for the remainder of her life. The defendant paid the annuity during Peter's lifetime but after his death failed to pay the agreed sum to Peter's widow. She brought a claim against the defendant for breach of contract in her personal capacity and also as administratrix of her husband estate.

Principle established

The court decided that:

- In her personal capacity she was not entitled to succeed for she was not a party to the agreement.

- In her capacity as administratrix she was entitled to an order of specific performance. The common law remedy of damages was inadequate to compensate her for the loss.

The remedy of specific performance, like all equitable remedies, is subject to the discretion of the court. But the exercise of this discretion is not precarious; instead, it is limited in scope in order to achieve fairness between the parties. The courts will take into consideration the conduct of the parties and the likely effect of the order on the defendant. A multitude of relevant factors are taken into account in deciding whether the order may be granted, including unreasonable delay or fault, such as non-disclosure, on the part of the claimant and hardship to the defendant. In *Patel v Ali*, the court adopted the exceptional step of taking into account circumstances that had taken place after the contract for the sale of land was entered into.

KEY CASE ANALYSIS: *Patel v Ali* [1984] 1 All ER 978

Background

The defendant exchanged contracts with the claimant for the sale of her house but before completion had contracted bone cancer, which resulted in the amputation of a leg. The defendant, a young married woman with three young children, relied on the assistance of family and friends living in the neighbourhood in order to keep the family together and was unable to complete the contract. The claimant applied to the court for an order of specific performance of the contract.

Principle established

The court refused to grant the order on the ground that such a course would have inflicted undue hardship on the defendant, even though such hardship was not caused by the claimant and was not related to the subject matter of the agreement.

During the period of development of this remedy, it was at one time believed that the court will not order specific performance of a contract that requires constant supervision, such as a contract to perform personal services. This was likely to involve a strain on the resources of the litigant and the courts by repeated applications. Often, the refusal of the order was due to difficulties in defining the obligations of the parties with precision or the inconvenience in administering the order has the effect of making an order for damages a more effective remedy. Thus, the courts have refused to enforce a covenant in a lease by a landlord to employ a resident porter or a tenant to repair a lease. The position today is that the need for supervision, by itself, is no longer a bar to the remedy, but is a factor to be taken into consideration by the court in exercising its discretion. If the contract is suitable for specific performance by reference to all the circumstances, the court may make such a decree. In *Wolverhampton Corp v Emmons* [1901] 1 KB 515, the court ordered specific performance of a contract to build new houses in a housing estate. The obligations of the defendant were clearly defined in the building plans. But in *Co-operative Insurance Society Ltd v Argyll Stores Ltd* [1998] AC 1, the court refused to grant an order to keep a supermarket open pursuant to a 'keep open' clause in a lease. On balance, the court decided that a one-off award of damages would achieve a more satisfactory result, as opposed to the prospect of making a series of orders requiring the defendant to carry on a business.

On-the-spot question

 What principles are applicable by the court in exercising its discretion to issue an order of specific performance?

INJUNCTIONS

An injunction is a court order directing the party named to discontinue an act stipulated in the order or to undo a transaction specified by the court.

There are several types of injunctions:

Prohibitory injunctions forbid the doing of a specified act, such as ordering the defendant not to build an extension to his property.

Mandatory injunctions have the effect of ordering a defendant to take positive steps to perform a particular act, such as the demolition of an unauthorised extension of his property.

Quia timet injunctions are issued where the claimant alleges that the defendant has threatened to infringe the claimant's rights without the actual infringement taking place, such as the threat from the defendant to trespass on the claimant's land.

Perpetual or **final** injunctions refer to court orders made after a full hearing of arguments by both parties. These may be perpetual or mandatory.

Interim injunctions (previously called **interlocutory** injunctions) are temporary injunctions intended to maintain the *status quo* of the parties pending a full hearing. The object of this type of injunction involves an emergency where the claimant requires urgent action by the court before the full merits of the case are considered. For example, the freezing of the defendant's assets where there is a strong likelihood of the defendant taking the assets out of the court's jurisdiction before the full hearing of the cause of action. In the case of interim injunctions, the application is made by the claimant *ex parte* (without notice to the defendant) based mainly on **affidavit** evidence and the principles applicable are essentially procedural, rather than equitable. These applications are subject to a different set of rules compared with perpetual injunctions.

Key Definition

Affidavit – A statement made in writing and on oath, sworn before someone who has the authority to administer the oath.

Perpetual injunctions

The general principles that are applicable to a final injunction are:

* The claimant in the first place is required to establish a right that is recognised either at law or in equity. Mere inconvenience suffered by the claimant is insufficient to justify the award of an injunction. In *Day v Brownrigg* the claimant failed to establish the existence of an interest in land.

KEY CASE ANALYSIS: *Day v Brownrigg* (1878) 10 Ch D 294

Background

The claimant sought an injunction to prevent the defendant from naming his house 'Ashford Lodge'. The claimant alleged that he had used that name for 60 years and that the defendant's conduct had caused him a great deal of inconvenience and materially diminished the value of his house.

Principle established

The court decided that defendant's conduct was not a violation of a legal right and dismissed the application.

- The injunction, as an equitable remedy like specific performance, will only be granted at the court's discretion. This requires the court to take equitable principles into account. The exercise of the discretion, however, is based on settled legal principles. Accordingly, the injunction will not be issued where it is likely to cause disproportionate hardship to the defendant or where the claimant did not act with 'clean hands' in failing to disclose relevant facts or delayed in bringing the claim. In *Wrotham Park Estate Co v Parkside Homes Ltd*, the High Court refused to issue a mandatory injunction for the demolition of newly built houses in an area where there was a shortage of housing.

KEY CASE ANALYSIS: *Wrotham Park Estate Co v Parkside Homes Ltd* [1974] 2 All ER 321

Background

The defendant, a developer, built houses on an estate in breach of a covenant. The claimant applied to the court for a final injunction, having omitted to petition the court for an interim injunction. Accordingly, the houses were completed at the time when the court was considering the merits of the case. The grant of the injunction would have required the defendant to demolish the houses.

Principle established

The court rejected the application on the ground that it would have amounted to an 'unpardonable waste of much needed houses'. Instead, the court ruled that the claimant was entitled to a sum of money by way of damages equivalent to the amount they would have been expected to receive for the suspension of the covenant (5 percent of the developer's profit).

A similar result was reached in *Jaggard v Sawyer* [1995] 1 WLR 269, where the defendant built a house in breach of a covenant with sole access over the claimant's land. The application for the injunction was rejected in favour of damages.

- An injunction will not be granted where the common law remedy of damages will adequately compensate the claimant for the loss suffered. The court will examine the circumstances of each case before ruling on the merits of injunctive relief. The defendant will bear the burden of establishing the case that the award of damages would be appropriate. This issue was considered in *Shelfer v City of London Electric Lighting Co*.

KEY CASE ANALYSIS: *Shelfer v City of London Electric Lighting Co* **[1895] 1 Ch 287**

Background

The defendant electricity company caused structural damage to the claimant's house. The claimant sought relief by way of an injunction.

Principle established

The High Court judge refused the claim and awarded damages as a substitute. On appeal, the Court of Appeal reversed the decision and granted the injunction. The court then gave guidelines as follows:

Smith LJ: 'In my opinion, it may be stated as a good working rule that:

(1) if the injury to the plaintiff's legal right is small, and
(2) is one which is capable of being estimated in money, and
(3) is one which can be adequately compensated by a small money payment, and
(4) the case is one in which it would be oppressive to the defendant to grant an injunction –
then damages in substitution for an injunction may be given.'

Section 50 of the Senior Courts Act 1981 broadens this principle by granting the court jurisdiction to award damages in addition to, or in substitution for, the award of specific performance or an injunction. This is a re-enactment of the Chancery Amendment Act 1858, known as Lord Cairns Act.

- The issue of an injunction requires the court to consider the conduct of both parties. The claimant would not be entitled to an injunction where he acts unconscionably or in breach of his duties. The maxim applicable here is 'he who comes to equity must come with clean hands'. The claim failed on this ground in *Littlewood v Caldwell*.

KEY CASE ANALYSIS: *Littlewood v Caldwell* (1822)
11 Price 97

Background

The claimant sought an injunction in proceedings for the dissolution of a partnership. The claimant, however, had wrongfully removed partnership books during the winding-up proceedings.

Principle established

The court refused the relief sought by the claimant because of his improper action.

On-the-spot question

 What factors should be taken into account by the court when deciding whether or not to grant an order for an interim injunction?

Interim injunctions

The interim injunction acts as a holding operation that maintains the position of the parties, so far as is possible, until the trial. Since the court is not in a position to determine the merits of the case, the court acts on a separate set of principles, mainly procedural rather than equitable. The grant of the interim injunction is discretionary and the court must be satisfied that it is probable that the claimant will be entitled to relief at the trial. Owing to the potentially disruptive nature of this relief, the claimant will be required to give an undertaking in damages if it turns out in the main trial that he was not entitled to interim relief.

The guidelines governing the principles underpinning interim injunctions were laid down by Lord Diplock in *American Cyanamid Co v Ethicon Ltd*.

KEY CASE ANALYSIS: *American Cyanamid Co v Ethicon Ltd* **[1975] AC 396, HL**

Background

The claimants owned a patent on absorbable surgical sutures. The defendants were about to launch on the British market a suture that the claimants alleged infringed their patent. The claimants applied for a *quia timet* interim injunction to stop the defendants marketing the product.

Principle established

The House of Lords, on appeal, granted the injunction on the ground that the balance of convenience justified the issuing of the injunction. The evidence disclosed the probability that the claimants could have been successful at the full hearing and damages would have been inadequate in the circumstances.

Lord Diplock in *American Cyanamid* issued guidelines in respect of applications for interim injunctions:

- The courts are required to decide whether the application is frivolous or vexatious.
- Does the balance of convenience favour the application? In particular, are damages an adequate remedy? Would the undertaking by the claimant as to damages be adequate to compensate the defendant in the event that the claimant fails at the full hearing?
- Are there other factors, including social and economic, which will favour the grant of the interim injunction?
- As a last resort, the court may consider the relative strength of each party's case.

In *Series 5 Software Ltd v Clarke* [1996] 1 All ER 853, the High Court did not regard the relative strength of each party's case as a last resort, but this should be avoided in cases where there is a serious dispute as to the evidence. In most cases where the court is entitled to do so, it may consider the strength of each party's case. In considering the relative strength of each party's case, the court should only do so on the basis of the affidavit and documentary evidence before it.

Recently, the courts were instrumental in the issue of 'super-injunctions'. These were injunctions issued to conceal from the public the existence of the injunction itself as well as the identity of the claimant. These cases involved celebrities who wished to suppress their identities and consequently promoted the existence of the 'gagging' order. The Neuberger

Committee recommended that such injunctions may only be used in very limited circumstances and in particular when they are strictly necessary in the interests of justice.

Two specific interim orders that warrant special consideration will now be outlined. These are **freezing** injunctions and **search** orders.

Freezing injunctions

These were originally called *Mareva* injunctions from the case of the same name (see below). A freezing injunction is an order from the court restraining the defendant from removing assets from the jurisdiction to prevent the frustration of the claimant's action. This type of injunction was originally created in *Mareva Compania Naviera SA v International Bulkcarriers SA*.

KEY CASE ANALYSIS: *Mareva Compania Naviera SA v International Bulkcarriers SA* [1975] 2 Lloyd's Rep 509

Background

The claimants, shipowners, sued the defendants for unpaid hire charges and damages for repudiation of a charter-party contract. The claimants applied for an injunction to restrain the defendants from removing moneys standing to the credit of the defendants in a London bank.

Principle established

The Court of Appeal decided that the injunction may be created until the date of the judgment at the full hearing.

Today, the authority to make such orders has been laid down in s 37 of the Senior Courts Act 1981 and the Civil Procedure Rules. The order is usually limited to the amount of assets not exceeding the value of the claim. The court may also make ancillary orders such as requiring the defendant to remain in the UK until he has made full disclosure of his assets.

Guidelines were issued by the Court of Appeal in *Third Chandris Shipping Corp v Unimarine SA* [1979] 2 All ER 972. These are:

- The claimant is required to make full and frank disclosure of all material matters within his knowledge. This is done *ex parte* by way of affidavit and documentary evidence.

- The claimant must have a 'good arguable case' to the effect that legal or equitable rights belonging to him require protection. Unlike general interim injunctions considered above, this type of injunction involves consideration of the merits of the case. He is required to state not only his case but also to anticipate the possible defences that may be raised by the defendant.
- The claimant is required to convince the High Court judge that the defendant has assets in this country. These assets are required to be identified with relative precision.
- The claimant must demonstrate that there are grounds for believing that there is a real risk the defendant may remove the assets from the jurisdiction.
- The claimant is required to give an undertaking in damages in the event of the claim failing at the full hearing.

On-the-spot question

On 12 April 2010, Charles made a loan to David of £50,000 in order to purchase 20,000 shares in Money Bags Ltd. The loan was repayable in five years' time and interest was payable at the rate of 10 percent per annum. Under the agreement, David was required to pay Charles £15,000 on 12 April each year for the next five years. In May 2012, Charles discovered that David had not purchased the shares from Moneybags Ltd and, more disturbingly, failed to repay any part of the loan. Charles's inquiries reveal that David left the UK in November 2011 for a 'short holiday' in Morocco. David was recently seen in Oxford Street, London. He was confronted by Charles about the non-payment of the first instalment of the loan. David told Charles that the money will be repaid after the sale of his restaurant in September 2012. Charles has lost trust in David and is very concerned that the money may never be repaid and that David may disappear if attempts are made to recover the money through the courts.

Advise Charles.

Search orders

Originally this order was called an *Anton Piller* order, derived from the case of a similar name. The order is a mandatory interim injunction requiring the defendant to permit the claimant to enter his premises in order to inspect and make copies of relevant documents.

KEY CASE ANALYSIS: *Anton Piller KG v Manufacturing Processes Ltd* [1976] 1 All ER 779

Background

The claimants applied for an order to enable them to enter the defendant's premises in order to view and take copies of documents in the possession of the defendant.

Principle established

The Court of Appeal granted the order under its inherent jurisdiction in order to preserve evidence relevant to the cause of action.

The elements required to be proved by the claimant are:

- there must be a strong *prima facie* case;
- the damage, actual or potential, must be very serious to the claimant;
- there was clear evidence that the defendant had documents in his possession that were relevant to the litigation and incriminating to the defendant, and there was a real risk that the latter was likely to destroy the documents;
- the orders should not be disproportionate and should not extend beyond what is necessary to achieve its purpose;
- the claimant may be required to give an undertaking in damages;
- the order is required to be executed during business hours, on business premises and on working days;
- the documents taken away are required to be covered in the order;
- a comprehensive record of the documents that have been taken from the defendant's premises is required to be completed by the claimant and served on the defendant as soon as is reasonably practicable.

CASE LAW SUMMARY

Beswick v Beswick – Mrs Beswick brought her claim in two capacities: in her personal capacity and as administratrix of her husband's estate. She succeeded in her claim and obtained specific performance on the second ground only. She was representing her husband who was a non-volunteer.

Patel v Ali – The court was entitled to refuse an order of specific performance of an agreement to sell a house based on the severe hardship that would have been endured by the defendant in granting the order.

Wolverhampton Corporation v Emmons – The court may order specific performance of building works provided that the terms of the building contract are clear.

Co-operative Insurance Ltd v Argyll Stores – specific performance will not be ordered where such order requires constant supervision and the common law remedy of damages is appropriate.

Day v Brownrigg – An injunction will not be granted where damages are considered to be an adequate remedy.

Wrotham Park Estate v Parkside Homes – The court, in its discretion, is entitled to decline an injunction on the ground that its grant may cause undue oppression on the part of the defendant.

Jaggard v Sawyer – The claimant may *prima facie* be entitled to an injunction, but the court retains the discretion to refuse the injunction on the ground that the loss to the defendant would be disproportionate to the loss that may be suffered by the claimant.

Shelfer v City of London Lighting – The court laid down guidelines for the granting of an injunction.

Littlewood v Caldwell – An injunction may not be granted where the claimant acted unconscionably.

American Cyanamid v Ethicon – The court laid down guidelines for the issue of an interim injunction including the notion of the balance of convenience.

Series 5 Software v Clarke – In deciding whether to grant an interim injunction, the court is entitled to consider the strength of the claimant's case and the balance of convenience.

Mareva Cia Naviera SA v International Bulkcarriers SA – An injunction may be granted to the claimant to prevent the defendant from removing assets from the jurisdiction.

Third Chandris Shipping v Unimarine – Guidelines were issued as to when a Mareva (freezing) order may be granted.

Anton Piller v Manufacturing Processes Ltd – An interim, mandatory injunction obtained *ex parte* with the object of preventing a defendant from concealing or destroying vital evidence relevant to the claimant's case.

ISSUES TO THINK ABOUT FURTHER

A freezing (Mareva) injunction is an order of the court obtained *ex parte* with the object of preventing the defendant from removing assets from the jurisdiction to avoid the risk of having to satisfy a final judgment. The elements that are required to be raised by the claimant were laid down by Lord Denning in *Third Chandris Shipping*.

In the scenario below, consider the extent to which Charles may successfully bring a claim for an interim order.

> On 12 April 2010, Charles made a loan to David of £50,000 in order to purchase 20,000 shares in Money Bags Ltd. The loan was repayable in five years' time and interest was payable at the rate of 10 percent per annum. Under the agreement, David was required to pay Charles £15,000 on 12 April each year for the next five years. In May 2012, Charles discovered that David had not purchased the shares from Moneybags Ltd and, more disturbingly, failed to repay any part of the loan. Charles's inquiries reveal that David left the UK in November 2011 for a 'short holiday' in Morocco. David was recently seen in Oxford Street, London. He was confronted by Charles about the non-payment of the first instalment of the loan. David told Charles that the money will be repaid after the sale of his restaurant in September 2012. Charles has lost trust in David and is very concerned that the money may never be repaid and that David may disappear if attempts are made to recover the money through the courts.
>
> Advise Charles.

SUMMARY

- We can see that the concurrent jurisdiction of equity satisfied the need to significant remedies in English law.
- The remedy of specific performance was a dynamic principle that may be mobilised to impose on the defendant to fulfil his obligations.
- Equitable principle of fairness manifesting itself in the discretion of the court underpinned this institution.
- The injunction serves the purpose of prohibiting the defendant from infringing the rights of the claimant.
- There are many varieties of injunctions that may be obtained by a claimant.
- Like specific performance, the injunction may be issued by the court in accordance with equitable principles.
- The injunction is not restricted to the maintenance of property rights but may be available in all walks of life outside property law, provided that the claimant has the *locus standi* to protect an interest.

FURTHER READING

Andoh B, 'The search order and the privilege against self-incrimination' (2006) 26 BLR 6.
[Commentary on the role of search orders including their jurisdictional basis and the impact on the privilege against self-incrimination.]

Chen M, 'Unjust factors and the restitutionary response' (2000) 20 OJLS 557.
[Unjust enrichment and the defence of change of position as part of the process of restitution.]

Collins L, 'The territorial reach of the Mareva injunction' (1989) 105 LQR 262.
[Considers the rationale and scope of the *Mareva* injunction (freezing order).]

Eady D, 'Injunctions and the protection of privacy' (2010) 29 CJQ 411.
[Explores the development of a right to privacy in the UK and the use of the injunction to protect it.]

Gee S, 'The undertaking in damages' [2006] LMCLQ 181.
[Considers the court's power to require undertakings in damages for claimants seeking interim injunctions.]

Harris D, 'Specific performance – A regular remedy for consumers' (2003) 119 LQR 541.
[Considers amendments to the Sale of Goods Act 1979 and the scope of the remedy of specific performance to repair breaches.]

Keay A, 'Whither American Cyanamid: interim injunctions in the 21st century' (2004) 23 CJQ 133.
[Analyses the law relating to interim injunctions and considers its operation after the introduction of the Human Rights Act 1998.]

Ramjohn M, 'Text, Cases and Materials on Equity and Trusts', 4th edn (Routledge–Cavendish, 2008).
[A combined text and casebook that examines the subject in more depth.]

Tinkler N, 'The bank, the thief and the freezing order (2005) 155 NLJ 82.
[Comments on the extent of the duty of care owed by a bank when a freezing order had been attached to the defendant's bank account.]

COMPANION WEBSITE

An online glossary compiled by the author is available on the companion website:
www.routledge.com/cw/beginningthelaw

Index

account, an 10, 20
action, forms of 16
Acts of Parliament 9
Administration of Estates Act 1925 34
administrative unworkability 53, 56
administrator of intestate's estate 35
advancement, power of/trustees 161
affidavits 181
agency 35
agriculture, as charitable purpose 106–7
Amnesty International 114
ancestral worship, trust for the performance of 81
animal welfare, as charitable purpose 106
animals: trusts for 80, 89; and unincorporated
    associations 86
Anton Piller order 187
any given postulant test 48, 50, 52–4, 56–7, 58
appointment, powers of 50, 51–4, 57–8
appointment of trustees 155, 156, 173
apportionment 95
armed forces, efficiency of/as charitable purposes 106
arts, as charitable purpose 104
assets, removal of/freezing injunctions 186–7, 190
Attorney General 80, 94
automatic resulting trusts 117, 118–20, 127

Baden test 48, 50, 53
bailment 36
balance of convenience 185, 189
beneficial interest, certainty of 46, 47–8, 57
beneficiaries 19, 30–1; and enforcing trusts 78, 89; as
    purposes 78
beneficiary principle 77, 88, 91; exceptions to 80–1
beneficiary trustees 19
benefit of covenant *see* covenant
binding precedent 42, 55
Birks, Professor 127
bona fide transferees of the legal estate for value
    without notice 31
breach of trust 6–7; and constructive trusts 133;
    defences to actions for 165–7; and terms of a trust
    162; by trustees 30, 155, 163–7, 172, 174
bribery: fiduciaries/constructive trusts 136–8, 151, 153;
    fourteenth century 16
Brightman, J. 85
Browne-Wilkinson, Lord 127, 163–4
buy-to-let transactions, constructive trusts 140

capital 3, 4, 161
certainty of beneficial interest 46, 47–8, 57

certainty of charitable objects 95
certainty of intention 4, 40–2, 45–6, 55, 57
certainty of objects 48–51, 56, 57–8, 90, 94–6
certainty of subject matter 46–7, 55, 56, 57
certainty of trust property 46, 47, 55, 56, 57
cestui que trust 2, 3
Chancellor 2, 3, 16, 25; *see also* Lord Chancellor
Chancery Amendment Act 1858 183
charitable intention, general 111–12
charitable objects, certainty of 95
charitable purpose(s) 99–107, 114; and public benefit
    97–8
charitable status, privileges enjoyed by 93–6
charitable trusts 5, 33, 80, 93, 94; *see also* charities
charitable unity 96
charities; *see also* charitable trusts: and excessive
    duration 96; and political campaigns 107
Charities Act 1601 99
Charities Act 1993 112
Charities Act 2006 5, 33, 93, 99, 114
Charities Act 2011 5, 33, 93, 94, 97, 99–107, 108, 110, 114
charity, a 94
Charity Commission 95, 97, 99, 103, 109; and activities
    outside the UK 107–8
Charity Tribunal 99
choses in action 68
circuit system 15
citizenship, as charitable activity 103–4
Civil Liability (Contribution) Act 1978 164
Civil Procedures Rules 186
claim *in personam* 168
claim *'in rem'* 168
class ascertainability test 48, 57
'clean hands' 122, 127, 182, 183
commercial transactions 44–5
common injunction 16, 18
common law 2, 15–17; remedy of damages 177, 182–3,
    189
common law courts 16, 17
community development, as charitable activity 103–4
Companies Act 2006 65
completely constituted trusts *see* express trusts
concession to human weakness 89, 90
concurrent jurisdiction, of equity 20–1
condition precedent, gifts subject to 54
conduct, past/relief in equity 22
conflict resolution, and Charities Act 2011 105
constitution of trusts 5
constructive trusts 6, 34, 131–4, 153; categories of
    134–51; and the family home 131; interim 65; sale

of land 138–9, 153; secret trusts 142–7, 152, 153; strangers as trustees 148–51
contempt of court 178
contract holding principle 128
contracts 35
Contracts (Rights of Third Parties) Act 1999 71, 75
contribution/indemnity, between trustees 164
conveyancing law 23
co-ownership/multiple ownership, property 84
corruption 16; see also bribery
Court of Chancery 2, 3, 16–17, 25
court of equity 20, 21, 139
Courts of Common Law 3
covenant 24, 68
creating trusts 74
Criminal Justice Act 1988 133
Cross, J. 83
culture, as charitable purpose 104
cy-près doctrine 93, 96–7, 109–12, 114

damages 16, 18; common law remedy of 177, 182–3, 189
death of testator/testatrix, trusts created by will on 28
deathbed gifts 72
debts enforceable at law 68
declaration of trust 5, 32, 39, 63
decree of specific performance 178
deeds 24
delay, and equity 22–3
delegable functions 159
Denley approach 81–2, 88
Denning, Lord 190
devisee, defined 144
dictionary approach 54
Diplock, L. 184–5
discretionary trusts 33, 49, 50–1, 52, 53, 57–8
dishonesty, test of 150, 152, 153
dispositions, meaning of 69
diversity, and Charities Act 2011 105
donatio mortis causa (DMC) 72, 75
Donovan, J. 102
duties, of trustees 159–60, 173, 174
duty of care, trustees 158–9
duty to account, and constructive trusts 133
duty to act impartially, trustees 159
duty to act personally, trustees 159
duty to act unanimously, trustees 159
duty to provide information/accounts, trustees 160

education, charitable purpose relating to 101–2, 113
enforceability: of imperfect trust 71; of perfect trust 70
environmental protection/improvement, and Charities Act 2011 105
equality, and Charities Act 2011 105
Equality Act 2010 122

equality is equity 95
equitable interest(s) 3; of fairness 190; inter vivos dispositions of 69–70; in property 2, 19, 73
equitable remedies 21
equity 2, 3, 18; and equality 96; equity aids the vigilant and not the indolent 166; equity considers as done that which ought to be done 137; equity will not allow a statute to be used as an engine for fraud 139, 153; equity will not assist a volunteer 71–2, 75; following the law 20, 151; he who comes to equity must come with clean hands 122, 127, 128, 183; historical development 15–18; and intent 23, 57; and law 16, 17, 25; maxims of 20–5, 26; rule(s) of 165, 177
European Convention on Human Rights 122
evidence, and interim injunctions 188, 189
evidential uncertainty 52–3
examination technique 10–13
exclusion clauses, and trustee liability 167
exclusive jurisdiction, of equity 20–1
executors 28, 35
express power, appointment of trustees 156
express trusts 5, 32–3, 55; creation of 36, 61–4, 70–1, 77; failure of 39, 46, 58, 119; imperfect 73; purpose trusts 93; and three certainties test 4

family home, and constructive trusts 131, 139–42, 151, 153
fiduciary duties: of personal representatives 36; of trustees 29
fiduciary power 51
fiduciary relationship 6–7; constructive trusts 134, 135, 136–8, 153
final injunctions 180
fire and rescue services, efficiency of/as charitable purposes 106
first in, first out (FIFO) 171, 173
fixed trusts 33, 48, 49–50, 57
Forfeiture Act 1982 22
form, and equity 23
forms of action 16, 17
Fountain of Justice, King as 16
fox hunting, trust for the promotion of 81, 89
freezing injunctions 186–7, 190
fully secret trusts 143–6, 152
future property 68

gagging orders 185–6
general charitable intention 111–12
gifts 36; charitable 95, 96–7, 112; and charitable/non-charitable purposes 94; failure of charitable 111; imperfect and equity 24–5; to incorporated/unincorporated associations 112; for political purposes 107; and secret trusts 142; subject to condition precedent 54; validity of 80, 82, 83–5, 87–8, 89, 90, 91

Goode, Roy 126
graves, trusts for the maintenance of 81

half-secret trusts 146–7, 152
he who comes to equity must come with clean hands
    122, 127, 128, 183
headnotes 9
health, charitable purpose relating to 103, 113
heritage, as charitable purpose 104
High Court, and charities 108
hospitals, charitable purpose relating to 103, 113
housing for the elderly, as charitable activity 105
Human Rights Act 1998 9
human rights, and Charities Act 2011 105
human weakness, concession to 89, 90
Hutton, Lord 153

imperfect gifts, and equity 24–5
imperfect trusts 70, 71, 73, 74, 75
implied trusts 5–6, 33–4, 117
impossibility, law on 110
impracticality, law on 110, 114
imputed intention 141
income 3, 4
incorporated associations, gifts to 112
indemnity: between trustees 164; of trustees 172
individual ascertainability test 48, 58
inferred intention 141
injunctions 16, 18, 20, 180–8, 189, 190
institutional constructive trusts 132
insurance, and powers of trustees 161
intended unlawful transactions 122
intent, and equity 23, 57
intention: certainty of 4, 40–2, 45–6, 55, 57; inferred/
    imputed 141
inter vivos dispositions, of equitable interests 69–70
inter vivos gifts 72
inter vivos trusts 28, 55
interim injunctions 181, 184–8
interlocutory injunctions 181
investment, and powers of trustees 160
is or is not test 48

joint tenants 84
judges, independence of 15
Judicature Acts 1873-75 3, 17, 25, 26, 177

Khoo Cheng Teow (1932) Straits Settlement Reports
    226 81
King: and the law 15; petitioning of 16, 25
King's Courts *see* Courts of Common Law

laches, doctrine of 22, 23, 166
land: and declaration of trust 62, 74; sale of/constructive
    trusts 138–9, 153

Langdale, Lord 40
last act theory 64–6
law: and equity 16, 17, 25; trusts 8–9; trusts/ and
    commerce 44–5
law of charities 5, 93; *see also* Charities Acts
Law of Property Act 1925 9, 13, 69, 121, 140
Law of Property (Miscellaneous Provisions) Act 1989 62
law reports, reading 9
Lawton, L.J. 83
legacies 28
legal title 2, 3, 19, 33, 64–5
legatee, defined 144
liability: broad test of 149; strangers/constructive trusts
    149–50, 152; of trustees 164, 167
Limitation Act 1980 23, 133, 166
limitation period: and claim for breach of trust 166;
    recovery of trust property 133–4
Lindley, L.J. 136
linguistic uncertainty 52
liquidation, and trust funds 44–5
list test 48, 49, 50, 56, 57
locus standi 78, 89, 94
Lord Cairns Act 183
Lord Chancellor 3; *see also* Chancellor

maintenance, power of/trustees 160–1
mandatory injunctions 180
Mareva injunctions 186
marriage consideration 71
masses, trust for the saying of in private 81
Matrimonial Causes Act 1973 140, 163
Matrimonial Proceedings and Property Act 1970 140–1
Maxwell, Robert 126
McNaghten, Lord 99
Megarry, J. 118, 127
Megaw, L.J. 54
memorials/monuments, trusts for 81, 89–90
Millett, Lord 127, 134
mixed-fund bank account, right to trace into
    170–1, 173
money/money's worth 71
moral obligations 2
multiple trustees 75

natural justice 16, 18
need, relief of/and Charities Act 2011 105–6
Neuberger, Lord 9
Neuberger Committee 185–6
next of kin 144
Nicholls, Lord 152
non-charitable trusts 88
non-discretionary trusts *see* fixed trusts
non-express trusts 33–4
non-volunteers, imperfect trusts 70
Normand, Lord 94

objects, certainty of 48–51, 56, 57–8, 90, 94–6
occupational pension schemes 124–6

parol evidence 121
Pension Law Review Committee 126
pensions 124–6, 128
Pensions Act 1995 126
Pensions Ombudsman 126
Pensions Regulator 126
perfect trusts 70, 74, 75
perpetual injunctions 180, 181–4
Perpetuities and Accumulations Act 2009 96
perpetuity rule 79–80, 96
personal power of appointment 51
personal remedies 7
personal representatives 35–6
personalty 19
petitioning of the King 16, 25
pets, trusts for 80; see also animals
police, efficiency of/as charitable purposes 106
political campaigns, and charities 107
political purposes, gifts to promote 107
poverty, charitable purpose relating to 99–101, 113
powers, of trustees 160–1
powers of appointment 50, 51–4, 57–8
preambles 99
precatory words 43–4, 55, 57
presumed resulting trusts 117, 119, 120–1, 127
presumption of advancement, abolition/rebuttal
    of 122
prima facie rule 85
private companies, transfer of shares in 65, 66
private purpose trusts 5, 77–9, 81–2, 89
private trusts 33
probate 72, 142
probity, want of/constructive trusts 152
profits, secret/constructive trusts 136–8, 151, 153
prohibitory injunctions 180
property; see also family home; Law of Property Acts:
    buy-to-let transactions 140; co-ownership/multiple
    ownership 84; duality of ownership in 19; equitable
    interest in 2, 19, 73; future 68; transfer of see
    transfer of property
proprietary claims 7, 174
proprietary estoppel 72, 75
proprietary remedies 21–2, 168–72
public (charitable) trusts see charitable trusts
public benefit, and charitable purpose 97–8
public benefit test 97, 113, 114; and trusts for relief of
    poverty 100, 101, 113
purchase in name of another 121
purpose trusts 93
purposes, beneficiaries as 77

quia timet injunctions 180

racial harmony, and Charities Act 2011 105
Radcliffe, Lord 74
receipts, powers of trustees 161
Recognition of Trusts Act 1987 27, 37
reconciliation, and Charities Act 2011 105
Recreational Charities Act 1958 104
recreational facilities, charitable 104
rectification 20
religion, charitable purpose relating to 102–3
religious harmony, and Charities Act 2011 105
remedial constructive trusts 131, 132–3, 151, 153
remedies 7; common law/damages 182–3, 189;
    equitable 21; proprietary 21–2; for specific
    performance 177
remedy of specific performance 179, 190
remote vesting 80, 96
representatives, personal 35–6
rescission 20
research, as education 101
resulting trusts 5–6, 117–21, 128
retirement, of trustees 157, 173
right to trace 168, 170, 171–2, 173
Romer, L.J. 69
rule of equity 165

Sachs, L.J. 54
saving of lives, charitable purpose relating to 103
science, as charitable purpose 104
search orders 187–8
secret trusts 142–7, 152, 153
self-dealing rule 158
self-declaration of trusts 5, 32, 62
Senior Courts Act 1981 183, 186
Settled Land Act 1925 163
settlors 29; creating trusts 67; declaration of trust
    63; intentions of 40; rights/powers of 28, 37; as
    trustees 75
shares, transfer of 65, 66
Smith, L.J. 183
social welfare, and recreational facilities 104
specific performance 178–80, 189; remedy of 177,
    179, 190
sport, as charitable head 104
Stamp, L.J. 54
Statute of Frauds 1677 9, 10, 13
Statute of Uses 1535 19, 26
statutory powers, appointment of trustees 156
statutory trusts 34
Stock Transfer Act 1963 65
strangers, as constructive trustees/accountable to
    innocent party 148–51, 152, 153
subject matter 4; certainty of 46–7, 55, 56, 57
sub-trusts 62
Sumner, Viscount 147
super-injunctions 185

taxation: and charities 96; and pensions 124
tenancy in common 84
terms of a trust, variation of 162–3
testators/testatrix 28
third-party trustees 67, 74, 75
'three certainties' test 4, 32, 33, 39, 40, 57; *see also*
    chapter 4
TOLATA 1996 *see* Trusts of Land and Appointment of
    Trustees Act 1996
trace, right to 168, 170, 171–2, 173
transfer and declaration 63
transfer of property 63, 64, 67, 73, 74, 118, 119, 128; in
    name of another 121, 128
transferees of the legal estate for value without notice 31
Trust of Land and Appointment of Trustees Act 1996
    141, 142
trust property 4; certainty of 46, 47, 55, 56, 57
Trustee Act 1925 6, 156–7, 161, 162, 163, 165, 166
Trustee Act 2000 9, 158, 159, 160
trustees 19; appointment of 155, 156, 173; beneficiary
    19; constructive 131, 132, 134, 148–51, 153;
    contribution/indemnity between 164; *de son tort*
    149; discretionary trusts 49; duty of care 158–9;
    lack of/equity 23; liability of 164, 167; mixing of
    trust funds 170–1; multiple 67–8, 73, 75; passive
    172; powers/duties of 3–4, 6, 7, 28, 29–30, 36,
    159–61, 172, 173, 174; removal of 155–7, 172, 173;
    retirement of 157, 173; role of 155, 158–60; settlors
    as 75; third-party 75
trust(s); *see also cestui que* trust; charitable trusts;
    constructive trusts; discretionary trusts; express
    trusts; fixed trusts; imperfect trusts; implied trusts;
non-express trusts; perfect trusts; presumed
    resulting trusts; private purpose trusts; purpose
    trusts; remedial constructive trusts; resulting
    trusts; secret trusts: characteristics of 27–31;
    classification of 32–4; constitution/formal
    requirements of 5; creation of 74; declaration of 5,
    32, 39, 63; development of 18–19; effect of creating
    70–1; *inter vivos* trusts 28, 55; law 8–9; nature of
    3–6, 27–37; origins of 1–3, 15–26; self-declaration
    of 5, 32, 62
Trusts of Land and Appointment of Trustees Act 1996 34,
    156, 157
Turner, L.J. 61–2

unconscionability 6, 65, 131, 132
unincorporated associations 77, 82–9, 90, 91, 112;
    winding-up of 124–6, 128
unlawful transactions, intended 122
use, the 2, 3, 19, 26

Vaisey, J. 105
valuable consideration 71
Variation of Trusts Act 1958 163
voluntary promise 24
voluntary transfer in name of another 121
volunteers: and equity 24; and imperfect trusts 71

Watson, Lord 158
Wilberforce, Lord 52, 101
wills 28, 43, 55, 142, 146
Wills Act 1837 28, 142, 143, 144, 147, 152
writs 15–16, 17